Praise for
MASTER PLANTS

"If you're looking for recipes that are easy yet exciting, healthy, and great tasting, this is the cookbook that you've been waiting for. Just as ancient civilizations thrived on a plant-based diet, so will you! As a physician and nutrition researcher, I have found low-fat vegan foods to pack enormous power. This is a great book for anyone, whether you're looking for help to get started or looking for new recipes and information. Read *Master Plants* and master your health!"

— **NEAL BARNARD, M.D.,** founding president of the Physicians Committee for Responsible Medicine, professor of medicine at the George Washington University School of Medicine and Health Sciences, author of 17 books and more than 70 published papers on nutrition and its impact on human health

"Margarita Restrepo and Michele Lastella have written a masterpiece of nutrition. You will become acquainted with the fascinating origin of the vegetables and fruit of the past and will be excited by the incredibly original and delicious recipes. The photography is so beautiful you will even want to take a bite of the soursop, peel and all. This is an extraordinary book that makes it clear there is no other way to eat than plant-based."

—**CALDWELL B. ESSELSTYN, JR., M.D.,** author of *Prevent and Reverse Heart Disease*, and Ann Crile Esselstyn, author with Jane Esselstyn of *The Prevent and Reverse Heart Disease Cookbook*

"What a beautiful book! Filled with valuable insights and helpful tips, and combining cutting-edge nutritional research with the nourishing traditions of ancient civilizations, *Master Plants* is the book that the food movement has been waiting for. It has my highest recommendation."

—**JOHN ROBBINS,** author of *The Food Revolution* and *Diet for a New America*

"Beauty is attractive. The brilliant colors used in the *Master Plants Cookbook* make us want to reach out to touch, taste, and smell foods that help us reach our highest potentials in life."

—**JOHN MCDOUGALL, M.D.,** founder of the McDougall Program, author, lecturer, and researcher

"The *Master Plants Cookbook* is first a feast for the eyes, then for the mind, and finally for the palate. It's gorgeous in every respect and organized like no other cookbook I've ever seen. Both user-friendly and gourmet, it's guaranteed to turn any veg-curious cook into a passionate and accomplished plant-based chef."

—**HOWARD JACOBSON, PH.D.,** co-author of *Whole: Rethinking The Science of Nutrition* and founder at PlantYourself.com

NAKED FOOD® MAGAZINE'S

MASTER PLANTS
Cookbook

THE 33 MOST HEALING SUPERFOODS FOR OPTIMUM HEALTH

With Over 100 Delicious Recipes

MARGARITA RESTREPO & MICHELE LASTELLA

RUNNING PRESS
PHILADELPHIA · LONDON

Published by Running Press Book Publishers,
An Imprint of Perseus Books, a Division of PBG Publishing, LLC,
A Subsidiary of Hachette Book Group, Inc.

Printed in China

Books published by Running Press are available at special discounts for bulk
purchases in the United States by corporations, institutions, and other organizations.
For more information, please contact the Special Markets Department at the Perseus
Books Group, 2300 Chestnut Street, Suite 200, Philadelphia, PA 19103, or call
(800) 810-4145, ext. 5000, or e-mail special.markets@perseusbooks.com.

ISBN 978-0-7624-6024-3

Library of Congress Control Number: 2016938267

E-book ISBN 978-0-7624-6025-0

9 8 7 6 5 4 3 2 1

Digit on the right indicates the number of this printing

Designed by Susan Van Horn

Edited by Jennifer Kasius

All photos taken by Margarita Restrepo and Michele LaStella, except where noted in
Photo Credits, page 289.

Illustrations on pages 5, 10, 54, 122, 256, 277, and 289 © Chantall/CreativeMarket.com

Typography: Futura, Archer, Cervo, and Nexa Script, Helvetica, Arial Unicode

Disclaimer: This book is intended only as an informative guide for those wishing
to know more about healthy diets. In no way is this book intended to replace,
countermand, or conflict with the advice given to the reader by her/his physician.
Information in this book is offered with no guarantees on the part of the author or the
publisher.

Running Press Book Publishers
2300 Chestnut Street
Philadelphia, PA 19103-4371

Visit us on the web!
www.runningpress.com

We dedicate this book to every human being who has passed away from a preventable chronic disease, and to those who have rediscovered the power of plants to reverse them.

To the organic farmer. To the fervent locavore. To the sustainable eater.

Contents

THE MODERN PARADIGM

Genes vs. Lifestyle 12
Understanding the Cause 13
Embracing Ancient Wisdom .. 13
The Hard Facts 14
Plant-Based Diet Facts 15

PLANT-BASED FOOD AND THE ANCIENT CIVILIZATIONS

Ancient Chinese Nutrition 16
Ancient Sumerian Nutrition 19
Ancient Indian: Veda Nutrition .. 19
Ancient Egyptian Nutrition 23
Ancient Maya Nutrition 23
Ancient Babylonian Nutrition ... 24
Ancient Inca Nutrition 24
Ancient Aztec Nutrition 25
Ancient Greek Nutrition 26
Ancient Roman Nutrition 27
Native American Nutrition 28

ORIGINS OF VEGETARIANISM

Ancient Religious Thinking & Beliefs about Nutrition 30
Hinduism 31
Buddhism 31
Islam 32
Jainism 33
Judaism 34
Christianity 36

THE ENLIGHTENED DIET

Common Questions 38
Why Organic? 38
Why GMO-Free? 40
Why Salt-Free? 40
Why Oil-Free? 41
Why Sugar-Free? 42

Getting Started 43
Sourcing Food 43
Protein and Calcium............ 44
Fish................................ 45
Omega-3s 46
Supplements 46
Vitamin B12 47
Organic, Grass-Fed Animal
    Products 47

The Shopping List 48
Plant-Based Substitutions for
    Common Foods.............. 50
Supplements..................... 51
Kitchen Essentials 51
Keeping Your Kitchen
    Sustainable................... 53

THE MASTER PLANTS

Arugula 56
Asparagus 58
Avocado 60
Beet................................. 62
Bell Pepper 64
Blueberry 66
Brazil Nut 68
Broccoli 70
Buckwheat 72
Cacao 74
Chia 76

Chickpea 78
Fig................................... 80
Fungi 82
Garlic 84
Ginger 86
Goji 88
Hemp 90
Kale 92
Kelp 94
Lemon 96
Lentil 98

Oats 100
Persimmon 102
Pomegranate 104
Quinoa 106
Rosemary 108
Soursop 110
Spinach 112
Sweet Potato 114
Tomato 116
Turmeric 118
Wheatgrass 120

THE MASTER PLANT RECIPES

Apulia Rucola Salad 124

Mediterranean Green
　　Lasagna 126

Damascus-Crusted
　　Asparagus 128

Ishtar's Asparagus 130

Aztec Avocado Boats 132

Cashew e Pepe 134

Cinque Terre Stuffed Ravioli ... 137

Marrakesh Beet Chips 138

Andean Pepper Boats 140

Columbus's Favorite Goulash ... 143

Apache Cheesecake 144

Blueberry Hopi Parfait 147

Amazon Nutty Steaks 148

Carioca Pear Crumble 151

Emperor's Broccoli Soup 152

Satay Broccoli Wings 155

Nepal's Buckwheat Wraps 156

The Monk's Cacao Porridge ... 158

Caribbean Cacao Pancakes ... 161

Olmec Fudge Brownies 162

Chichén-Itzá Blackberry
　　Mousse 164

Incan Mango Pudding 167

Lebanese Chickpea Stew 168

Jordanian Roasted
　　Chickpeas 171

Babel Fig Pie 172

Goddess Baked Onion Tarts ... 175

Kyoto Fungi Risotto 176

Tibetan Creamy Caps 178

Agrodolce Fig Bruschetta 180

Kazakh Sautéed Veggies 183

Ming's Roasted Cauliflower ... 184

Holy Anti-Inflammatory Tea ... 187

Himalayan Goji Rice 188

Ningxia Goji Macaroons 191

Qi Carrot Wraps 192

Steps to Heaven Hemp Bars ... 195

Mesopotamian Kale Pesto 197

Persepolis Kale Salad 199

Keobab Kelp Pâté 200

Madagascar "Tuna" Salad ... 203

Bhutan Lemon Smoothie 205

Tantric Lemon Bliss Tarts 206

Demeter's Harvest Burgers 209

Plato's Lentil Risotto 210

Nile's Pan-Seared Oatmeal ... 213

Pharaoh's Holy Bites 214

Ming's Raw Crumble
　　Cream 217

Zen Persimmon Pico
　　de Gallo 218

Fabulous Mediterranean
　　Pkhali 220

Shiva's Antioxidant Pudding ... 222

Machu Picchu's Quinoa
　　Cookies 225

Quechua Quinoa Bowl 226

Valle d'Itria's Roasted Onions ... 228

Sumerian Rosemary Roast 230

El Dorado's Golden
　　Ice Cream 233

Tayrona's Secret Smoothie ... 234

Armenian Spinach Rice 237

Persian Green Antioxidant
　　Smoothie 238

Polynesian Layered Bake 241

Samoa Sacred Potatoes 242

Mayan Stuffed Tomatoes 245

Sunday's Italian Ragù 246

Mumbai Curcuma Healing
　　Smoothie 249

Vedic Turmeric Croquettes 250

Manna Quinoa Breakfast
　　Bowl 253

The Essenes Gazpacho 254

ESSENTIAL RECIPES

Dressings 258

Lemon Dressing 258

Ranch Dressing 258

Turmeric Date Dressing 258

Drinks 259

All-Star Pregnancy Smoothie ... 259

Cancer Fighter Smoothie 259

Classic Almond Milk 260

Classic Hemp Milk 260

Digestion Booster Smoothie ... 261

Green Protein Smoothie 261

Heart-Thriving Smoothie 261

Kidney and Liver Cleansing
    Smoothie 262

Man-Power Smoothie 262

Whole Grains and
Legumes 263

Brown Rice 263

Buckwheat 263

Millet 264

Beans 264

Quinoa 265

Chickpeas 265

Lentils 266

Sides and Soups 267

Spicy Baked Plantain Chips ... 267

Crackers 268

Kale Chips 268

Potato Salad 269

Sweet Potato Hummus 270

Traditional-Style Yucca 270

Chilled Watermelon Soup 271

Classic Potato Soup 271

Spreads and Dips 272

Cashew Cheese 272

Fig Pâté 272

Naked Mayo 272

Naked Guacamole 273

Pico De Gallo 273

Sofrito 274

Sweets 275

Chocolate Spread 275

Carrot Cookies 275

Date Sauce 275

Chia Pudding 276

Naked Pie Crust 276

Three-Ingredient
    Oat Cookies 276

Acknowledgments *page 277*
Glossary *page 278*
References *page 284*
Photo credits *page 289*
Index *page 290*

The Modern Paradigm

IF YOU WANT TO KNOW WHAT YOU SHOULD BE EATING FOR OPTIMAL HEALTH AND WELL-NESS, LOOK NO FURTHER THAN OUR CLOSEST RELATIVES, THE CHIMPANZEES.

These creatures are probably the best living example of what our diet looked like before modern agriculture . . . and what it *should* look more like today. Chimpanzees eat plants and fruit all day, but eat meat only about nine days out of the year. For a long time, we humans followed suit. For one hundred thousand years, in fact, humans evolved with a diet that was primarily the same as that of our chimpanzee brethren: low-fat and plant-based, with infrequent forays into meat. After all, our bodies were not designed to capture prey, and our tools for hunting and fishing were primitive.

These eating habits weren't just a primitive phenomenon. Even as recently as two hundred years ago, Americans seldom ate meat. In the early 1800s, meat was simply too expensive and too impractical for the average household. Only the rich ate meat on a regular basis, which is why gout, caused by the breakdown of protein, was called the "rich man's disease." Most Americans would only eat meat on special occasions such as Easter and weddings.

Historically, plants weren't just for eating. They were also for healing. The first healing doctors relied on herbs and substances derived from natural sources as an important cure for diseases. Ancient doctors found ways to cure ailments by testing the plants available to them, and through trial and error treatments. In most cultures, the women who cared for the health of their families were in charge of gathering and doling out plants.

This wealth of knowledge was then passed down through the generations orally.

It is believed that another source of medicine was the earth. Soils and clays may have provided prehistoric peoples with some of their first medicines. Early humans may have learned about the use of various healing clays by observing animal behavior. Such clay was used both internally and externally, for things like treating wounds and after surgery.

Obviously, this is not the world we live in today. So, what changed? It's no secret that humankind has seen rapid-fire technical advances over the course of the past century, which have had a major impact on how we live our day-to-day lives and *especially* how we eat and medicate ourselves. When you step back and look at the numbers, it's shocking how quickly and completely things have changed. By 1910, advances in farming and transportation increased annual meat consumption to 100 pounds per capita. Less than a century later, in 2007, this number rose to an astounding *220 pounds of meat per person, per year*. It goes without saying that this is a long way from those nine days a year our chimpanzee ancestors were eating meat. Not only that, but in the past 200 years, sugar consumption has also skyrocketed from 15 pounds per year to 160. Looking back, all of this happened very quickly, but because this change in diet occurred over the course of many generations, it went largely unnoticed. After all, the dietary habits we learn early in life are rarely questioned.

Just as our eating habits changed, so too did our healthcare practices. In 1903, Thomas Edison said that the doctors of the future would give no medicine. Instead, doctors would use diet as a primary mode of establishing wellness, healing, and disease prevention. If good ol' Edison is, in fact, right, he's speaking about a future that has not yet come. As humans began to eat more and more meat in the past hundred years, doctors simultaneously started using drugs to treat whatever ails us. As a society, we have become used to trusting that a small pill is, or can be, the solution to all of our health problems.

Although many doctors still prescribe drugs when necessary, it is vital we understand that the leading causes of disability and death in the United States are brought on mostly by lifestyle, and that knowledge about what we put in our mouths is essential. An impressive number of studies have shown that lifestyle is the root cause of disease. This means that taking care of ourselves through the basic forms of prevention—food, exercise, and stress-reduction—will keep us healthy, strong, and feeling good.

Genes vs. Lifestyle

Some people believe that they have little control over their own health and well-being, and that they are pre-determined from their birth thanks to DNA. But the scientific and medical worlds have known for a long time that our genes are responsible for only 10% to 20% of risk for most of the leading causes of death. Interestingly, while the rates of big killers like heart disease and cancer differ vastly from one population to the next, when people migrate from low- to high-risk countries, their disease rates almost always change to those of the new environment. For example, at least 70% of strokes and colon cancer are avoidable, as are

more than 80% of coronary heart disease and more than 90% of type-2 diabetes. The bottom line here? It's time we stop blaming our genes and focus on the large percentage of our health that is under our control and based on the decisions we make. This may very well be the real solution to the health care crisis we are experiencing worldwide.

Most people already know what they need to do to be healthy. Adhering to just a few simple healthy lifestyle practices can go a long way toward preventing chronic diseases: not smoking, maintaining a healthy weight, exercising 30 minutes a day, and eating more healthfully (more fruits, vegetables, whole grains, legumes, tubers, and less processed foods, dairy, and meats). What many people might not know is how profoundly these lifestyle decisions can positively impact our health. These simple practices cut our risk of developing a chronic disease by 78%, of developing diabetes by 95%, and of a heart attack by 80%.[1] They may decrease our chances of having a stroke by one-half and cut cancer risk by one-third. Clearly, we're not yet doing what we need to be to prevent disease. As it stands now, each year a million Americans experience their first heart attack or stroke, a million develop diabetes, and another million get diagnosed with cancer.

Not only will eating right and exercising prevent disease, but these decisions will also help us live a better life for a longer amount of time. The Center for Disease Control recently conducted a 6-year study in which they followed more than 8,000 Americans 20 years of age or older. They discovered that just three lifestyle choices exerted an enormous impact on mortality. People who follow the federal dietary guidelines, don't smoke, and engage in physical activity for at least 21 minutes or more a day substantially reduce their risk of early death. Not only that, but those who managed at least one of the three guidelines reduced their chances of dying by

40%. Those who performed two out of three cut their chances of dying by more than half. And, finally, those who scored all three reduced their chances of dying during those six years by 82%!

Understanding the Cause

So, how did we get here? Our grandparents didn't have the obesity rates we do today, nor did they suffer from the high occurrence of cancer or other obesity-related ailments that we are all too familiar with. It turns out that our habits have changed. We don't have the time to grow our food; most of what we eat is the product of huge multimillion-dollar industries, our soils are depleted, and our food's DNA is now the property of a pesticide-producing corporation. Not only that, but turn on your TV, walk into your local bookstore, or log on to Pinterest and you will see *thousands* of cooking shows, cookbooks, and recipes. Unfortunately, the majority of these meals are built around meats, fats, flours, and sugars. Mainstream media constantly features food challenges, cook-offs, celebrity chefs, and comfort foods, all with one common denominator: they are all based on unhealthy ingredients. It isn't surprising that these same ingredients are the basis of most of the food consumed in America. Meats, dairy, sugar, flour, fat, and salt are all the essence of the Standard American Diet.

We don't even know what healthy is anymore. There are many issues threatening our food supply—and, thus, our health and the health of our planet. It's a scary thought, but the answer isn't to be frustrated, or to be scared and run away from the problem. Each and every one of us has the opportunity to do something about this. Maybe you're only making small changes in your own life and diet. But even *that* can have a major impact. Eating a sustainable diet will inspire others around you. It will also make you a

more conscious individual, benefit the animals that are being abused and slaughtered every minute, and help heal the environment.

Knowledge is key. It is impossible to get a driver's license if we aren't able to drive a car. Is it dangerous to drive? Sure, it is. So we learn to be cautious, protect our kids, get insurance, and drive carefully. Our food sources are no different (minus the bad license picture). We source from our local farmer, we know where our food comes from, and choose plant foods. You'll be shocked at how rapidly the many benefits of these three actions will affect not only your health, but also the health of everything and everyone around you.

Maybe all of this still sounds overwhelming. If so, know this: Eating in a way that will keep you healthy and better the world around you will not only make you feel phenomenal, but it will also taste amazing! As Naked Food chefs, it is our goal to make you fall in love with plant foods. But before we get to the delicious recipes, we want to help you understand *why* the foods and recipes included in this book are so incredible, and how deeply entrenched in our collective history of food and medicine they are. In *Master Plants*, we're taking you on a great journey of discovery that involves our ancestors and the richness of their heritage from the perspective of good health, healing, and eating habits.

Embracing Ancient Wisdom

As you may know, one of the most beneficial aspects of ancient nutrition is that our ancestors' food was locally grown and sourced—after all, there were no big rigs to transport food from region to another. Every community benefited from and subsisted on the foods that were available to them. The only way food crossed boundaries was when local trades were made over short distances. As a result, the food of our ancestors was always fresh. It was also what we call "real" food, as opposed to the "food products" we know today. It was not processed, and it was not chemically preserved or transformed. In the farmlands, crops weren't treated with pesticides or herbicides, and all the seed species were completely pure.

Although the food in ancient times varied from civilization to civilization (much as it does today), the array of available foods was vast. The average farmer was able to grow and source many types of fruits and vegetables and to feed his or her family on staple crops. In fact, many of the powerful whole foods we know today, such as cacao, turmeric root, or chia seeds, are some of the most ancient foods found on planet Earth. These Master Plants date back thousands of years to the pre-Columbian era, and ancient humans benefited from these plants in the same way we benefit from them today. Both scientists and archaeologists have found that some of the main ancient civilizations consumed large amounts of vegetables, fruits, whole grains, seeds, and nuts. For instance, one of the latest studies analyzing the diet of ancient Egyptians has revealed they were largely vegetarian and their diet was primarily wheat- and barley-based.[1]

In *Master Plants*, we will highlight these cultures and the foods they grew, ate, and thrived on. Our ancestors didn't think of food *as* medicine from a learned concept. Food *was* inherently medicine. *Master Plants* links the knowledge that our ancestors acquired with the magnificent power of foods we still enjoy today. Whether you are already well on the road to a healthier way of eating or just starting and need a little push, *Master Plants* will inspire and empower you to stay on track.

The Hard Facts

As we already know, there's good news: The chronic diseases that plague the United States today—such as heart disease, stroke, cancer, diabetes, obesity, and arthritis—are some of the easiest to solve and even *prevent* because they are linked to nutritional deficiencies. The bad news is that, currently, these diseases run rampant in our society.

- As of 2012, about half of all adults—117 million people—have one or more chronic health conditions. One of four adults has two or more chronic health conditions.[1]

- Seven of the top 10 causes of death in 2010 were chronic diseases. Two of these chronic diseases—heart disease and cancer—together accounted for nearly 48% of all deaths.[2]

- From 2009–2010, more than one-third of adults—about 78 million people—were obese (defined as body mass index [BMI] ≥30 kg/m^2). Nearly one of five youths aged 2 to19 was obese (BMI ≥95th percentile).[3]

By addressing our eating habits, we can also help the economy. The majority of U. S. health care and economic costs associated with medical conditions involve some of these same chronic diseases and conditions. Think of all the other areas we could filter all of these massive amounts of money into!

- Eighty-four percent of all health care spending in 2006 was for the 50% of the population who have one or more chronic medical conditions.[4]

- The total costs of heart disease and stroke in 2010 were estimated at $315.4 billion. Of this amount, $193.4 billion was for direct medical costs, and don't include the costs of nursing home care.[5]

- Cancer care cost $157 billion in 2010 dollars.[6]

- The total estimated cost of diagnosed diabetes in 2012 was $245 billion, including $176 billion in direct medical costs and $69 billion in decreased productivity, which includes people being absent from work, being less productive while at work, or not being able to work at all because of diabetes.[7]

Plant-Based Diet Facts

- *Vegetarians live longer and better.* Compared to omnivores, vegetarians have a lower overall mortality rate and a lower rate of non-communicable diseases, such as heart disease, type 2 diabetes, and cerebrovascular disease.[1]

- *Plants make your heart happy.* Large-scale studies show that mortality from coronary heart disease is 30% lower among vegetarian men and 20% lower among vegetarian women than in non-vegetarians.[2] There's a clear reason for this: Plant-based diets offer lower levels of saturated fat, cholesterol, and animal protein, and higher levels of carbohydrates, fiber, magnesium, potassium, folate, and antioxidants, such as vitamins C and E and phytochemicals.[3]

- *Plan your plants.* Eating a plant-based diet doesn't mean eating the same berries or salads every day, just like eating an omnivorous diet doesn't mean you should subsist solely on steak and pasta. The goal here is a well-rounded, nutritional diet that provides you with all of the vitamins and minerals you need to flourish. A well-planned plant-based diet will provide all the same nutrients as meat-eater's receive,[4] except

for the damaging ones, such as cholesterol (bad fat), which is not found in plants. Cholesterol is only found in animal-derived foods! The human body produces the adequate amount of fat it needs on its own, so there is no reason to consume it in our diets.

- *Do away with diabetes.* As a testament to the medicinal power of plants, plant-based diets can actually meet the guidelines for the treatment of diabetes, and some research suggests that diets that are more plant-based reduce the risk of type-2 diabetes. Studies conducted in religious communities such as the Seventh-Day Adventists (SDA), which encourage a vegetarian diet, have found that diabetes rates are *less than half* of those in the general population. Also among SDA, vegetarians have lower rates of diabetes than non-vegetarians. This might well be attributed to the lower BMI of vegetarians and higher fiber intake, both of which improve insulin sensitivity.[5]

- *Cut out the bad, bring on the good.* On average, vegetarians consume a lower proportion of calories from fat (particularly saturated fatty acids), fewer overall calories, and more fiber, potassium, and vitamin C than do non-vegetarians.

- *Bring down the BMI.* Vegetarians generally have a lower body mass index. This may contribute to the positive health outcomes that have been identified among vegetarians.[6]

Plant-Based Food and the Ancient Civilizations

AS WE SPEAK, THOUSANDS OF AMERICANS ARE CURRENTLY ON A DIET, WHILE MANY OTHERS HAVE GIVEN UP ON THEIR DIETS AND ARE ON A BINGE. COLLECTIVELY, WE ARE OVERWEIGHT, SICK, AND STRUGGLING. OUR CHOICES ABOUT WHAT AND HOW MUCH TO EAT HAVE GONE VERY WRONG. THE TIME HAS COME TO RETURN TO A MORE SENSIBLE WAY OF EATING AND LIVING . . . BUT HOW? THE ANSWER LIES IN THREE MAGIC WORDS: *BACK TO BASICS*. AND THE SIMPLEST WAY TO EAT INCLUDES PLANTS IN THEIR RAW STATE OR LIGHTLY COOKED, MINIMALLY PROCESSED, AND WHOLE.

For many, it seems like plant-based eating is simply too restrictive, but rest assured, there is a vast and wonderful world of foods to be rediscovered. A whole food, plant-based diet does, indeed, exclude processed foods such as refined flours and sugars, oils, and all animal-derived foods. But it does include all fruits and vegetables (sea vegetables and fungi, too!), whole grains, legumes, nuts, and seeds. Together, we will rediscover the diet our ancestors knew: a mainly vegetarian diet, which was the natural off-shoot of *their* ancestors' diet. The diets of nearly all monkeys and apes (except the leaf-eaters) are composed of fruits, nuts, and leaves. With agriculture, human bodies changed and adapted to digest other plant starches, other leaves, other nuts, other fruits and vegetables, and to benefit from their amazing protective nutrients.

As we think back to how our ancestors ate, remember that until very recently there was no way of processing food. In the absence of that, they learned to utilize the soil, sun, and water to grow food, preserve produce for the winter or dry periods, and to treasure the earth. Therefore, people needed to be innovative and willing to create new ways of preparing one plant that maximized and utilized its flavor, skin, pulp, stem, and leaves. Plants were also the primary mode for treating ailments and afflictions. Earth gave humans every instrument we need to generate and maintain life—how awesome is that? These natural tools and resources are how every ancient civilization relied on just a handful of plants as their main staples—and thrived on them. Let's explore together what our ancestors ate and how their food choices came to be.

Ancient Chinese Nutrition

As one of the oldest and longest lasting civilizations in the world, the history of ancient China can be traced back more than 4,500 years. It is said that Shennong (神农), also known as the Emperor of the

Five Grains, ruled prehistoric China back then. He was viewed as a cultural hero for revolutionizing the lives of his people (and, over time, the world) by teaching them the practices of agriculture, how to cultivate grain, and to avoid killing animals. Appropriately, his name means "the Divine Farmer."

As if all of this wasn't enough, Shennong also discovered hundreds of herbs and tested their medical value. His most well-known work is *The Divine Farmer's Herb-Root Classic* (神农本草经), which was first compiled several thousand years after his death. Considered to be the earliest Chinese pharmacopoeia, the book includes 365 medicines derived from minerals, plants, and animals. Acting as his own guinea pig, Shennong identified hundreds of medicinal (and poisonous) herbs by personally testing their properties, which was crucial to the development of traditional Chinese medicine. If you want to talk about a long-lasting influence, according to legend, Shennong also discovered tea around 2737 BCE as an antidote against the poisonous effects of nearly seventy herbs. Though, historically, the earliest records of tea drinking in China dates back to the Han dynasty (206 BCE–220 BCE). Even some 2,000 years after Shennong tea was still used as medicine.

There's more. Shennong is also credited with cultivating the "five grains" or (WǔGǔ), a grouping of five farmed crops that were all-important in ancient China. The crops themselves were regarded as a sacred boon from a mythological or supernatural source. Most of us don't think of food as divine today, but back then the five grains were attributed to the saintly rulers who were believed to create Chinese civilization. So these were viewed not merely as five crops chosen from many options, but as the source that gave birth not only to agrarian society, but also to civilization. This was serious business; squandering the five grains

was seen as a sin worthy of torment in *Diyu*, the Chinese hell.

So what are these almost mystical five grains? *The Book of Rites*, which was compiled by Confucius in the 6th and 5th centuries BCE, lists soybeans (豆), wheat (麦), broomcorn (黍), foxtail millet (稷), and hemp as the five grains. The "Hei'anzhuan," an ancient Chinese poem, lists millet, rice, adzuki bean, soybean, barley and wheat together, and sesame as Shennong's "five" grains, although these make up a list of six. Another list replaces hemp with rice (稻). You might notice that Shennog's initial list is the only one that doesn't include rice. There's a reason for this, which was pointed out by the Ming encyclopedist Song Yingxing: Rice was not counted among the five grains cultivated by Shennong because southern China had not *yet* been settled or cultivated by the Han. Rice was the first grain farmed by the Chinese. Archaeological evidence points to rice farming along the Yang-tse River as early as about 5000 BCE. People cooked their rice by boiling it in water or making it into wine, the latter of which has been popular in the southern regions of China since prehistory. It wasn't until the Han dynasty, in about 100 CE, that the Chinese people began crafting their wheat and rice into long noodles.

Meanwhile, those in northern China gathered wild millet and sorghum. By 4500 BCE, people in northern China were farming millet, and ate it boiled into a kind of porridge. During the Han dynasty, millet wine became even more popular than tea. Rounding out the main carbohydrates in China during ancient times is sorghum.

Later on, during the Zhou dynasty (1046–476 BCE), Chinese imperial cuisine took shape, and both staple and non-staple foods were plentiful. The imperial system included supervising the royal food and developing grades for the emperor, princes and dukes. According to the Book of Rites, "There were 26 bowls for the emperor, 16 for the princes and dukes, 13 for the marquis, 8 for the senior officials, and 6 for the junior officials." Among the food choices, there were abundant quantities of rice, corn, millet, beans, and vegetables, which are the basis of many famous Chinese dishes.

A fascination with exotics from the diverse range of the Tang empire and the search for plants that promoted health and longevity were two of the main factors that gave rise to variety in the Chinese diet.[1] With this, some foods were also *off-limits* because the Tang court encouraged people not to eat beef. As time went on, some exotic foreign foods, including dairy products, were imported to China from abroad during the Song dynasty (960–1279). Until that point, dairy products were a foreign concept to the Chinese, which explains the previous absence of cheese and milk in their diet.[2] Not surprisingly, the Han Chinese developed an aversion to dairy products and abandoned dairy foods.[3]

Finally, during the Ming dynasty (1368–1644), China became involved in the Columbian Exchange, a global trade of goods, plants, animals, and food crops. Although the bulk of imports to China were silver, the Chinese also purchased and imported New World crops from the Spanish empire, such as sweet potatoes, maize (corn), and peanuts—foods that could be cultivated in lands where traditional Chinese staple crops like wheat, millet, and rice couldn't grow. This led to a massive agricultural surplus that became the basis of a market economy. Furthermore, the highly productive corn and potatoes diminished famines and spurred population growth.[4]

CHINESE FOOD THERAPY

Also called nutrition therapy and dietary therapy, Chinese Food Therapy is a mode of dieting rooted in the Chinese understanding of the effects of food on humans,[5] and centered around concepts like eating in moderation. Its basic precepts are a mix of folk views and ideas drawn from Traditional Chinese Medicine (TCM). Food therapy has long been a common approach to health among the Chinese both in China and overseas, and was popularized for Western readers in the 1990s with the publication of books like *The Tao of Healthy Eating* and *The Wisdom of the Chinese Kitchen*.[6]

Traditional Chinese Medicine "holds that the body's vital energy (*chi* or *qi*) circulates through channels, called meridians, which have branches connected to bodily organs and functions." The doctrines of Chinese medicine are rooted in books like the *Yellow Emperor's Inner Canon* and the *Treatise on Cold Damage*, as well as in cosmological principles like yin-yang and the five phases. Starting in the 1950s, these precepts were standardized in the People's Republic of China, including attempts to integrate them with modern ideas such as anatomy and pathology. In the 1950s, the Chinese government even promoted a systematized form of Traditional Chinese Medicine.[7]

TCM's view of the body places little emphasis on anatomical structures, and is mainly concerned with functional entities that regulate important life functions like digestion, breathing, aging, etc. With this, health is viewed as the harmonious interaction of these entities and the outside world and disease is seen as disharmony. A TCM diagnosis traces symptoms back to disharmonious interactions by measuring the pulse, inspecting the tongue, skin, and eyes, and looking at the eating and sleeping habits of the person, in addition to many other factors.

Ancient Sumerian Nutrition

The Mesopotamians farmed all types of crops but most valuable were their staple whole grains, which could be grown in abundance and packed the most nutritional and caloric punch. They also lent themselves to soups and enriched bread. Of the grains, barley was probably the most common. Not only could it be ground into flour for bread and made into soups, but it could also be fermented and turned into beer. Sumerians also combined barley with other local vegetables, including beans, lentils, chickpeas, mustard, and lettuce. Lamb, goat, pork, and fish were favorites of the city-dwelling Sumerians, but rural farming communities didn't eat meat often, living instead on a mostly vegetarian diet.[1] Sumerians often dried their fruits (apples, figs, dates, and grapes) or preserved them in honey, a favorite treat that was added to almost all types of food.

Ancient Indian: Veda Nutrition

India is not only the home of vegetarian cooking, but also of the science of healthful *living*. The scripture known as the *Ayur-veda*, is the oldest known work on biology, hygiene, medicine, and nutrition. This branch of the Vedas was revealed thousands of years ago by Sri Bhagavan Danvantari, an incarnation of Krishna. Some of the *Ayur-veda*'s instructions are the guideline for today's modern nutritional teachings—or just for plain old fashioned common sense.

From a Western standpoint, it might seem odd to see physical health discussed in spiritual writings. The Vedas consider the human body to be a divine *gift*, a chance for the imprisoned soul to escape from the cycle of birth and death. The importance of healthful living in spiritual life is also mentioned by Lord Krishna in the *Bhaga-*

> Sumerian cities had food stalls, a type of "fast food" establishment where pedestrians could order any type of food and be on their way with a fully cooked meal in a matter of minutes.

In many ways, the food culture in ancient Sumer was much like it is today. Sumerian cities had food stalls, a type of "fast food" establishment where pedestrians could order any type of food and be on their way with a fully cooked meal in a matter of minutes. The civilizations of Mesopotamia also placed great value on the written word and, once writing was invented in the mid- to late-3000s BCE, the scribes were almost obsessed with recording every facet of their cities' lives. In fact, Sumerians are responsible for the first written recipes, the oldest of which date back to 2200 BCE.[2]

vad-gita: "There is no possibility of becoming a yogi, O Arjuna, if one eats too much or eats too little, sleeps too much or does not sleep enough. One who is temperate in his habits of eating, sleeping, working, and recreation can mitigate all material pains by practicing the yoga system."[1] Good advice, right?

According to the Vedas, proper eating is important for two reasons. Besides its role in maintaining bodily health, proper eating can also help the aspiring transcendentalist attain mastery over his or her senses. Eating in a disturbed or anxious state of mind or eating unclean foods causes indigestion, which is considered "the parent of all diseases." "Of all the senses, the tongue is the most difficult to control," says the *Prasada-sevaya*, a song composed by Srila Bhaktivinoda Thakura, "but Krishna has kindly given us this nice *prasada* to help us control the tongue." The prasada is usually an edible food offered to a deity, saint, Perfect Master, or an avatar, and then distributed in His or Her name to followers as a good sign.

SPIRITUALIZING THE ACT OF EATING

Culinary wisdom is said to have evolved from the Vedas, which provide a common sense approach to eating that is very easy to incorporate into modern life. It provides delightful tips for better cooking and eating, all of which hold a healthy lifestyle as the underlying goal.

The Vedas explain both the techniques of healthy vegetarian cooking and the art of eating, which nourishes our soul, body, and mind. There's no doubt they were on to something; modern science has recently verified the Vedic philosophy as it pertains to vegetarian cooking and foods. The Vedas also link the act of cooking with human spirituality because cooking demands purity of mind, or *sattva*. Sattva infuses mindfulness, awareness, and love in the human soul, and helps us stay engrossed in our cooking. According to the Vedas, if we are not present in what we do, it is difficult to be spiritually engaged, and cooking becomes a mundane day-to-day job. In the Veda tradition, cooking offers an ideal, everyday, and priceless opportunity to be spiritual that satisfies both personal and social obligations. A sense of spirituality is bound to influence the daily activities of someone who cooks for family and friends, since the day begins with a spiritual outlook derived from cook-

ing. This same outlook is maintained until the next dawn and has the possibility to grow and continue day by day.

Whether they come from cooking the food or from the food itself, negative emotions certainly do not result in a delightful and delicious meal, and thus deprive us and those we love of happiness, harmony, mental and physical well-being, and transmission of Vedic wisdom about food. Cooking is both a personal and social affair. When we cook for ourselves, we develop a sense of belonging for and with the food. When cooking for others, we extend this belonging to them.

The purpose of food is not only to increase longevity and bodily strength, but also to purify the mind and consciousness. Therefore, the spiritualist offers his food to the Lord before eating. Food offerings, in turn, clear the way for spiritual progress. There are millions of people in India and around the world who would not consider eating unless their food was first offered to Lord Krishna.

The *Bhagavad-gita* divides food into three classes known as Gunas, which exist together in equilibrium: Sattva (purity and goodness); Rajas (activity, passion, the process of change); and Tamas (darkness, inertia, and ignorance). Most healthful are the foods of Sattva, which stands for pure essence. Sattvic foods include sprouted whole grains, fresh fruit, land and sea vegetables, pure fruit juices, legumes, nuts, seeds, sprouted seeds, and herb teas. They are sweet, juicy, fatty, and palatable; they are naturally and organically grown, and as unrefined as possible. Modern food processing takes the Prana (or life force) out of many foods and makes them heavy, impotent, and lifeless—or, more simply, it makes them "dead food." A Sattvic diet thus leads to true health: a peaceful mind in control of a fit body, with a balanced flow of energy between them. All of this increases the duration of life, purifies one's existence, and results in strength, health, happiness, and satisfaction.

Foods that are too bitter, sour, salty, pungent, dry, or hot are Rajasic, the quality of passion, and cause distress. Too much Rajasic food will over-stimulate the body and result in strong emotions and passions, making the mind restless and uncontrollable. Rajasic foods include hot substances, such as sharp spices or strong herbs, and stimulants, like coffee and tea, salt, and chocolate. Rajastic foods can destroy the mind-body equilibrium by feeding the body at the expense of the mind. Nonetheless, ancient Rishis teachers did see *some* value in this, and recommend a combination of Sattvic and Rajasic foods for those who practice demanding disciplines such as martial arts.

Foods of the quality of ignorance, or Tamasic, are described as "putrid, decomposed, and unclean," and produce only pain, disease, and bad karma. Tamasic items include meat, poultry, fish, eggs, alcohol, tobacco, and stale leftover food, contaminated or overripe substances, and other intoxicants including drugs. Overeating is also regarded as Tamasic. The Vedas believe that there is much needless suffering in the world today because most people have no criterion for choosing food other than price and sensual desire.

EATING AT FIXED TIMES

Whenever possible, the main meal should be eaten midday, when the sun is highest. This is the time when the digestive power is strongest. One must wait at least three hours after a light meal and five after a heavy meal before eating again. Eating at fixed times without snacking between meals helps the mind and tongue attain a peaceful state.

EATING IN A PLEASANT ATMOSPHERE

A cheerful mood helps digestion; a spiritual mood helps even more. According to the *Ksema-kuntuhala*, a Vedic cookbook from the 2nd century CE, a pleasant atmosphere and good mood are as important to proper digestion as the quality of food is. Vedic philosophy recommends eating in pleasant surroundings and discussing spiritual topics at mealtimes. One must look upon food as Krishna's mercy. Food is a divine gift, so it should be cooked, served, and eaten in a spirit of joyful reverence.

COMBINING FOODS WISELY

Foods should be combined for taste, efficient digestion, and assimilation of nutrients. For instance, the Vedas' recommend avoiding combining vegetables and raw fruits; vegetables with rice and grains, on the other hand, are a good choice. Fruits are best eaten as a separate meal, and acidic and alkaline fruits should not be mixed. The typical Vedic lunch of rice, split-lentil soup, vegetables, and chapatis (unleavened flatbread) is a perfectly balanced meal.

SHARING PRASADA WITH OTHERS

In the *Upadesamrita*, a five-hundred-year-old classic about devotional service, Srila Rupa Gosvami explains that, "One of the ways for devotees to express love is to offer prasada and accept prasada from one another." A gift from God is too good a thing to keep to oneself, so the scriptures recommend sharing prasada with others, whether they be friends or strangers. Even in modern India, many householders will open their doors at mealtimes and call out, "Prasada! Prasada! Prasada! If anyone is hungry, let him come and eat!" After welcoming his guests and offering them all the comforts at his disposal, he will feed them to full satisfaction before eating his own meal.

CLEANLINESS

Vedic culture places great emphasis on cleanliness, both internal and external. One can internally cleanse the mind and heart of material contamination by chanting Vedic mantras, particularly the Hare Krishna mantra. External cleanliness includes maintaining a high standard of hygiene when cooking and eating. This includes the usual good habits of washing one's hands before eating, and the hands and mouth after.

consequently, the urge to overeat. Drinking moderately while eating helps the stomach do its job. But drinking afterward dilutes the gastric juices and reduces the fire of digestion. The Veda says that we should not drink for at least an hour after eating, and if need be, a drink is advised every hour after that until the next meal.

WASTING FOOD

The scriptures say that for every bit of food wasted in times of plenty, an equal amount will be lacking in times of need. One must put only as much as he can eat on a plate, and save any leftovers for the next meal. If prasada has to be discarded for some

Vitality and strength depend not on how much food is eaten, but on how much of it is digested and absorbed into the system.

EATING MODERATELY

Vitality and strength depend not on how much food is eaten, but on how much of it is digested and absorbed into the system. Vedics believe the stomach needs working space, so they fill it halfway rather than completely. This leaves a fourth of the space for liquid and another fourth for air. Moderate eating will also satisfy the mind and harmonize the body. Overeating makes the mind agitated or dull, and the body heavy and tired.

ALLOWING THE FIRE OF DIGESTION

The Vedas believe that a fire called *Jatharagni*, or "the fire in the belly," is responsible for digesting food. Therefore, because we often drink with our meals, the effect of liquid on fire becomes an important consideration in the art of eating. Drinking before a meal tempers the appetite and,

reason, it should be fed to animals, buried, or put in a body of water. Prasada is sacred and should never be put in the garbage.

OCCASIONAL FASTING

According to the *Ayur-veda*, fasting strengthens both willpower and physical health. An occasional fast gives the digestive system a rest and refreshes the senses, mind, and consciousness. In most cases, the *Ayur-veda* recommends water fasting. Juice fasting is popular in the West because Western methods encourage long fasts. In Ayur-vedic treatment, however, most fasts last for only one to three days. While fasting, one should not drink more water than is necessary to quench thirst. Because *Jatharagni*, or the fire of digestion, doesn't have to work on digesting food, it can instead incinerate accumulated waste in the body, and too much water inhibits that process. Devotees of Krishna observe another kind of fast on Ekadasi, the eleventh day after the full moon and the eleventh day after the new moon, by abstaining from grains, peas, and beans. The *Brahma-vaivarta* scripture says, "One who observes Ekadasi is freed from all kinds of reactions to sinful activities, and thereby advances in pious life."

Ancient Egyptian Nutrition

Egyptian cuisine relies heavily on vegetable dishes for the practical reason that meat in Egypt has been very expensive throughout history. A great deal of vegetarian dishes have been developed to work around this economic reality.

The ancient Egyptians regularly utilized a wide variety of foods in their diets. They cultivated emmer and barley, as well as several other cereal grains. The roots and seeds of aquatic plants like the lotus were also eaten, although generally only when other vegetables were scarce.

Vegetables and fruits were watered by hand since they were grown in garden plots, close to habitations, and on higher ground. Egyptians liked strong-tasting vegetables such as garlic and onions (two of their favorites according to Egyptian writings and images, along with leeks), and thought these were good for health.[1] They also ate peas, beans, lettuce, and cucumbers.[2] Much like today, the Egyptians often served their veggies with oil and vinegar dressing.

Figs, dates, pomegranates, and grapes (some of which were made into wine, although this was something only the rich could afford) were the only fruits that could be grown in the hot climate. Other grown crops included melons, squashes, pulses, and lettuce. The Egyptians were very secure in their knowledge that the Nile valley always yielded enough to feed the country, even when nearby parts of the world were experiencing famine.[3]

Staple fruits included the fruit of the sycamore tree or wild fig, associated with the goddess Hathor, and Persea fruit, which has a taste similar to an apple and was eaten fresh or ground to make flour. Egyptians considered figs to be one of nature's most nutritious fruits, as they provided protein, fiber, and potassium.[4] Figs aided digestion and helped prevent the digestive diseases that were common in ancient times due to contaminated food and foodborne illnesses such as listeria and salmonella. Along with dates and fruit juices, figs were eaten fresh or used to sweeten food. For the rich, honey was the principal sweetener until sugar was introduced to Egypt from the Middle East and India during Greco-Roman times. Jujubes, carob pods, doum palm fruit, and dates all had medicinal uses.

Egyptians didn't only use their plant resources for food. Flax plants, grown for the fibers of their stems, were uprooted before they started flowering and the fibers were split along their length and spun into thread, which was used to weave sheets of linen and to make clothing. The papyrus plants that grew on the banks of the Nile River were used to make paper.

Ancient Maya Nutrition

The Maya diet focused on four domesticated crops: maize, squash, string beans, and chili peppers. The first three of these are commonly referred to in North America as the "Three Sisters." Together, they nutritionally complement one another.[1]

Of the three, maize was the central component of the Maya diet and also figured prominently in mythology and ideology. Maize was used and eaten in a variety of ways, but always *nixtamalized*, a procedure in which maize is soaked and cooked in an alkaline solution. This releases niacin, a necessary B vitamin (vitamin B3, specifically) that prevents vitamin deficiency diseases (pellagra) and reduces incidents of protein deficiency. Once nixtamalized, maize was typically ground up on a mortar, cooked on a smooth, flat griddle (comal), and used to wrap other foods, including as tortillas or tamales. Though these dishes could be consumed plain, other ingredients like chili peppers, cacao, wild onions, and salt were added to diversify flavor. Some believe that maize was actually harder to grow than other crops, which is why it was revered and even considered prestigious.

Unlike maize, yuca was easily grown, and a staple crop of the Maya.[2] Several different varieties of beans were grown, including pinto, red, and black. The Mayans are believed to be the first to discover and cultivate the cacao plant for food.[3] Cacao beans were ground up and mixed with chili peppers, cornmeal, and honey to create a drink called *xocolatl*, which only the rich and noble could indulge in. Cacao beans were also used as ceremonial sacrifices to the gods.

Ancient Babylonian Nutrition

The average ancient Babylonian market (circa 1894 to 539 BCE) provides us with a lot of fascinating information about the daily lives of the Mesopotamian kingdom's inhabitants, including their dining habits. These vibrant markets were filled with accessories, attire, and food staples.

Ancient Babylonians regularly consumed large amounts of legumes and leafy greens. Salads were a typical dish, and often included beans, lentils, and pears. The Babylonians created vinegar-based "dressings" for their salads using sesame oil, pepper, salt, and various herbs like mint, tarragon, and saffron, a particularly beloved dressing herb.[1] Fresh vegetables and fruits were also often savored with unleavened bread. Thick soups were pretty common in Babylonian times, and often featured lentils and onions, honey, and carrot leaves. That's right: In this culture, carrots were commonly grown for their fragrant leaves rather than their edible roots.

Various fruits were also a big part of the ancient Babylonian diet, and were consumed both boiled and raw.[2] Dates were especially beloved by the ancient Babylonians and offered a way of obtaining a sugary flavor. Babylonians would often pickle their fruits and vegetables to conserve them because of the region's extremely hot weather.

Ancient Inca Nutrition

Would you believe that food storage is actually thought to be one of the reasons behind the mighty growth of the Inca Empire? That's right: They created a storehouse of foods throughout their empire that was stocked with three to seven years' worth of food. Back then, this sort of access to sustenance was an extremely rare and powerful asset that offered the Incas a type of security others simply didn't have. For instance, they stored potatoes and other tubers (roots) by setting them out on dry days and cold nights, essentially freeze-drying them. Techniques like this helped combat droughts and allowed them to feed the standing army for years.

The Inca cropland stretched from north to south, and had different climate zones and altitudes, which resulted in a great variety of vegetables. Food grown in the mountain zone was entirely different from the food grown in the coastal zone. Potatoes were one of the main foods of the Incas, and they grew several hundred varieties, which were used in many different dishes, including the stews and soups they frequently ate.

Ullucu and *arracacha*, which were roots similar to carrot, were also used in soups and stews. Maize and *oca* were also popular. Oca is a root vegetable similar to yams, which the Incas used as a starch base for sweet and bitter flavors. The sweet oca was preserved and used as a sweetener until sugar cane arrived on the scene. Another sweet, starchy root named *achira* was baked in a kind of earth oven before being eaten.

Chili peppers were an important part of Inca cuisine, and *aji amarillo*, or yellow pepper, was a favorite ingredient. Some varieties of seaweed were also popular, and they were consumed dried or even fresh. Blue algae was eaten raw and processed raw for storage; it was also used in desserts.

Last but not least, one of the Inca's favorite staples was grain amaranth. Amaranth was also used to make sculptures of animals and in different religious ceremonies. Later on, the Spaniards would ban amaranth for these very reasons.

Ancient Aztec Nutrition

Aztec cuisine includes that of the Aztec Empire and the Nahua people of the Valley of Mexico prior to European contact in 1519. Their most important food staple was corn, a crop so important to Aztec society that it also played a central role in their mythology. Just like wheat in Europe and rice in most of East Asia, it was the food without which a meal was not complete. Corn came in an inestimable number of varieties that differed in color, texture, size, and prestige, and was eaten as corn tortillas, tamales or *ātōlli*, maize porridge.[1] Tortillas, tamales, casseroles, and the sauces that went with them were the most common Aztec dishes.[2] Chili and salt were both abundant, and the most basic meal was usually just corn tortillas dipped in

ground chilis. In fact, chili and salt were *such* constants in the Aztec diet that their basic definition of fasting was to abstain from these two flavors.

The other major foods were beans, squash, and New World varieties of the grains amaranth (or pigweed) and chia.[3] The combination of maize and these basic foods would have provided the average Aztec with a balanced diet without any significant vitamin or mineral deficiencies. Maize grains were cooked in alkaline solutions, which significantly bolstered its nutritional value.

The Aztec diet also included a variety of fungi, which, along with beans and squash, were often added to chilis and tomatoes, all still prominent in the Mexican diet to this day. They harvested spirulina algae, which was made into a sort of cake rich in flavonoids.[4] Although the Aztecs' diet was mostly vegetarian, they consumed insects such as grasshoppers (*chapulín*), maguey worms, ants, and larvae.

The Aztecs prepared most of their food by boiling or steaming it in two-handled clay pots or jars called *xoctli* in Nahuatl and *olla* in Spanish ("pot"). The olla was filled with food and heated over a fire. Sometimes they would steam their food by pouring a little water into the olla and then placing tamales wrapped in maize husks on a light structure of twigs in the middle of the pot. Spanish chroniclers make several references to frying food, but the only specification about the Aztec style of frying appears to be some kind of cooking that was done with syrup, rather than cooking fat.[5] This is corroborated by the fact that no evidence of large-scale extraction of vegetable oils exists, and that archaeologists have not found cooking vessels suited for frying.

In major Aztec towns and cities, vendors sold street food of all kinds, catering to both the rich and poor. Other than ingredients and prepared food, every imaginable type of maize porridge could be bought, either as a thirst quencher or as an instant meal in liquid form. Water, maize gruels, and pulque, the fermented juice of the century plant (*maguey* in Spanish), were the most common drinks, and there were also many different fermented beverages made from honey, cacti, and various fruits. The elite took pride in drinking cacao, which was among the most prestigious luxuries available. Favored by rulers, warriors, and nobles, the cacao drinks were flavored with chili peppers, honey, and a seemingly endless list of spices and herbs.

Ancient Greek Nutrition

Food was a big part of life in ancient Greece. Most people's diets consisted mainly of breads, vegetables, and fruits. These staples are what we now consider to be integral parts of the Mediterranean Diet.

The Greeks ate three to four meals a day. Breakfast consisted of barley bread dipped in wine, and sometimes complemented by figs or olives. They also ate pancakes called *tagenites* or *tagēnias*. Cereals formed the staple diet. The Greek's two main grains were wheat and barley. Wheat grains were soaked to soften, then either reduced into gruel or ground into flour, kneaded, and formed into loaves or flatbreads, either plain or mixed with honey. The Greeks later used an alkali or wine yeast as a leavening agent.

A simpler method of leavening involved putting lighted coals on the floor and placing a dome-shaped cover over the heap. When it was hot enough, the coals were swept aside, dough loaves were placed on the warm floor, the cover was put back in place, and the coals were gathered on the side of the cover. This method is still traditionally used in Serbia and elsewhere in the Balkans. The first stone oven did not appear until the Roman period. Solon, an Athenian lawmaker of the 6th century BCE, prescribed that leavened bread be reserved for feast days. By the end of the 5th century BCE, leavened bread was sold at the market, though it was expensive.

Barley was easier to produce than wheat, but more difficult to make bread from. It provided nourishing but very heavy bread. Because of this, it was often roasted before milling to produce a coarse flour that was used to make μᾶζα (maza), the basic Greek dish. In *Peace*, Aristophanes employs the expression ἐσθειν κριθὰς μόνας, literally "to eat only barley." The English equivalent of this would be a "diet of bread and water." Many recipes for maza are known; it could be served cooked or raw, as a broth, or made into dumplings or flatbreads. Like wheat breads, it could also be augmented with honey.

FRUIT AND VEGETABLES

Greek cereals were often accompanied by what was generically referred to as ὄψον opson, or relish. The word initially referred to anything prepared on the fire, and by extension, anything that accompanied bread. In the classical period it came to refer to fruit and vegetables: cabbage, onions, lentils, sweet peas, chickpeas, etc. In the cities, fresh vegetables were expensive, and therefore, the poorer city dwellers used dried vegetables.

Legumes were eaten as a soup, boiled or mashed, and seasoned with olive oil, vinegar, or herbs. According to Aristophanes, mashed beans were a favorite dish of Heracles, who is always represented as a glutton in comedies. Lentil soup was the workman's typical dish, while poor families ate oak acorns. Raw or preserved olives were commonly used as appetizers. Other legumes were available at the time, such as bitter vetch (ὄροβος orobos), a flowering plant in the legume family that is a relative to lentils and peas. This legume was one of the first domesticated crops, and was grown in the Near East about 9,500 years ago. During the famine of 1124-26, Bernard of Clairvaux shared a bread of vetch meal with his monks, though, eventually, the bitter vetch was dropped from human

all qualities, from common table wine to vintage. General opinion held that the best wines came from Thásos, Lesbos, and Chios.

Food was no joke in Greek society. They believed that the types of food eaten played an important role in a person's overall composition.

> The Greeks were water sommeliers of sorts, and would describe water as robust, heavy or light, dry, acidic, pungent, wine-like, etc.

use and saved as a crop of last resort in times of starvation. Broad beans remained prominent in the Near East, where the seeds are mentioned in Hittite and Ancient Egyptian sources dating back more than 3,000 years ago.

Fresh or dried fruits and nuts were eaten for dessert. Important fruits included figs, raisins, and pomegranates. Dried figs were also eaten as an appetizer or when drinking wine. In the latter case, grilled chestnuts, chickpeas, and beechnuts often accompanied them.

The most widespread drink was water, so fetching water was a daily task for women. Though wells were common, spring water was preferred: it was recognized as nutritious because it caused plants and trees to grow. The Greeks were water sommeliers of sorts, and would describe water as robust, heavy or light, dry, acidic, pungent, wine-like, etc. One of the comic poet Antiphanes's characters claimed that he could recognize Attic water by taste alone. Athenaeus states that a number of philosophers had a reputation for drinking nothing but water, a habit combined with a vegetarian diet. Milk was not consumed, as it was considered barbaric.

The Greeks are thought to have made red as well as rosé and white wines. These wines came in

Classicist John Wilkins notes that "in the *Odyssey* for example, good men are distinguished from bad and Greeks from foreigners partly in terms of how and what they ate. Herodotus identified people partly in terms of food and eating."

Ancient Roman Nutrition

Ancient texts have plenty to say about lavish Roman feasts. The wealthy could afford exotic fruits and vegetables, as well as shellfish and snails. A formal feast could last for hours; it involved multiple dishes, and was eaten from a reclined position. Ancient Roman writers have less to say about the poor, other than directions for landowners about the appropriate amount to feed slaves, who made up about 30 percent of the city's population.

Ancient Italians were locavores. For example, those who lived in Rome ate less fish compared to people living on the coasts of the empire. The ancient Roman diet resembles a classic Mediterranean diet, but without several familiar foods common in Italian cuisine today. The ancient Romans did not consume spinach or eggplant, which later became common thanks to an influence from the Arab world, or tomatoes or bell peppers, which only appeared in Europe following the discovery of the New World and the Columbian Exchange. There were also few citrus fruits.

However, other items that are staples of modern Italian cooking were present in ancient Rome. Pliny the Elder discussed more than 30 varieties of olives, 40 kinds of pears, figs (both native and imported from Africa and the eastern provinces), and a wide variety of vegetables. Historian Jacques André listed 54 cultivated and 43 wild vegetables in ancient Rome. Some of these vegetables are no longer present in the modern world, while others have undergone significant changes. For example, carrots existed in old Rome, but they weren't orange.

Butcher's meat was an uncommon luxury. John E. Stambaugh writes that meat "was scarce except at sacrifices and the dinner parties of the rich." Fish was more common thanks to sophisticated aquaculture. Large-scale industries were devoted to oyster, snail, and oak grub farming.

Fruit was eaten fresh when in season, and dried or preserved in the winter. One of the most used vegetables was cabbage, which was eaten both raw (sometimes dipped in vinegar) and cooked. The emperor Cato held cabbage in great esteem, believing it to be good for the digestion. Not only that, but he also thought that if a sick person ate a great deal of cabbage and bathed in his urine, he would recover. Legumes were limited, although Romans often ate several varieties of chickpeas cooked down into a broth and roasted as a snack. The Roman gourmet Apicius gives several recipes for chickpeas. They also ate walnuts, almonds, hazelnuts, pine nuts, and sesame seeds, which they sometimes pulverized to thicken spiced, sweet wine sauces for food flavoring.

Native American Nutrition

The new settlers in North America had a difficult time learning how to grow food and harvest crops to sustain their colonies through the land's harsh winters. Native Americans, on the other hand, were accustomed to the climate and the land's nuances, and familiar with the types of food available to them during different times of the year. They did not go hungry as the settlers did. The Native Americans were skilled agriculturists, nomadic hunters, and food gatherers who lived in relatively egalitarian communities where women and men had equal responsibilities. To put their agricultural expertise into perspective, consider this: It is estimated that 60% of modern agricultural production in the United States involves crops domesticated by Native Americans.

The diets of Native Americans varied by geographic region and climate. The most widely grown and consumed plant foods were maize in the mild climate regions and wild rice in the Great Lakes region, which they prepared in a variety of ways to make porridges and breads. Native Americans also used the process of *nixtamalizacion* (soaking dry corn in lime water) to soften corn into dough. Many tribes grew beans and enjoyed them as *succotash*, a dish made mainly of beans and corn. Tubers, also widely eaten, were cooked slowly in underground pits until the hard, tough root became a highly digestible gelatin-like soup. Maple sugar cane served as a basic seasoning for grains and breads, stews, teas, berries, and vegetables.

Origins of Vegetarianism

EARLY LACTO-VEGETARIANISM (A VEGETARIAN DIET THAT INCLUDES DAIRY PRODUCTS) WAS ROOTED IN DIFFERENT IDEALS AND PHILOSOPHIES FROM ONE REGION TO THE NEXT. AS DISCUSSED, IN SOME AREAS PEOPLE ATE VEGETARIAN DIETS BY DEFAULT, SIMPLY DUE TO A LACK OF ACCESS TO MEAT OR THE RESOURCES TO ACQUIRE IT. IN ASIA, THE VEGETARIAN DIET WAS CLOSELY CONNECTED TO THE IDEA OF NONVIOLENCE TOWARD ANIMALS (CALLED AHIMSA IN INDIA), AND WAS PROMOTED BY RELIGIOUS GROUPS AND PHILOSOPHERS. AMONG THE HELLENES, EGYPTIANS, AND OTHERS, VEGETARIANISM WAS BASED ON MEDICAL OR RITUAL PURIFICATION PURPOSES.

The earliest records of vegetarianism come from ancient India and Greece in the 5th century BCE.[1] The Greek philosopher Pythagoras was reportedly vegetarian (and studied at Mt. Carmel, where some historians say there was a vegetarian community), and his followers were expected to be as well. The common Greek beliefs of Orphism (a religion) and Pythagoreanism (a philosophy) both suggested practitioners adopt a different way of life based on the concept of purity and purification (κάθαρσις katharsis), a form of asceticism. Because of this, vegetarianism was a central element of both belief systems. Vegetarianism was also a consequence of a dislike for killing: "For Orpheus taught us rights and to refrain from killing." Later on (1st–2nd century), Plutarch elaborated on the barbarism of blood-spilling by inverting the usual terms of debate, and asking the meat-eater to justify his choice.

Also in ancient Greek philosophy, Empedocles (5th century BCE) justified vegetarianism through his belief in the transmigration of souls: who could guarantee that a slaughtered animal did not house the soul of a human being? In addition, the Neoplatonic Porphyrius associates vegetarianism with the Cretan mystery cults, and gives a census of past vegetarians, starting with the semi-mythical Epimenides. For him, the origin of vegetarianism was Demeter's gift of wheat to Triptolemus so that he could teach agriculture to humanity. His three commandments were: "Honor your parents," "Honor the gods with fruit," and "Spare the animals."

Vegetarianism and the idea of ascetic purity were closely associated with and often accompanied by sexual abstinence.

Roman writer Ovid concluded his magnum opus *Metamorphoses*, in part, with an impassioned argument (uttered by the character of Pythagoras) that in order for humanity to change into a better, more harmonious species, it must strive toward more humane tendencies. He cited vegetarianism as the crucial key to this metamorphosis, explaining his belief that human and animal life are so entwined that to kill an animal is virtually the same as killing a fellow human: "Everything changes; nothing dies; the soul roams to and from, now here, now there, and takes what frame it will, passing from beast to man, from our own form to beast and never dies . . . Therefore lest appetite and greed destroy the bonds of love and duty, heed my message! Abstain! Never by slaughter dispossess souls that are kin and nourish blood with blood!"[2]

Following the Christianization of the Roman Empire, vegetarianism practically disappeared from Europe as it did on other continents, with the exception India. In fact, several orders of monks in medieval Europe restricted or banned the consumption of meat for ascetic reasons, but none of

other, and the world. The Christian Communion, Hindu deity feedings, and everyday eating according to the kashrut or halal codes of Judaism and Islam, are just some examples of this connection. Some religions even prohibit specific foods. For instance, Hindus do not eat beef and Muslims do not eat pork, whereas Christians eat both. Although some of these practices date back to ancient times, food remains an important fixture in religious discourse, and much of people's relationship to food can be explained through religious thoughts, ideals, and codes. Throughout history, food has been categorized as natural or unnatural, good or bad. Good foods are whole, real, clean, and natural. Bad

> Much of people's relationship to food can be explained through religious thoughts, ideals, and codes.

them eschewed fish. Vegetarianism re-emerged during the Renaissance,[3] becoming more widespread in the 19th and 20th centuries. In 1847, the first Vegetarian Society was founded in the United Kingdom; Germany, the Netherlands, and other countries followed. The International Vegetarian Union, a union of the national societies, was founded in 1908. In the Western world, the popularity of vegetarianism grew during the 20th century as a result of nutritional, ethical, and more recently, environmental and economic concerns.

Ancient Religious Thinking & Beliefs about Nutrition

Food and religion have been linked since the beginning of time. From the moment Adam and Eve were driven out of paradise because of an apple, food has allowed humankind to relate to their gods, each

foods are usually described as deliciously "sinful," "guilty" pleasures and are fake, unnatural, and processed. Bad foods harm us, and good foods cleanse us. Pope Francis recently denounced pesticides and genetically engineered (GE) crops, declaring, "the spread of these crops destroys the complex web of ecosystems, decreases diversity in production and affects the present and the future of regional economies."[4] He is not at all alone in approaching food production through the lenses of nature and the past. We, as a world society, are experiencing one of the biggest challenges of our time, and we must not only think about how food can benefit us, but also about how our choices can benefit the planet. Even at that, we clearly see the vast difference between how we respect nature and how our ancestors did. For them, Mother Nature was the *only* source of food, and it was therefore considered sacred. Fertility was a gift from the gods.

Theories about our relationship to food and the social meanings encoded in religious dietary laws have come to shape the study of food. They have even influenced the study of religion. In fact, the first reliable evidence of ancient communities following a plant-based diet dates back to roughly the sixth century BCE and is associated with the birth of the first great religious movements. In this chapter we'll take a more in-depth look at the relationship between food and religion, focusing on Hinduism, Buddhism, Islam, Jainism, Judaism, and Christianity.

HINDUISM

Hinduism *is the dominant religion or way of life in South Asia and India, with more than 900 million followers worldwide. It is the world's third-largest religion after Christianity and Islam. Unlike other religions,* **Hinduism** *has no single founder, no single scripture, and no commonly agreed upon set of teachings. Although Hinduism contains a broad range of philosophies, it is a family of linked religious cultures bound by shared concepts, rituals, cosmology, textual resources, pilgrimages to sacred sites, and questioning of authority. It includes Shaivism, Vaishnavism, and Shaktism, among other denominations, each with interwoven beliefs and practices.*

For those who practice Hinduism, vegetarianism is an ideal for three main reasons: the principle of nonviolence (*ahimsa*) as applied to animals; the intention to offer only "pure" (plant) food to a deity, and then to receive it back as *prasad*; and the conviction that a plant-based diet is beneficial for a healthy body and mind, and that non-vegetarian food is detrimental for both the mind and spiritual development.

Although Hinduism includes a wide variety of practices and beliefs that have changed over time,

an estimated 20% to 30% of all Hindus are vegetarians.[5] The earliest Hindu scriptures belong or refer to the Vedic period (c. 1500–500 BCE), during which people did not approve of cow slaughter or meat eating in general.[6]

BUDDHISM

Buddhism *is a nontheistic religion or philosophy (Sanskrit: dharma; Pali: dhamma) that encompasses a variety of traditions, beliefs, and spiritual practices largely based on teachings attributed to Gautama Buddha, who is more commonly known as the Buddha ("the awakened one"). According to Buddhist tradition, the Buddha lived and taught in the northeastern part of the Indian subcontinent sometime between the 6th and 4th centuries BCE. He is recognized by Buddhists as an awakened or enlightened teacher who shared his insights to help sentient beings end their suffering through the elimination of ignorance and craving. Buddhists believe that this is accomplished through the direct understanding and perception of dependent origination and the Four Noble Truths.*

In the earliest recording of his teachings, the *Tripitaka*, the Buddha did not categorically forbid his disciples from eating meat, which tells us it is unlikely that the historical Buddha was a vegetarian. According to the *Vinaya Pitaka*, when Devadatta urged Buddha to make complete abstinence from meat compulsory, the Buddha refused, maintaining that "monks would have to accept whatever they found in their begging bowls, including meat, provided that they had not seen, had not heard, and had no reason to suspect that the animal had been killed so that the meat could be given to them."

Having said that, the First Precept of Buddhism is "do not kill."[7] The Buddha told his followers not to kill, participate in killing, or cause any living thing to be killed. Some argue that eating meat is taking part in killing by proxy. The counter-argument to this is that if an animal is already dead and not slaughtered specifically for food, it is not quite the same thing as killing the animal. The latter argument seems to be how the historical Buddha understood eating meat. However, the Buddha also listed certain types of meat that were not to be eaten, including horses, elephants, dogs, snakes, tigers, leopards, and bears. Because only some meat was specifically forbidden, we can infer that eating other meat was allowed.

However, certain Mahayana sutras (Buddhist scriptures) strongly denounce eating meat. According to the Mahayana *Mahaparinirvana Sutra*, the Buddha revoked permission to eat meat and warned of a dark age when false monks would claim that they were allowed meat. The historical Buddha and the monks and nuns who followed him were homeless nomads who lived on the alms they received. Buddhists did not begin to build monasteries and other permanent communities until some time after the Buddha died. Monastic Buddhists do not live on alms alone, but also on food grown by, donated to, or purchased by monks. Because it is hard to argue that meat provided to an entire monastic community did not come from an animal specifically slaughtered on behalf of that community, many sects of Mahayana Buddhism in particular began to emphasize vegetarianism. In fact, some of the Mahayana sutras, such as the *Lankavatara*, include decidedly vegetarian teachings.

Buddhists practice *metta*, which means extending loving kindness to all beings without selfish attachment. Buddhists refrain from eating meat out of loving kindness for living animals, and not because there is something unwholesome about an animal's body. In other words, the meat itself is not the argument, and under some circumstances compassion might cause a Buddhist to break the rules. In several Sanskrit texts of *Mahayana Buddhism*, Buddha instructs his followers to avoid meat, but each branch of Mahayana Buddhism selects which sutras to follow. Some branches, including the majority of Tibetan and Japanese Buddhists, eat meat, while many Chinese Buddhist branches do not.

Although vegetarianism is encouraged in all schools of Buddhism, in most it is a personal choice and not a strict requirement. Buddhism discourages fanatical perfectionism. The Buddha taught his followers to find a middle way between extreme practices and opinions. For this reason, Buddhists who do practice vegetarianism are discouraged from becoming fanatically attached to the idea of it.

ISLAM

Islam is a monotheistic, Abrahamic religion that adheres to the Qur'an, a religious text considered by its adherents to be the verbatim word of God (Allāh). It is based on the teachings and normative example of Muhammad (c. 570-632 CE), considered by most to be the last prophet of God. Muslims believe that God is one and unparalleled, and that the purpose of existence is to worship God. Muslims also believe that Islam is the complete and universal version of an ancient faith that was revealed many times before through prophets including Adam, Noah, Abraham, Moses, and Jesus. Although a large majority of Muslims do believe that the previous messages and revelations have been partially misinterpreted over time,[8] according to the Qur'an they are nonetheless obliged to treat the older scriptures with the utmost respect. Religious concepts and practices include the five pillars of Islam, which are essential

concepts and obligatory acts of worship that follow Islamic law, which touches on virtually every
aspect of life and society, and provides guidance
on various topics from banking and welfare, to
family life and the environment.

Followers of Islam, or Muslims, have the free-
dom to choose a vegetarian lifestyle for medical
reasons or if they do not personally like the taste
of meat. However, the choice to become vegetarian for non-medical reasons can sometimes
be controversial.

Islam explicitly prohibits eating some kinds
of meat, especially pork. However, one of the most
important Islamic celebrations, *Eid ul-Adha*, involves
animal sacrifices. According to the Qur'an, a large
portion of the meat of a sacrificed animal has to be
given to the poor and hungry, and every effort must
be made to see that no impoverished Muslim is left
without sacrificial food during days of feast.

Nonetheless, vegetarianism has been practiced
by some influential Muslims, including the Iraqi
theologian, Râbi'ah al-'Adawîyah of Basrah, and the
Sri Lankan Sufi master Bawa Muhaiyaddeen, who
established the Bawa Muhaiyaddeen Fellowship of
North America. Former Indian President Dr. A. P. J.
Abdul Kalam is also famously a vegetarian. Certain
Islamic orders, such as Sufis, are mainly vegetarian.
Though some more traditional Muslims may keep
quiet about their vegetarian diet, the number of
vegetarians within the religion is increasing. In 1995,
a Muslim Vegetarian/Vegan Society was formed
in the United Kingdom, which promotes vegetarianism in accordance with the Qur'an's teachings
and demonstrates how kindness and compassion
to animals are virtues practiced by Islam. Iran is
also home to the Iranian Vegetarian Society, which
is very active in promoting the benefits of a pure
vegetarian diet in the modern Islamic world, both in
terms of health and the well-being of animals.

JAINISM

Jainism, *traditionally known as the Jina śāsana or
Jain dharma, is a South Asian religion. It belongs
to the śramaṇa tradition and is one of the oldest
Indian religions. The three main principles of Jainism are nonviolence, non-absolutism, and non-
possessiveness. Followers of Jainism take five major
vows: nonviolence, not lying, not stealing, chastity,
and non-attachment. They believe that this nonviolence (ahinsa) toward all living beings, together
with self-control, are the means to liberation. The
word "Jain" is derived from the Sanskrit word jina
(conqueror). It refers to the concept that a human
being who has conquered all inner passions, like
attachment, desire, anger, pride, greed, etc., possesses pure, infinite knowledge.*

Ahimsa, in the Indian religions of Jainism,
Hinduism, and Buddhism, is the ethical principle
of not causing harm to other living things. In Jainism, ahimsa is the standard by which all actions
are judged. Every act in which a person directly
or indirectly supports killing or injury is seen
as violence, which creates harmful karma. The
object of *ahimsa* is to prevent the increase of bad
karma. Nonviolence is practiced first and foremost
during interactions with other human beings, and
Jains believe in avoiding harm to others through
actions, speech, and thoughts.[9]

Jains believe that all living organisms, even
microorganisms, are living, have a soul, and have
one or more of the five senses. Because of this
belief, Jains go to great lengths to minimize causing any harm to any living organism. Not surprisingly, vegetarianism is considered mandatory for
all practitioners, and Jains are either lacto-vegetar-
ians or vegans. Products obtained from dead animals are not allowed, because when a living being
dies, a large quantity of microorganisms (called
decomposers) reproduce in their bodies. Therefore,

in eating the dead bodies, violence toward the "decomposers" is unavoidable.

More devout Jains also do not eat root vegetables because they believe that they contain many more microorganisms than other vegetables, and that by eating them they are committing violence toward these microorganisms. This includes tubers such as potatoes, garlic, and anything that involves uprooting (and hence eventually killing) a plant to obtain food. Instead, they focus on eating beans and fruits, whose cultivation does not involve killing a great quantity of microorganisms. Honey is forbidden, because honey is a collection of eggs, excreta, dead bees, and saliva. Some particularly dedicated Jains are fruitarians.

You will probably not be surprised to learn that Jains do not practice animal sacrifice because they consider all sentient beings to be equal. Their conscientious and thorough way of applying nonviolence to everyday activities, and especially to food, shapes their entire lives and is the most significant hallmark of Jain identity. Fasting is very common among Jains and as a part of Jain festivals. However, a Jain may fast at any time, especially if he or she feels an error has been committed. Variations in fasts encourage Jains to do what they can to maintain whatever self-control is achievable for the individual.

JUDAISM

Judaism *is an ancient monotheistic religion, with the Torah as its foundational text. Yahadut, the distinctive characteristics of the Judean ethnos, encompasses the religion, philosophy, culture, and way of life of the Jewish people. Religious Jews consider their religion to be the expression of the covenantal relationship God established with the Children of Israel. The religion includes a large body of texts, theological positions, practices, and forms of organization. There are a variety of movements within Judaism, most of which emerged from Rabbinic Judaism, which holds that God revealed his laws and commandments to Moses on Mount Sinai in the form of both the Written and Oral Torah.*

While Jews are neither required to nor prohibited from eating meat, a number of medieval scholars of Jewish religion (e.g., Joseph Albo and Isaac Arama) regard vegetarianism as a moral ideal, not just because of a concern for the welfare of animals, but because the slaughter of animals might cause the individual who performs such acts to develop negative character traits.[10]

One modern-day academic who is in favor of vegetarianism is the late Rabbi Abraham Isaac Kook, the Chief Rabbi of Mandate Palestine. In his writings, Rabbi Kook speaks of vegetarianism as an ideal, and points to the fact that Adam did not partake of the flesh of animals because God originally commanded that all humans and animals only eat plants.[11] Rabbi Kook makes these comments in his portrayal of the Eschatological (Messianic) era. However, he personally refrained from eating meat except on the Sabbath and during festivals. One of his leading disciples, Rabbi David Cohen, known as the "Nazirite" of Jerusalem, was a devout vegetarian. Several other members of Rabbi Kook's circle were also vegetarians.

According to some Kabbalists, only a mystic, who is able to sense and uplift the reincarnated human souls and "divine sparks," is permitted to consume meat, though eating the flesh of an animal might still cause spiritual harm to the soul. A number of Orthodox Jewish vegetarian groups and activists promote these ideas and believe that the halakhic permission to eat meat is only a temporary tolerance for those who are not ready yet to accept the vegetarian diet. Jewish law also commands people to ritually slaughter animals when killing them, and goes into precise detail on the rituals of both animal sacrifice and ordinary slaughter (*shechita*). According to medieval sage Rabbi Shlomo Ephraim Luntschitz, author of the Torah commentary Kli Yakar, the complexity of these laws was intended to discourage the consumption of meat.[12]

Genesis 1:29 states, "And God said: Behold, I have given you every herb yielding seed which is upon the face of all the earth, and every tree that has seed-yielding fruit—to you it shall be for food." According to Richard H. Schwartz, president emeritus of Jewish Vegetarians of North America and author of the book *Judaism and Vegetarianism*, God's original plan was for mankind to be vegetarian, and He only later gave man permission to eat meat in a covenant with Noah (Genesis 9:1–17), and as a temporary concession because of man's weak nature.[13] This concessionary view of meat-consumption is based on the scriptural analysis of several Rishonim, the leading rabbis, and Poskim, who lived at some point between the 11th and 15th centuries.

Jewish vegetarians use several religious and philosophical arguments when debating the ethics of eating meat. One *mitzvah* cited by vegetarians is *tza'ar ba'alei hayyim*, the injunction not to cause "pain to living creatures."[14] As discussed, the laws of *shechita* are meant to prevent the suffering of animals. Hence, factory farming and high-speed mechanized kosher slaughterhouses have been criticized. Another mitzvah often cited by Jewish vegetarians is *bal tashchit*, the law that prohibits waste.[12] They suggest that an omnivorous diet is wasteful, since it uses 5 times more grain, 10 times more water, 15 times more land, and 20 times more energy than a vegan diet. According to some, vegetarianism is consistent with the sacred teachings and highest ideals of Judaism, including compassion, health, life, and conservation of resources, tzedakah, kashrut, peace, and justice. In contrast, the mass production and consumption of meat and other animal products contradicts many Jewish values and teachings, and gravely harms people, animals, communities, and the environment.[15] Others point out that Jews are required to eat the Paschal Offering (Passover sacrifice) during the Temple period. In addition, the Talmud states that a holiday meal should consist of meat and wine, however, today there is no obligation to consume meat when there is not a sacrificial offering.

One of the sects from the Second Temple Judaism is the Essenes. This group flourished from the 2nd to 1st century BCE and lived in various cities but congregated in communities dedicated to asceticism, voluntary poverty, and daily

> According to some, vegetarianism is consistent with the sacred teachings and highest ideals of Judaism.

immersion.[16] Members of the ancient community of Essenes were also called Yessenes, Iessenes, Nazarites, and Nazirs. Members wore white and followed a vegetarian diet.[17] According to the 4th century church historian, Epiphanius, and Jewish philosopher, Philo, the Essenes were Jews who kept all the Jewish observances, but were nonviolent toward all living creatures and considered it unlawful to eat meat or offer animal sacrifices.[18] Essenes are essentially lacto-vegetarian, with an emphasis on raw foods and a sprouted wheat bread known as "Essene" or "manna bread."

CHRISTIANITY

Early Christianity *is considered to be the period preceding the First Council of Nicaea in 325. As described in the first chapters of the Acts of the Apostles, the first Christians were Jewish. They are thus referred to by historians as "Jewish Christians." The early Gospel message was spread orally; probably in Aramaic,[19] and later in Greek.[20] The New Testament's Book of Acts and Epistle to the Galatians records the first Christian community as being centered in Jerusalem. Its leaders included Peter, James, and John. After his conversion to Christianity, Paul of Tarsus claimed the title of "Apostle to the Gentiles." Paul's influence on Christian philosophy is said to be more significant than any other New Testament author. By the end of the 1st century, Christianity began to be recognized as a religion separate from Judaism, which was also refined and further developed in the centuries following the destruction of the Second Temple of Jerusalem.*

In his book, *Food for the Spirit*, Steven Rosen writes: "The early Christian fathers and groups adhered to a meatless regime." In fact, the writings of the early Church indicate that meat eating was not officially allowed until the 4th century, when the emperor Constantine decided that his version of Christianity would be the version for everyone. Some groups that claim spiritual descent from the ancient Essenes believe that the 27 books we now call the New Testament of the Bible and even some translations of books considered canonical were changed to censor certain beliefs, such as transmigration, the feminine aspect of Divinity, and vegetarianism. These groups use the *Nazarean Bible of the Essene Way*, the *Dead Sea Scrolls*, the *Nag Hammadhi Library* manuscripts, and other recently discovered gospels as the basis for much of their beliefs.

Although the Bible is not complete and its many inconsistencies about meat eating and vegetarianism require thoughtful interpretation, countless passages refer to vegetarianism. Many Christian scholars have concluded that vegetarianism is more consistent with the spirit of Christ's teachings. According to the Dead Sea Scrolls, discovered in 1946 in a place where the Essenes lived, the angel said to Mary: "You do not eat meat or drink strong drinks because the child will be consecrated to God from the womb of his mother." In the same text, Jesus says: "Be respectful and compassionate, not only to your likes but toward all creatures placed under your protection." Also of note is a passage where Jesus rebukes fishermen, saying: "Maybe the fish come to you to ask for the land and its fruits? Leave your nets and follow me, I will make you fishers of souls."

Christianity does not forbid any sort of food upon religious principle, so eating meat is neither encouraged nor discouraged. According to Canon Law, Roman Catholics are required to abstain from meat (defined as all animal flesh, but excluding water animals) as an act of penance on Ash Wednesday and all Fridays. Some monastic orders also follow a vegetarian diet, and members of the Orthodox Church follow a vegan diet during fasts.[21] The protestant Christian church of Seventh-day Adventists (who live an average of 10 years longer than the American life expectancy of about 79 years), are encouraged to engage in healthy eating practices. The General Conference of Seventh-day Adventists Nutrition Council (GCNC) recommends ovo-lacto-vegetarian diets (a vegetarian who does not eat animal flesh of any kind, but consumes dairy and egg products). They also have sponsored and participated in many scientific studies to explore the impact of dietary decisions upon health outcomes, and live one of the healthiest lifestyles of any community in the world.

The Enlightened Diet

AN ENLIGHTENED DIET IS ACTUALLY THE SIMPLEST, MOST BASIC FORM OF NUTRITION. IT'S COMPRISED OF WHOLE PLANT FOODS, WHICH ARE VEGETABLES, FRUITS, LEGUMES, WHOLE GRAINS, NUTS, AND SEEDS. IN THIS BOOK, WE HAVE PINPOINTED 33 OF THESE INCREDIBLE PLANTS FOR THEIR AMAZING PROPERTIES. BELIEVE US, NARROWING A LIST DOWN TO JUST 33 OF THE THOUSANDS OF FASCINATING AND EXTREMELY HEALING PLANTS ON PLANET EARTH IS QUITE A DIFFICULT TASK! *ALL* WHOLE FOODS—NOT JUST THE ONES IN THIS BOOK—ARE PACKED WITH LIFE-SAVING PROPERTIES, ANTIOXIDANTS, PHYTONUTRIENTS, MINERALS, VITAMINS, AND OTHER NUTRIENTS.

Mother Nature provides the richest sources of nutrients for humans and animals alike. We consider all plants to be superfoods, and they all contain the perfect combination of protectants for those who eat them. Not only are the oxygen, nitrogen, and water they provide essential, but, even more than that, *plants are responsible for the fact that life on Earth is possible*. It's incredible, when you think about it. Here's how it works: Oxygen generates reactive molecules, called free radicals, throughout all of the body's tissues. These free radicals are dangerous to the body's cells because they can damage essential molecules like DNA and the enzymes necessary for proper cell functions. Antioxidants capture these reactive free radicals and safely convert them back to normal. Although the body *does* produce antioxidant molecules on its own, they must work together with the antioxidants delivered through our diet, which come mainly from fruits and vegetables.

Antioxidants can be divided into several groups. In addition to the "classic" antioxidants vitamin C, vitamin E, and selenium, there is another group, which includes the carotenoids, such as beta-carotene, lycopene, lutein, and astaxanthin. Another subgroup comprises the flavonoids, which are found in most fruits. All of these antioxidants are molecules that plants use to protect themselves against environmental factors like solar radiation, heat, toxic chemicals, and molds. These antioxidants also protect all life on earth—including plants, animals, and humans—against the damaging effects of oxygen radicals, which are always formed in an oxygenated environment. Over eons of time, all forms of life evolved together and thus depend on each other for survival. Fruits and vegetables, both of which are especially rich in antioxidants, are absolutely necessary for the health of humans and animals.

A low-fat, whole-food, plant-based diet is based on on whole, unprocessed, or minimally processed plants. It consists of vegetables, fruits, tubers/

roots, whole grains, legumes, seeds, and nuts, and it excludes or minimizes animal-based foods such as meats (including chicken and fish), dairy products, and eggs, as well as refined flour, refined sugar, and oil. The Naked Food philosophy also excludes gluten and genetically modified foods.

fact that they are vegan. It may surprise you that vegan foods can also contain genetically modified ingredients, chemicals, refined sugars and flours, oils, and lots of sodium. In fact, some common processed potato chips, cookies, and cereals are vegan.

The goal of the plant-based lifestyle is to

> The goal of the plant-based lifestyle is to choose real, minimally processed, organic, animal-free foods.

Contrary to what many people think, plant-based eating doesn't consist solely of eating vegetables. Although lots of leafy greens—such as chard, kale, spinach, and cabbage—are essential nutrients, plant-based nutrition is not a raw-only diet, and should actually include a wide variety of all sorts of plant foods. It's important to understand that leafy greens are very poor foods in terms of obtaining calories (which we *need*). It is virtually impossible to get enough calories to form a sustainable diet from leafy vegetables alone. Trying to live solely on leafy vegetables is probably the most common reason people fail at the plant-based lifestyle. It's a sure-fire way to be left feeling hungry, which, over time, may result in decreased energy, feelings of deprivation, cravings, and even binges. These issues are not caused by switching to a plant-based diet in and of itself but, rather, from not eating *enough*.

Another misconception about healthy eating, whether it's a hundred-percent plant-based or not, is falling into the belief that organic processed products are inherently healthy. Organic ingredients are certainly ideal, but we must not base our purchasing-decisions on this factor alone. (We'll get into this in depth in the next section.) We also don't recommend vegan foods based solely on the

choose real, minimally processed, organic, animal-free foods. Our calorie sources become plant starches; our sweeteners become whole foods; and all of our nutrients, including protein, come from plants. In the United States and many other parts of the world, meals are built around meat as the main dish. In a plant-based diet, starchy foods become the superstars. You will be building your meals around plants that may be more commonly known as "side dishes." Tubers like potatoes and sweet potatoes; starchy vegetables like corn and peas; whole grains like brown rice, millet, quinoa, and buckwheat; and legumes like chickpeas, lentils, and all types of beans.

Common Questions

WHY ORGANIC?

Today's crops are heavily sprayed with a chemical concoction of synthesized pesticides, fungicides, herbicides, and fertilizers. Some of these chemicals are highly toxic to humans and have a very long half-life (the time it takes for the concentration of a substance in the body to decrease by half). DDT, for example, has been banned from use in the United States since 1972, yet this very dangerous pesticide is still showing up today in the placenta of birthing mothers. This is bad news, considering the fact that girls exposed to DDT before puberty are five times more likely to develop breast cancer in middle age, according to the President's Cancer Panel.[1] This is just one of the 85,000 chemicals we humans have created in the last 150 years that now pollutes our environment.

The practice of spraying crops with artificial chemicals upsets the balance of our natural ecosystem. Crops treated this way become increasingly dependent on artificial substances, which weakens the plant's natural growth and defense mechanisms. Organic crops use only natural methods and products that are harmless to humans and to the environment for fertilization, pest control, fungus control, and weed suppression. Unfortunately, because of several generations of unsustainable farming practices, the topsoil on most factory farms has been depleted of minerals. Most of the food that is mass-produced for commercial consumption is grown on three minerals: nitrogen, potassium, and phosphorus (NPK). These three nutrients are significant because they help the plants sprout up fast so that farmers can turn the quickest profit possible. The downside is that the iron, calcium, magnesium, zinc, copper, and every one of the other 92 minerals humans need for good health are missing. If they are missing from the soil, they will also be missing from the plants. And if they are missing from the plants, they will be missing from the human body.

Another problem is that plants that are fed high concentrations of nitrogen grow too quickly before they are harvested, and are not given the time necessary to soak in whatever few minerals may still be present in the soil. According to a UCLA study[2] conducted on the iron content of spinach, we would have to eat 43 bowls of spinach in 1997 to equal the iron in just 1 bowl from 1953. Not only was the spinach deficient in iron, but other minerals as well. When mineral levels are insufficient, the body cannot use the vitamins. The best organic farming practices focus on more sustainable growing methods, such as composting, crop rotation, rock dust, permaculture, and other approaches that all help restore and preserve the minerals in the soil and produce more mineral-rich crops.

Phytonutrients like chlorophyll, beta-carotene, and lycopene are natural defense substances that plants produce to help protect themselves from germs, fungi, bugs, and diseases found in nature. Organic fruits and vegetables have far more phytonutrients than nonorganic plants because nonorganic plants become dependent upon the artificial, chemically synthesized pesticides and fungicides. Consequently, the plants stop producing many of the antibodies they need to naturally combat these challenges. Phytonutrients are also very sensitive to heat and destroyed by the cooking process. Therefore fresh, ripe, raw, and organic whole fruits, vegetables, and sprouts are the best sources of these powerful immune system defenders.

When organic food isn't available, conventional whole foods can be scraped with a natural-fiber brush and washed with a homemade formula made of 1 part sea salt and 9 parts water. Natural fiber brushes can be found in natural health stores (we use a coconut fiber brush) and used for solid foods such as potatoes, eggplant, carrots, etc. The salt-water formula has been tested and proven to be as effective as apple cider vinegar, and more effective than commercially sold vegetable washes. Food should be rinsed and submerged in the salt-water formula. Be sure to rinse the food thoroughly with filtered water afterward to avoid salty-tasting food.

WHY GMO-FREE?

The practice of creating GMOs in food involves injecting the DNA of one species into the DNA of another species in an effort to develop certain characteristics. For example, the DNA of fungus, mold, bacteria, viruses, fish, humans, and jelly-fish have been injected into corn, potatoes, and strawberries in an effort to increase crop yields. Unfortunately, this genetic manipulation creates unintended consequences in our food, such as twisted proteins and carbohydrates, as well as toxins. GMOs have been linked to serious health challenges such as a weakened immune system, autoimmune diseases, food allergies, gastrointestinal problems, childhood learning disorders, leaky gut syndrome, autism, and cancer.

In 2009, The American Academy of Environmental Medicine (AAEM) released its position paper on Genetically Modified foods, stating that "GM foods pose a serious health risk" and calling for a moratorium on them. The paper cited several animal studies, and concluded, "there is more than a casual association between GM foods and adverse health effects" and that "GM foods pose a serious health risk in the areas of toxicology, allergy and immune function, reproductive health, and metabolic, physiologic, and genetic health."[3]

Twenty-six countries outside of the United States have already banned GMOs at least partially. But the most common GMO foods in the United States are conventional corn, soy, canola, sugar beets, Hawaiian papaya, zucchini, and yellow squash, as well as any processed products that contain any one of these foods. The best defense to avoid GMOs in the U.S. is to eat only organic food. According to the USDA, the use of GMOs is prohibited in organic products. This means that an organic farmer cannot plant GMO seeds, an organic cow cannot eat GMO alfalfa or corn, and an organic soup producer cannot use any GMO ingredients. To meet the USDA organic regulations, farmers and processors must show they aren't using GMOs and that they are protecting their products from contact with prohibited substances such as GMOs from farm to table.

When purchasing food, we recommend choosing certified organic foods and foods certified with the Non-GMO Project label as much as possible. Local produce farmers may also offer organic foods that are not certified organic but that are grown organically and honestly. The rigorous organic certification process can be discouraging for small farmers; however, knowing your farmer and where your food comes from can make the task of choosing sustainably grown food much easier.

WHY SALT-FREE?

Eighty percent of the salt consumed in Western diets is irreversibly intermingled with processed foods. Scientific research, and especially studies about the eating habits of specific populations, incriminates salt as the cause of many diseases. However, when people transition to a naturally low-sodium diet, free of cholesterol, refined flour, and sugar, they also decrease their sodium intake. The large amounts of sodium found in these foods are the real cause of our society's high-sodium levels.

Eating salt is not harmful or unhealthy when it's added in small amounts to otherwise healthful ingredients, like whole foods and plant starches. The basic ingredients of the Master Plants recipes are very low in sodium, so they will still be perfectly healthy with a sprinkle of salt added right before eating. During the actual cooking process, we recommend flavoring meals with miso, tamari, shoyu, spices, and herbs, instead of salt. When you *do* use salt, try a sea salt like pink Himalayan salt. A diet of whole plant starches, vegetables, and fruits can even counteract the negative effects of common salt. Plant foods are inherently low in sodium, chloride, and fat (with the exception of nuts, seeds, avocados, and coconut), and high in potassium.

Plants contain thousands of ingredients, some of which are identified and many others that have yet to be discovered, that keep blood pressure low, the blood vessels strong, and the body healthy. A basic diet of plant starches and whole foods with no added sodium provides less than 500 mg of

which is a major risk factor for declining kidney function. There is also increasing evidence that a high salt intake may increase deterioration of the kidneys in people already suffering from kidney problems. Sensitive people can develop swelling (edema) from salt, which is reported as swollen feet after a meal or on a long airplane ride. It has been suggested that consumption of salty foods causes stomach cancer (the second leading cause of cancer death worldwide); however, current

> Plants contain thousands of ingredients, some of which are identified and many others that have yet to be discovered, that keep blood pressure low, the blood vessels strong, and the body healthy.

sodium daily. Adding a half teaspoon of salt to the surface of your meals daily adds about 1,100 mg of sodium, making the total daily intake 1,600 mg, the recommended maximum daily intake.

Low-sodium diets allow our intestines to increase their sodium absorption and the kidneys to reduce the loss of sodium into the urine. Healthy bodies never mismanage this life-sustaining regulation. The human body removes unwanted fluid by filtering blood through the kidneys via osmosis to draw excess water out of the blood. Human kidneys efficiently conserve sodium and excrete potassium, although a high salt diet will alter this sodium balance, which causes the kidneys to have reduced functionality and to remove less water. The end result of this is higher blood pressure. This puts a strain on the kidneys and can lead to kidney disease.

Too much sodium has been blamed for causing hypertension, osteoporosis, kidney stones, and cancer. A high salt intake has also been shown to increase the amount of protein in the urine,

research does not support this belief.[4] Consumption of animal foods and lack of fruits and vegetables have been well established as the real cause of this cancer.[5, 6]

WHY OIL-FREE?

This is one of the most questioned elements of a plant-based diet. We've all heard that oils are healthful foods, and especially olive oil, canola, and coconut oils. We are aware that the Mediterranean diet in particular considers oils to be a healthy source of nutrients; however, olive oil is not a "health" food. Neither is coconut, grape seed, flaxseed, avocado, or any other oil you may have heard of.

The Mediterranean diet has been identified as a way of reducing the risk of cardiovascular disease; however, the benefits of the diet actually come from its legumes, whole grains, fruits, and vegetables, not from the oils.[7, 8] In fact, olive oil has been found to reduce blood flow in the arteries by 31%,[9] which is significant in terms of blood clots, heart attacks, and angina. Though, the issue of oil doesn't refer only to olive oil. Another study reports that other types of oils can also result in a significant and constant decrease of endothelial function for three hours after each meal, independent of the type of oil, and whether it is fresh or deep fried.[10] This is the same effect caused by smoking one cigarette. This endothelial layer is the thick lining of all of our blood vessels, and its function is to manufacture a protective molecule of gas called nitric

mote lung cancer. "Better" monounsaturated fats like olive oil may still lead to diseased arteries.

The rule of thumb is that highly concentrated fat just isn't healthy, whether it comes from a plant or any other source. All oils have a negative impact on blood vessels and promote heart disease.[11] Furthermore, they may also lead to increased bleeding by thinning the blood, negative effects on lung function and oxygen exchange, suppression of cer-

> Oil is nothing but fat—just a single tablespoon contains about 14 grams of fat—and it has more calories per gram than any other food.

oxide. Nitric oxide is vital for us because it protects the blood vessels, and keeps our blood flowing smoothly. Nitric oxide is the strongest dilator (widener) of our blood vessels, so when we exercise, for example, nitric oxide is doing its job by dilating the blood vessels so we get enough blood flow in our brain, lungs, heart, and organs.

Also, all vegetable-based oils, which pretty much follow the same model as processed sugar, are pressed from plants. All of the nutrients, including protein, carbohydrates, vitamins, minerals, fiber, and water, have been stripped away. Oil is nothing but fat—just a single tablespoon contains about 14 grams of fat—and it has more calories per gram than any other food.

Foods like olive oil that are rich in monounsaturated fats may be better than foods full of saturated and trans fats, but remember: Just because something is "better" doesn't mean it's good. Replacing some or all of the butter in our diet with vegetable oil will lower our cholesterol numbers, which is *better*, but it's still not *good* in either the short or long run. "Better" cigarettes (those with less nicotine and toxic chemicals like benzo(a)pyrenes) still pro-

tain immune system functions, and an increased risk of cancer.[12] Not to mention the fact that excess calories from fat get stored as fat, no matter what type of fat calories are consumed.

WHY SUGAR-FREE?

Back in the sixteenth century, Americans consumed about 4 pounds of sugar per person each year. By the 1800s, this number rose to 20 pounds, and by 1994 it had skyrocketed to 120 pounds. Today, we are closer to 160 pounds. Half of this can be attributed to processed sugar, which makes up about 10% of our diet.

Research suggests that sugar calories may be worse than just empty calories. A growing body of scientific evidence suggests that large enough amounts of sucrose and fructose in the form of table sugar and high fructose corn syrup can trigger processes that lead to liver toxicity and other chronic diseases. Much like alcohol, fructose corn syrup increases the fat in our liver and, subsequently, the risk for nonalcoholic fatty liver disease. The effect of fructose corn syrup in the liver is one of the most remarkable medical developments over the past 30 years, not only in America but also around the globe.

Let's talk about fructose for a second. Fructose is a simple sugar that occurs naturally in foods like honey, tree and vine fruits, flowers, berries, and most root vegetables. Fructose in fact is what gives fruit their sweet taste, however, it is important to differentiate the intake of fructose from a whole food, with the intake of fructose from a processed food. Just like we discussed before about oil, the problem with fructose starts when one of the properties or molecules of a plant is extracted from it to create a concentration of that single nutrient. Many commercially used plants such as corn and sugar beets are being genetically modified, which already brings the first issue, though, furthermore, the extraction of their fructose content is what becomes the concentrated sugar that gets added to most commercial foods. Fructose corn syrup is added to many processed foods and drinks to enhance their taste. This type of fructose is far from the same fructose that we find naturally in a berry, for example.

In the same way that excess fat or excess salt create health problems and imbalances, excessive fructose consumption causes insulin resistance, obesity, elevated LDL cholesterol and triglycerides, leading to metabolic syndrome, type 2 diabetes, and cardiovascular disease. Though here is the difference. Even the sweetest of fruits when eaten whole, has the adequate balance of nutrients and a molecular equilibrium that makes that food healthful.

Does this apply for diabetics who need to eat fruit? Yes, the same basic concept remains. A whole food, plant-based diet rich in vegetables, plant starches, and fruits is ideal for all of us, diabetic or not; fruit, in particular, is beneficial in almost any amount. To prove this, in a recent study, seventeen people were made to eat 20 servings a day of fruit. Despite the extraordinarily high fructose content of this diet (presumably about 200 grams per day, or the equivalent of 8 cans of soda), researchers reported no adverse effects on body weight, blood pressure, and insulin. Furthermore, lipid levels demonstrated an astounding 38-point drop in LDL cholesterol. The side effect found during the study, however, was that this amount of fruit combined with other whole vegetables resulted in the largest bowel movements ever documented in a dietary intervention.[13]

Rather than sugar, the Naked approach to eating uses whole foods like dates, figs, prunes, cranberries, and apples, to sweeten recipes. We stay away from processed sweeteners of all kinds. If this doesn't sound good to you, you might just be in for a treat. To add sweetness, try adding some whole dates to smoothies, desserts, and other dishes, and date paste (blended dates) or date sugar (dried dates pulverized into powder) as liquid sweeteners. We bet you'll be pleasantly surprised.

Getting Started

As you begin this journey (or delve further into it), you may have questions about your food sources, nutrient intake, approved ingredients, and the best way to prepare your food. Here are some helpful answers for some of the questions we hear most.

SOURCING FOOD

In an ideal world, we would all have a parcel of land where we could grow our food. We would know exactly what we are adding to it, the nutrient quality of our soil, and where our food came from. We would also have the advantage of eating all fresh foods, all of the time. If this describes your situation, fantastic! For the rest of us, the next best thing is our local farmer. Depending on where you live, you may have the ability to source local food quite easily. Most farmers prepare for weekend sales and have a regional or city venue where they gather . . . so find your local market, and get to know your farmer. Be aware that not all local farmers' markets source organic food, so make sure you let your farmer know that you want them. If we all create a demand for it, more and more organic foods will be grown. Even if not all farmers are currently able to switch over to organically grown foods, they will certainly start looking into it.

Even when living in urban environments, we can still grow at least some of our food. Start a windowsill box and pack it with fresh, fragrant herbs. You can even use this same windowsill strategy to grow delicious foods like pineapple, celery, ginger, and potatoes.

PROTEIN AND CALCIUM

Some of the most common questions about plant-based diets involves nutrient intake. Most people are particularly concerned about getting enough protein and calcium. We have been led to believe that protein is such an essential nutrient that we must actively pursue foods that contain high amounts of it, even when those foods, such as meat and dairy, compromise our health in many ways.

We have also been led to believe that only animal-based foods contain sufficient protein and, furthermore, that we *need* to eat those foods to avoid becoming protein deficient. The reality is that protein deficiency is almost exclusively seen in people suffering from a *calorie* deficiency. In this case, there will be an overall nutrient deficiency, not just a specific protein deficiency. If this happens, the concern should be getting more calories and *all* nutrients, and not just more protein.

As for how much protein we need, the answer is that we need the amount a diet of whole, plant-based foods provides. All whole, plant-based foods have protein. People thrive on plant-based diets without ever going out of their way to seek out protein sources. Think about it this way: We've evolved over millions of years without ever aiming for a "source" of protein or any other nutrient. Nonetheless, the mistaken notion that we need to go out of our way to consume certain individual nutrients is widespread, and protein is the nutrient most commonly identified as the one we have to hunt down.

With a diet based on fruits, vegetables, tubers, whole grains, and legumes, about 10% of total calorie intake comes from protein. This is to say, you shouldn't concern yourself with how much protein you're getting any more than you should worry about the perfect number of breaths to take per day. If you're worried that 10% isn't adequate, know there's evidence that consuming *too much* protein is harmful—especially when it comes from animal sources.

In terms of calcium, many believe it's important to get enough from excellent sources, especially milk and other dairy products. As with protein, it is *not* difficult to get enough calcium when eating whole, plant-based foods. Calcium, like iron, magnesium, and copper, is a mineral. It is found in the soil, where it is absorbed into the roots of plants. In fact, because it comes from the earth, it is abundant in *all* whole foods. Animals get their calcium by consuming mineral-abundant plants and metabolizing that calcium into their bodies.

There are two major contributing factors to the leaching of calcium from bones, which leads to their weakening and may increase the risk of osteoporosis. The first is consuming a highly acidic diet. Our bodies are alkaline. It is vital that the acidity level of our diet is not so high that our bones have to leach calcium to keep the body's alkaline levels balanced. The levels of acidic compounds in plant foods are lower so they won't draw the calcium from your bones the way animal foods will. Eating a whole-food, plant-based diet gives your body the acid/alkaline balance it needs for optimal bone health. The second factor is consuming a high-sodium diet. The diet we recommend is naturally low-sodium because it relies so little on processed foods, which tend to be very high in salt.

Once a certain threshold for calcium has been met (which, again, you *will* achieve by eating a whole-food, plant-based diet), the formula for strong bones relies on two other factors: First, that you get sufficient vitamin D from exposure to the sun. Vitamin D is a key factor in calcium absorption, and the sun is the best way to meet this requirement. The key is getting sufficient sun exposure on our bare skin without getting burned. The vitamin D found in milk is added to it, and we do not recommend getting vitamin D from milk or any other fortified foods in which the vitamin does not naturally occur. The second factor in having strong bones is that you practice strength training and impact exercise. When you lift weights or do resistance exercises, not only do you build muscle, but you also stress your bones, which makes them stronger. Walking, jogging, and running are examples of impact exercises that will also help with bone strength.

As with protein, many will suggest the need to consume a specific amount of calcium per day for strong bones; however, good bone health has nothing to do with achieving an arbitrary amount of calcium. This only leads to a reduction-ist approach whereby individuals target specific nutrients. Following a sustainable way of eating inherently includes receiving the right amount of *all* nutrients.

FISH

Not surprisingly, many people don't consider fish to be "meat." They have a perception that fish flesh is not as unhealthy as the flesh of a mammal or bird. Much of this perception comes from study after study that has found fish to be "heart healthy" or "good for our brains." Most of this data has been misinterpreted and faulty conclusions have been drawn from otherwise reasonable research.

The levels of acidic compounds in plant foods are lower so they won't draw the calcium from your bones the way animal foods will.

The frequently referenced studies of Okinawan and Mediterranean populations have followed this pattern. The benefits of diets that are also high in fruits, vegetables, and whole grains are frequently credited to small amounts of fish, much like they are often credited to olive oil and wine. In the case of the famous Okinawan Centenarian Study, for example, only 1% of calories consumed by the residents came from fish; 69% of the diet came from sweet potatoes.[1] Yet the perception from this very study is that Okinawans are healthy as the result of a fish-heavy diet.

The problem here is that meaningful long-term studies are pored over by individuals or organizations who are often selecting data to reinforce a specific agenda. As Dr. John McDougall says, "A muscle is a muscle, whether it comes from a chicken, cow, or fish." In other words, the nutrient profile of all animal products, (i.e., high in fat, acid, and cholesterol, and low in fiber and carbohydrates) is as true for fish as it is for beef and other meats. In fact, although fish are often marketed as a wise, heart-healthy food choice, they have as much cholesterol as beef, chicken, and pork.

Ideally, 1 to 3 percent of your calories should come from the essential fats. Adequate omega-3 intake is 1.1g for adult women and 1.6g for adult men.[3] That's ¼ to ⅓ teaspoon per day. If you meet all of your caloric needs with a low-fat, whole-foods diet full of fruits, vegetables, whole grains, and

> The nutrients in whole foods work together much like a symphony; extract and consume those nutrients apart from the whole and their effects are compromised.

OMEGA-3 FATTY ACIDS

Every whole plant food has fat, and there's no evidence that we need any more fat than that which occurs naturally in a low-fat, whole-food, plant-based diet. Just as is the case with protein and calcium, you should not target specific foods to get enough of a particular kind of fat. Omega-3 and omega-6 fatty acids appear to be involved in a variety of important bodily functions, including cell membrane stabilization, nervous system function, immune system function, and blood clotting, as well as impacting triglyceride levels, blood pressure, inflammation, cancer, and heart disease. Although they are both essential in general, these two essential fatty acids should be consumed in a healthy ratio to one another. Omega-6 fats are found mostly in animal and processed foods, and excess consumption of it impairs the absorption of omega-3.[2] The solution, however, is not simply to eat more omega-3 fats. The answer is to eliminate or minimize processed and animal-based foods and, instead, eat a whole-food, plant-based diet, which restores a healthy omega-6 to omega-3 balance and, more importantly, leads to positive health outcomes.

legumes, you will easily consume enough essential fatty acids, *and* those fatty acids will be in good balance with one another. Nuts and seeds are whole plant foods with higher concentrations of essential fatty acids, although there's no evidence that we actually need to eat these foods to get the proper amount of any kind of fat. Most whole plant foods have small amounts of essential fats. Over the course of a day full of these foods, we will achieve the necessary amounts, which aren't that much to begin with. In fact, it is significantly more important to worry about *not* consuming excess fat than it is to worry about consuming sufficient omega-3.

SUPPLEMENTS

As T. Colin Campbell, PhD, describes it, when it comes to nutrition, the whole is greater than the sum of its individual parts. The nutrients in whole foods work together much like a symphony; extract and consume those nutrients apart from the whole and their effects are compromised. The relationship between whole food and the human body is very intricate and has come about as a result of millions of years of evolution. Our food contains countless nutrients and substances that lead to thousands of metabolic reactions when consumed.

The hardworking supplement industry has not been able to produce beneficial products, despite decades of effort and billions of dollars. With the *exception of vitamin B12* and unless a specific deficiency arises that cannot be corrected with whole, plant-based foods, this is the only supplement you will need (see the next section for more information on B12). It has been demonstrated that, in general, supplements do not offer any benefits. On the contrary, they may cause harm.[4] A review of twenty-four randomized controlled trials showed "no consistent evidence that the vitamin and mineral supplements affected cardiovascular disease, cancer, or other causes of mortality in healthy individuals."[5] Single-vitamin supplements have shown similarly negative results. For example, vitamin A, beta-carotene, and vitamin E, while all healthy when consumed in food, have been shown to significantly increase death when consumed as supplements.[6]

In the event we need a particular nutrient, that doesn't mean we need a high dose of it or that we should consume it separately from all the other nutrients and substances it's designed to work with. The best way to achieve a complete and safe amount of nutrients is by eating whole foods.

VITAMIN B12

As for that one supplement we *do* need: Vitamin B12 is important for the development and protection of nerve cells and red blood cells and helps in the production of DNA. Insufficient B12 can lead to many health issues, including weakness, fatigue, difficulty concentrating, increased irritability, gastrointestinal distress, anemia, and nervous system dysfunction. B12 is the one nutrient that cannot be sufficiently obtained from today's plant-based diet. Animal products themselves don't always contain enough B12[7] because *neither plants nor animals naturally synthesize B12*. It is made from bacteria. Animals consume dirt, which is full of bacteria, through the unwashed plants and non-chlorinated water they consume. B12 accumulates in the animals' tissues, which becomes a source of the vitamins for humans when they eat the animal.

We humans, on the other hand, rarely eat anything unwashed. We remove the dirt that contains B12-producing bacteria from our foods. There is enough research about B12 that shows, when taken appropriately, it is beneficial.

ORGANIC, GRASS-FED ANIMAL PRODUCTS

The nutrient makeup of animal foods (high in fat and cholesterol, low in fiber and antioxidants) is the main reason that consuming them will increase your chances of getting chronic diseases like heart disease and type 2 diabetes. This nutrient profile exists whether animal foods are organic or grass-fed. Replacing animal foods with whole plant-based foods is a significant change that will greatly improve your chances of achieving good health, whereas the change between organic and conventional animal foods is relatively small and unlikely to make much of a difference.

The Shopping List

A balanced plant-based diet should include a wide range of vegetables, fruits, whole grains, herbs, seeds, nuts, legumes, spices, roots and tubers, fungi, and sea vegetables. Plant foods should include a variety of the following:

VEGETABLES

- Artichoke
- Arugula
- Asparagus
- Bok Choy
- Broccoli
- Brussels Sprouts
- Cabbage
- Cauliflower
- Celery
- Chard
- Collard Greens
- Eggplant
- Endive
- Kale
- Lettuce
- Mustard Greens
- Okra
- Parsley
- Radicchio
- Rhubarb
- Spinach
- Water Chestnut
- Watercress
- Wheatgrass

LEGUMES

- Alfalfa Sprouts
- Adzuki Beans
- Bean Sprouts
- Black Beans
- Black-Eyed Peas
- Chickpeas (Garbanzos)
- Green Beans
- Kidney Beans
- Lentils
- Lima Beans
- Navy Beans
- Pinto Beans
- Soy Beans
- Peas

WHOLE GRAINS
*(*Gluten-free whole grains)*

- Amaranth*
- Barley
- Bulgur
- Corn*
- Kamut
- Millet*
- Gluten-free Oats*
- Brown Rice*
- Rye
- Sorghum/Milo*
- Spelt, Teff*
- Whole Wheat
- Wild Rice*

FRUITS

- Acorn Squash
- Apple
- Apricot
- Avocado
- Banana
- Banana Squash
- Blackberry
- Blackcurrant
- Blueberry
- Butternut Squash
- Cantaloupe
- Cherry
- Chili Pepper/Capsicum
- Clementine
- Cucumber
- Date
- Dragonfruit
- Eggplant
- Gem Squash
- Goji Berry
- Grape
- Grapefruit
- Green Pepper
- Guava
- Honeydew Melon
- Jackfruit
- Kiwi Fruit
- Lemon
- Lime
- Lychee
- Mandarin
- Mango
- Melon
- Nectarine
- Orange
- Peach
- Pear
- Pepper
- Physalis/Tomatillo
- Pineapple
- Pitaya
- Plum/Prune (dried plum)
- Pomegranate
- Pumpkin
- Raisin
- Raspberry
- Red Pepper/Bell Pepper/Pimento
- Rock Melon
- Squash
- Soursop
- Spaghetti Squash
- Squash
- Star Fruit
- Strawberry
- Tangerine
- Tomato
- Watermelon
- Yellow Pepper
- Zucchini

ROOTS AND TUBERS

- ○ Beet
- ○ Carrot
- ○ Chives
- ○ Garlic
- ○ Ginger
- ○ Green Onion/Scallion
- ○ Horseradish
- ○ Jicama
- ○ Jerusalem Artichoke
- ○ Leek
- ○ Maca
- ○ Onion
- ○ Potato
- ○ Parsnip
- ○ Radish
- ○ Shallot
- ○ Sweet Potato
- ○ Turnip
- ○ Yam

HERBS AND SPICES

- ○ Allspice
- ○ Anise
- ○ Basil
- ○ Bay Leaf
- ○ Cayenne
- ○ Celery Seed
- ○ Chamomile
- ○ Chili powder
- ○ Cilantro
- ○ Cinnamon
- ○ Cloves
- ○ Coriander
- ○ Crushed Red Pepper
- ○ Cumin
- ○ Curry Powder
- ○ Dill
- ○ Dry Mustard
- ○ Fennel
- ○ Lemon Grass
- ○ Nutmeg
- ○ Oregano
- ○ Paprika
- ○ Parsley
- ○ Rosemary
- ○ Sage
- ○ Tarragon
- ○ Thyme
- ○ Turmeric
- ○ Vanilla

NUTS AND SEEDS

- ○ Almond
- ○ Brazil Nut
- ○ Buckwheat
- ○ Cacao
- ○ Cashew
- ○ Chestnut
- ○ Chia
- ○ Coconut
- ○ Flax
- ○ Hazelnut
- ○ Hemp
- ○ Macadamia
- ○ Pine Nut
- ○ Pistachio
- ○ Pumpkin
- ○ Quinoa
- ○ Sesame
- ○ Sunflower
- ○ Walnut

FUNGI

- ○ All edible varieties of mushrooms, including, but not limited to Button, Crimini, Oyster, Porcini, Portabello, Shiitake, and Wood Ear

SEA VEGETABLES

- ○ Chlorella
- ○ Dulse
- ○ Kelp
- ○ Kombu
- ○ Nori
- ○ Spirulina
- ○ Wakame

Plant-Based Substitutions for Common Foods

MILK SUBSTITUTES

Opt for unsweetened non-dairy milks such as rice, oat, hemp, nut, and grain milks. Coconut milk is also acceptable, but because of its fat content, it should be used sparingly.

SUGAR SUBSTITUTES

Use fresh fruit as natural sweetener, or dried fruit such as dates, figs, cranberries, apricots, prunes, and raisins. For liquid sweeteners, use organic date paste (see Essential Recipes, page 257) or 100% pure maple syrup.

OIL SUBSTITUTES

Baking without oil: Replace the oil called for in the recipe with half the amount of another moist food, such as applesauce, mashed bananas, mashed potatoes, mashed pumpkin, or tomato sauce.

Sautéing without oil: Replace the oil with vegetable broth, water, apple cider, sherry, rice vinegar, white or red wine, or lemon juice.

PASTA SUBSTITUTES

Use gluten-free, whole grain quinoa, buckwheat, rice, and plant-based varieties free of gluten. Whole foods such as carrots, zucchini, and squash also make great raw or cooked pasta substitutes.

EGG SUBSTITUTES

Baking without eggs:
- 1 egg equals ½ banana, or ¼ puréed fruit
- 1 egg equals 1 tablespoon ground flaxseed + 3 tablespoons water
- 1 egg equals 1 teaspoon ground chia seeds + 3 tablespoons water

Cooking without eggs: For quiche, non-egg scrambles, and frittatas, use organic, non-GMO soft tofu.

MEAT SUBSTITUTES
(Tofu, Seitan, and Tempeh)
Both tofu and tempeh are soybean-based; therefore, if used, they should come from organic and non-GMO sources. These are both high in protein, omega-3s, iron, and fiber. Seitan is made of wheat protein, or gluten, so it should be avoided if you are gluten intolerant.

CHEESE SUBSTITUTES

Nuts and seeds make great cheese alternatives. Sunflower and pumpkin seeds, as well as cashews, pine nuts, macadamia, or almond nuts blended with onion, garlic, miso, soy sauce, herbs, legumes, and cooked potatoes can satisfy any cheese craving.

Nutritional yeast is yeast that is cultured from molasses and sugar cane. It is also a good source of B12 and protein, and can be used as a cheese-flavoring ingredient.

SALT SUBSTITUTES

Low-sodium, non-GMO miso paste and rice miso, salt-free seasoning, shoyu, and tamari, are good salt alternatives for a wide variety of recipes.

Supplements

- *Vitamin B12:* The recommended dosage of vitamin B12 is 2,500 mcg of cyanocobalamin once per week, ideally as a chewable, sublingual, or liquid supplement. The daily recommendation is 250mcg.

- *Vitamin D:* The recommended dosage is exposure to sunlight for 25-30 minutes daily, or a daily vitamin D3 supplement made from Cholecalciferol.

Kitchen Essentials

❶ LARGE KITCHEN TOOLS

Besides the usual refrigerator and oven/stove, you will need:

- *High-powered Blender:* We recommend the brands Vitamix® and Blendtec®. For a less expensive option, we recommend the Ninja® brand.

- *Food Processor:* According to the brand manufacturers, these are BPA, PVC, Phthalate-free: Dex Products® Baby Food Processor, Vitamix® Professional, Vortex® Blender Manual Blender, DeLonghi® Food Processor, and Philips® Food Processor.

- *Dehydrator:* We recommend Excalibur®. It's great for drying fruits and veggies.

- *Ice Cream Maker:* We usually make our ice cream by using silicone molds and storing them in the freezer. However, we also use the Yonana® Ice Cream Maker, which we use with frozen fruit.

- *Crock Pot/Slow Cooker:* As an option, you may prefer to get a slow cooker to cook grains and vegetables in low temperatures. Hamilton Beach® offers lead-free slow cookers.

- *Water Filter:* There are many available in the market, although we recommend ones that are metal and plastic free, PBA and lead-free.

❷ COOKWARE

Use non-stick, Teflon®-free and chemical-free cookware. Acceptable cookware materials include glass, non-stick coated pans and bake ware, silicone-coated bake ware, solid silicone bake ware, and ceramic.

- Ceramic cookware is ideal. We recommend ceramic skillets such as Xtrema® Cookware and Le Creuset®. There are many other good brands for more affordable prices; however, we recommend buying only one or two pieces at a time if cost is an issue. It is considerably better to get one good ceramic pot or pan than compromising with a full set of a toxic brand.

- Iron, aluminum, copper, and any other metal cookware should be avoided.

- Use parchment paper sheets or silicone mats such as Silpat® in between cooking trays and food, unless you are using silicone, ceramic, or glass. Avoid contact between food and aluminum foil. All soft and heavy metal cooking or kitchen storage materials should be avoided.

- Glass- or silicone-based baking dishes are great for everyday cooking and baking.

- We do not recommend using a microwave at all. Although cooking more quickly is time-efficient, microwave ovens are not healthy. Take a couple of minutes and reheat your food in the stove or oven.

A few general tips on cookware:

- If your nonstick coating is chipped, scratched, or damaged you must dispose of it immediately.

- Never use metal utensils with your cookware.

- Never use steel wool to clean the non-stick coating. Use sponges, and let the cookware soak in water to loosen burnt food.

- Don't exceed temperatures of 450°F, as this could cause the coating to break down.

- When storing cookware, do not pile them on top of each other as this could damage the coating.

❸ SMALL KITCHEN TOOLS

You will need:

- A set of quality knives

- A julienne peeler

- A mandoline slicer to grate, slice, or cut

- Bamboo cutting boards

- Bamboo or silicone cooking utensils

- A fermentation crock

- A spiralizer for making vegetable and fruit noodles and a variety of creative slices

❹ JARS

We use jars for everything, so they have a category of their own. We use them for storage, drinking glasses, fermenting things like beet kvass, water kefir, and salsa, as well as for second ferments of kombucha. We love glass jars and have a collection of sorts in our kitchen:

- Quart-size and pint-size mason jars: Use for drinking glasses, storing food in the fridge, packing salads and foods for lunch, etc.

- Silicone or BPA-free lids: Convert mason jars into drinking cups for hot or cold beverages.

- Sprouting lids for mason jars: Great for covering open ferments.

- Storage jars with glass lids.

- BPA-free plastic bags for occasional food storage.

❺ OTHER ITEMS

- Cheesecloth for nut milks. You can also use a teakettle filter to drain the pulp.

- Cloth napkins

- Bamboo or silicone bowls for mixing and serving

- Glass containers

- Silicone mitts

Keeping Your Kitchen Sustainable

When recycling old cookware, keep in mind that most recycling programs do not accept china or ceramic plates and bowls. The most sustainable way to get rid of old crockery is to simply donate it to a thrift store, charity, or friend in need.

recent study estimates an average of about eight million tons of plastic—including everything from water bottles to garbage bags to food packaging—is improperly disposed of every year. The amount of debris in the Great Pacific Garbage Patch has accumulated because much of it is not biodegradable. For instance, many plastics do not wear down; they simply break into tinier and tinier pieces.

> The most sustainable way to get rid of old crockery is to simply donate it to a thrift store, charity, or friend in need.

Metal pots, pans, and flatware can be recycled if your program accepts "scrap metal," but these items are usually not collected at the curb. Pans lined with Teflon or another non-stick compound are usually not recyclable.

When recycling old knives, make sure to cover them in cardboard and write "SHARP" on the outside so sanitation workers are not injured.

Plastic kitchen tools, cookware, plates, utensils, or glasses should not be used, and should be discarded properly. Remember that one of the biggest problems in our oceans is the amount of discarded plastic we have tossed into it over the years. A

When discarding plastic cartons, jars, and containers: Before dumping anything into the recycling bin, mosey over to your state or municipality's website to scope out which varieties of plastics are acceptable. The Plastics Industry Trade Association created the "Resin Identification Code" system, in which numbers one through seven identify grades of plastic. Look on the bottom of any container for the number inside the triangular recycling symbol to know whether it will be accepted for recycling in your area. Some places may not accept certain recycling numbers, so be sure to check the piece before recycling.

THE MASTER PLANTS

"Let food be thy medicine and medicine be thy food."
—Hippocrates, c. 460– c. 370 BCE

BEFORE TODAY'S PHARMACEUTICALS, THERE WERE THE ANCIENT MASTER PLANTS: VEGETABLES, FRUITS, LEGUMES, NUTS, SEEDS, AND GRAINS THAT NOURISHED AND STRENGTHENED CIVILIZATIONS FOR THOUSANDS OF YEARS. ALTHOUGH LITTLE WAS KNOWN AT THAT TIME ABOUT VITAMINS, MINERALS, OR ANTIOXIDANTS, THE ANCIENT PEOPLES KNEW WHICH EDIBLE PLANTS TO USE TO PREVENT AND HEAL DIFFERENT AILMENTS. WHAT IF WE LOOKED BACK TO THE WISDOM OF THOSE ANCIENT CIVILIZATIONS AND THE USE OF THE MASTER PLANTS TO HELP HEAL US? WE PINPOINTED 33 OF THESE ANCIENT FOODS THAT CAN REAP THE MOST BENEFITS, WHICH ARE DETAILED IN THE PAGES TO COME.

ARUGULA

ERUCA SATIVA is an edible annual plant, commonly known as salad rocket, rucola, rucoli, rugula, colewort, roquette and, in the United States, arugula.

ANCIENT HISTORY

Grown as an edible herb in the Mediterranean area since Roman times, arugula was celebrated as an aphrodisiac, most famously in a poem long ascribed to Virgil. This reputation may have been why it was forbidden to grow rocket in monasteries during the Middle Ages. In 802, however a decree by Charlemagne made arugulaone of the pot herbs suitable for growing in gardens. Gillian Reilly, author of the *Oxford Companion to Italian Food*, states that because of its reputation as a sexual stimulant, it was "prudently mixed with lettuce, which was the opposite."

BENEFITS

- It is a rich source of certain phytochemicals such as indoles, thiocyanates, sulforaphane, and iso-thiocyanates. Together, these compounds have been found to counter carcinogenic effects of estrogen and thus help protect against prostate, breast, cervical, colon, and ovarian cancers by virtue of their cancer-cell growth inhibition and cytotoxic effects on cancer cells.

- In addition, di-indolyl-methane (DIM), a lipid soluble metabolite, has immune modulator, anti-bacterial, and anti-viral properties DIM has been used to treat recurring respiratory papillomatosis caused by the Human Papilloma Virus (HPV) and is in Phase III clinical trials for cervical dysplasia.

- 100 g (3½ ounces) fresh leaves contain 1424 micrograms (mcg) of beta-carotene, and 2373 IU of vitamin A. Carotenes convert into vitamin A in the body, which help protect from skin, lung, and oral cavity cancers.

- 100 g of fresh greens contain 97 mcg or 24% of the recommended daily amount (RDA) of folic acid. When given to anticipant mothers around the time of conception, folate can help prevent neural tube defects in the newborns.

- 100 g provides about 90% of RDA of Vitamin C. Promotes osteotrophic (bone formation and strengthening) activity. It also limits neuronal damage in the brain, an important role in the treatment of Alzheimer's patients.

NUTRIENTS
(per 1 cup)

Vitamin A ······· 24 mcg RAE

Vitamin A ············· 474 IU

Beta Carotene····· 284 mcg

Vitamin K··········· 21.8 mcg

Lutein + Zeaxanthin ···711 mcg

Calcium ················ 32 mg

Phosphorous ········10.4 mg

Potassium·············7.4 mg

ASPARAGUS

ASPARAGUS OFFICINALIS is a spring vegetable; a flowering perennial plant species in the genus **ASPARAGUS**. It is native to most of Europe, northern Africa, and western Asia, and is widely cultivated as a vegetable crop.

ANCIENT HISTORY

A distant cousin of the onion, its history goes back as far as that of the leek and has been consumed for over 2,000 years. This garden plant originated in the eastern Mediterranean countries, and traces of wild varieties have been discovered in Africa. Archaeologists believe that it also was cultivated in Egypt. In ancient Greece, asparagus was considered to be an aphrodisiac, as well as a medicine to cure certain afflictions.

Hippocrates used it to treat diarrhea and pains of the urethra. This plant, in fact, contains asparagine, which is known for it diuretic properties. The Romans, in contrast, seemed to just appreciate asparagus' pure deliciousness, as they often ate it as an entrée or as a vegetable accompanying fish.

Starting in the 16th century, asparagus was served in the royal courts of Europe, and in the 17th century it was cultivated in France for Louis XIV who was so fond of this delicacy that he had special greenhouses built so that he could enjoy aspargus throughout the year. It wasn't until the 18th century that asparagus was made available in the local marketplaces.

BENEFITS

- Fresh asparagus spears are a good source of anti-oxidants such as lutein, zea-xanthin, carotenes, and crypto-xanthins. Together, these flavonoid compounds help remove harmful oxidant free radicals from the body, protecting it from possible cancer, neuro-degenerative diseases, and viral infections.

- The shoots are also rich in B-complex groups of vitamins such as thiamin, riboflavin, niacin, vitamin B6 (pyridoxine), and pantothenic acid. These groups of vitamins are essential for optimum cellular enzymatic and metabolic functions.

- Asparagus is rich in minerals, especially copper and iron. In addition, it has small amounts of some other essential minerals and electrolytes such as calcium, potassium, manganese, and phosphorus.

- 100 g provide 2.1 g of fiber, which helps control constipation conditions, decrease (LDL) cholesterol levels by binding to it in the intestines, and regulate blood sugar levels.

- 100 g of spears provide about 54 mcg or 14% of RDA of folic acid. Folates are one of the important co-factors for DNA synthesis inside the cell.

- Asparagus have long been used to treat conditions like dropsy and irritable bowel syndrome.

NUTRIENTS
(per 1 cup)

Folate ················· 70 mcg

Phosphorus ············· 70 mg

Potassium ············· 271 mg

Beta Carotene ······ 602 mcg

Lutein +
Zeazanthin ······· 951 mcg

Choline ··············· 21.4 mg

Vitamin C ············· 7.5 mg

Vitamin K ············· 55.7 mcg

AVOCADO

PERSEA AMERICANA, or the avocado, is believed to have originated in Mexico, around 10,000 BCE, though fossil evidence suggests similar species were much more widespread millions of years ago, occurring as far north as California at a time when the climate of that region was more hospitable to them.

ANCIENT HISTORY

Ancient Aztec civilization thought the avocado was a powerful symbol of fertility and offered the fruit to the dead as a gift in the afterlife. In the native tongue of the Aztecs, the name for avocado translates to "testicle." When the Spanish conquered the Aztecs, they brought avocado to the rest of the world, promoting it as a rare a fruit, with a pleasant buttery taste that strengthened the body with lust.

BENEFITS*

- Avocados offer nearly 20 vitamins and minerals in every serving, including potassium, lutein, folate, and plenty of fiber.

- 100g (3.5 ounce) serving contains 14% of the RDA of potassium, compared to 10% in bananas, which are a typical high-potassium food. High potassium intake is linked to reduced blood pressure.

- A 100g (3.5 ounce) serving of avocado contains 7 grams of fiber, which is 27% of the recommended daily amount.

- Avocados are high in monounsaturated fat. HDL cholesterol helps lower LDL (bad cholesterol), when consumed in moderation.

Doctor's Note: The consumption of some nuts and avocado are acceptable for people with no heart disease who are able to achieve a cholesterol of 150 and LDL of 80 or under, without cholesterol-lowering drugs.

NUTRIENTS
(per 1 avocado)

Protein · · · · · · · · · · · · · · · · · 4 g

Total Fat · · · · · · · · · · · · 29.47 g

Fiber · · · · · · · · · · · · · · · · 13.5 g

Omega-3 · · · · · · · · · · · · 221 mg

BEET

BETA VULGARIS is grown for their edible taproots and their greens. These varieties have been classified as *B. Vulgaris* a subspecies of the **VULGARIS CONDITIVA** group.

ANCIENT HISTORY

The wild beet, the ancestor of the beet with which we are familiar today, is thought to have originated in prehistoric times in North Africa and grew wild along Asian and European seashores. In these earlier times, people exclusively ate the beet greens and not the roots.

In ancient times, beet leaves were used to cure fever and constipation, though the ancient Romans were one of the first civilizations to cultivate beets to use their roots as food and as medicine. Both white and black beet roots were used as curative broths to treat fevers and other ailments. The tribes that invaded Rome were responsible for spreading beets throughout northern Europe, where they were first used for animal fodder and later for human consumption, becoming more popular in the 16th century.

BENEFITS

- Beets are a unique source of phytonutrients called betalains, which have been shown to provide antioxidant, anti-inflammatory, and detoxification support.

- The betalin pigments in beets support the body's Phase 2 detoxification process, which occurs when broken-down toxins are bound to other molecules to be excreted from the body. Traditionally, beets are valued for their support in detoxification and helping to purify the blood and liver.

- Beets are known to lower blood pressure, boost stamina, and protect from various forms of cancer. Beet greens actually have more iron than spinach as well as a higher nutritional value overall than the beetroot itself. Beets are high in immune-boosting vitamin C, fiber, and potassium (essential for healthy nerve and muscle function), and high in manganese (beneficial for bones, liver, kidneys, and pancreas).

- Nitrates in beets are converted into nitric oxide in the body, which in turn helps to relax and dilate blood vessels, improving blood flow and lowering blood pressure.

- Beet greens boost bone strength, help fight Alzheimer's disease, and stimulate the production of antibodies and white blood cells.

NUTRIENTS

(for beetroot) (per 1 cup)

Potassium········518.50 mg   Magnesium········39.10 mg   Protein················2.86 g

Phosphorus·······64.60 mg   Calcium·············27.20 mg   Beta-Carotene·····35.70 mcg

BELL PEPPER

CAPSICUM ANNUUM is a cultivar group of plants that produce fruits in different colors, including red, yellow, orange, green, chocolate/brown, vanilla/white, and purple. Bell peppers are sometimes grouped with less pungent pepper varieties as "sweet peppers." Peppers are native to Mexico, Central America, and northern South America.

ANCIENT HISTORY

Bell peppers have been cultivated for more than 9,000 years, with the earliest cultivation having taken place in South and Central America. But it was Christopher Columbus who introduced peppers to Europe. This was sort of a "happy accident," as Columbus had mistaken the pepper plants for the plants that produce peppercorns. Today, though bell peppers are botanically fruits, they are generally considered in culinary contexts to be vegetables.

BENEFITS

- Capsicum peppers are rich sources of antioxidants and vitamin C. Compared to green peppers, red peppers have more vitamins and nutrients. The level of carotene, like lycopene, is nine times higher in red peppers. Red peppers have twice the vitamin C content of green peppers.

- A cup of chopped peppers of any color provides more than 100% of the daily value of the antioxidant vitamin C, which supports tissue health and immunity. Green bell peppers provide 551 international units, IU, of vitamin A, per 149 g, or 1 cup chopped. Red bell peppers are higher in this vitamin, which is essential to healthy eyesight, with 4,666 IU; almost a day's worth, based on a 2,000-calorie diet.

- Lycopene, the nutrient that gives red bell peppers their color, helps fight free radicals acquired from natural exposure to environmental toxins, and helps prevent certain types of cancer, especially prostate cancer.

- One cup of green pepper contains 261 mg of potassium, while red and yellow varieties offer more than 300 mg per cup. Bell peppers provide 3 g of fiber per cup, which can help regulate digestion and cholesterol levels.

- One cup of chopped pepper contains between 30 and 40 calories. Peppers offer a sweet flavor and satisfying crunch, which makes them a good substitute for high-calorie chips in dips such as hummus or salsa.

NUTRIENTS
(per 1 cup)

GREEN PEPPER, RAW

Vitamin A · · · · · · · · · · · · 551 IU

Vitamin C · · · · · · · · · · · · 120 mg

Vitamin B6 · · · · · · · · · · 0.3 mg

Iron · · · · · · · · · · · · · · · · 0.5 mg

Magnesium · · · · · · · · · 14.9 mg

Phosphorus · · · · · · · · · 29.8 mg

Potassium · · · · · · · · · · · 261 mg

Manganese · · · · · · · · · · 0.2 mg

RED PEPPER, RAW

Vitamin A · · · · · · · · · · · 4666 IU

Vitamin C · · · · · · · · · · · · 190 mg

Vitamin E · · · · · · · · · · · · 2.4 mg

Vitamin K · · · · · · · · · · · 7.3 mcg

Riboflavin · · · · · · · · · · · 0.1 mg

Niacin · · · · · · · · · · · · · · · 1.5 mg

Vitamin B6 · · · · · · · · · · 0.4 mg

Folate · · · · · · · · · · · · 68.5 mcg

YELLOW PEPPER, RAW

Vitamin A · · · · · · · · · · · · 372 IU

Vitamin C · · · · · · · · · · · · 341 mg

Vitamin B6 · · · · · · · · · · 0.3 mg

Folate · · · · · · · · · · · · 48.4 mcg

Calcium · · · · · · · · · · · · 20.5 mg

Potassium · · · · · · · · · · · 394 mg

Copper · · · · · · · · · · · · · · 0.2 mg

Manganese · · · · · · · · · · 0.2 mg

BLUEBERRY

CYANOCOCCUS are perennial flowering plants with indigo-colored berries within the genus **VACCINIUM**, a genus that also includes cranberries and bilberries. They are native to North America, but were introduced into Europe in the 1930s.

ANCIENT HISTORY

The American Indian held the wild blueberry in very high esteem, due to the fact that the blossom end of each blueberry forms a five-pointed star. It was believed the "Great Spirit" sent these star berries to relieve the hunger of children during a famine. Indians also used blueberries for medicinal purposes and made a strong aromatic tea from the root. It was used as a relaxant during childbirth. Blueberry juice was used for "old coughs" and tea made from wild blueberry leaves was believed to be a good tonic to help purify the blood.

BENEFITS

- Blueberries contain resveratrol, which reduces damage from over-exposure to the sun, and can naturally darken the skin. They also help prevent macular degeneration and improve vision.

- Being a natural source of soluble and insoluble fiber, blueberries can help regulate the gastrointestinal track by eating just a couple of handfuls a day.

- Blueberry health benefits have also been shown to lower LDL cholesterol, raise HDL cholesterol, and lower blood pressure.

NUTRIENTS

(per 1 cup)

Beta Carotene ······ 47.4 mcg	Choline ················· 8.9 mg	Copper ················· 0.1 mg
Vitamin C ············· 14.4 mg	Calcium ··············· 8.9 mg	Manganese ·········· 0.5 mg
Vitamin K ··········· 28.6 mcg	Potassium ············ 114 mg	

BRAZIL NUT

BERTHOLLETIA EXCELSA is a South American tree in the family Lecythidaceae. Indigenous names include **JUVIA** in the Orinoco area. Despite their name, the most significant exporter of Brazil nuts is not Brazil but Bolivia, where they are called **NUEZ DE BRASIL**. Though it is commonly called the Brazil **NUT**, in botanical terms it is the seed from the fruit of this tree.

ANCIENT HISTORY

Native Amazonians cherished these delicious nuts, which provided them much-needed protein, fats, and other essential nutrients. It has also been used as "carrier or base oil" in traditional medicines and aromatherapy, as well as in the pharmaceutical and cosmetic industries.

BENEFITS

- A single ounce of Brazil nuts (6 to 8 nuts) provides 774% of the daily recommended value of selenium. Selenium is an important antioxidant that can protect from the harmful effects of free radicals, which are highly reactive particles that can oxidize and thereby damage the body cells and tissues. Selenium is also required for the proper functioning of the thyroid gland.

- Brazil nuts can also assist in controlling weight as its high protein and fiber content of these nuts help to control hunger. They are a very rich source of omega-6 fatty acids that can help lower the risk of cardiovascular diseases.

- A one-ounce serving of Brazil nuts contains 27% of the RDA for magnesium, which helps with the functioning of muscles, the production of protein, and absorption of energy from food.

- They also offer 25% of the RDA for copper which can help the body use iron, maintain bone and connective tissue health, promote thyroid function, support the production of melanin, and protect and repair tissues.

NUTRIENTS
(per 1 cup)

Protein	19 g	Magnesium	500 mg	Selenium	2,550 mcg
Fiber	10 g	Phosphorus	964 mg	Copper	2.3 mg

BROCCOLI

BRASSICA OLERACEA is an edible green plant in the cabbage family, whose large flowering head is used as a vegetable. The word broccoli comes from the Italian plural of **BROCCOLO**, which means "the flowering crest of a cabbage."

ANCIENT HISTORY

Originally, broccoli was mainly used to treat gynecological disorders, digestive problems, tetanus, and possibly dropsy. In the 1st century CE, skin infections and digestive issues were the most important illnesses treated with broccoli. The ancient Roman Cato advised all Roman citizens to grow broccoli in their orchard as all-purpose medicine. Greek physician Galen prescribed broccoli to treat a medical condition that was most probably colon cancer.

BENEFITS

- Broccoli contains the compound glucoraphanin, which can be processed into an anti-cancer compound called sulforaphane. These compounds from broccoli and broccoli sprouts play a major role in the protection against cancer and other oxidative and degenerative diseases.

- Broccoli is also an excellent source of indole-3-carbinol, a chemical which boosts DNA repair in cells and appears to also block the growth of cancer cells. The anti-cancer benefits of broccoli are greatly reduced if the vegetable is boiled. Boiling broccoli reduces the levels of suspected anti-carcinogenic compounds, such as sulforaphane, with losses of 20 to 30% after five minutes, 40 to 50% after ten minutes, and 77% after thirty minutes. Consuming steamed, lightly sautéed, or raw are recommended ways to keep the beneficial nutrients intact.

- Broccoli is high in vitamin C and dietary fiber. A single serving provides more than 135% of vitamin C and 9% of dietary fiber.

- Broccoli contains high levels of both calcium and vitamin K, both of which are important for bone health and prevention of osteoporosis.

- Sulforaphane, one of the isothiocyanates (ITCs) in broccoli, may be able to prevent, or even reverse, damage to blood vessel linings caused by inflammation due to chronic blood sugar problems.

NUTRIENTS
(per 1 cup)

Folate · · · · · · · · · · 168.48 mcg	Choline · · · · · · · · · · · · 62.56 mg	Protein · · · · · · · · · · · · · · · 3.71 g
Fiber · · · · · · · · · · · · · · · · · · 5.15 g	Potassium · · · · · · · · · 457.08 mg	Calcium · · · · · · · · · · · · 62.40 mg
Phosphorus · · · · · · · 104.52 mg	Magnesium · · · · · · · · · 32.76 mg	

BUCKWHEAT

FAGOPYRUM ESCULENTUM is a plant cultivated for its grain-like seeds, and also used as a cover crop. Despite its name, buckwheat is not related to wheat, as it is not a grass. While resembling a grain, buckwheat is actually a fruit seed related to rhubarb (and it's naturally gluten-free!).

ANCIENT HISTORY

Buckwheat is native to Northern Europe as well as Asia. From the 10th through the 13th century, it was widely cultivated in China. It spread to Europe and Russia in the 14th and 15th centuries, and was introduced in the United States by the Dutch during the 17th century. Since ancient times, the many parts of the buckwheat plant have been used as a staple food, incorporated in porridges, teas, beer, and medicine, as well as bedding and upholstery filling.

BENEFITS

- Buckwheat is a high-fiber seed. Studies have shown that it helps slow down the rate of glucose absorption after a meal, making it a healthy choice for people with diabetes.

- Buckwheat is also high in manganese, magnesium, copper, and zinc. It also contains all nine essential amino acids, including lysine, which plays a key role in collagen production and is not produced by the human body.

- Lysine is also beneficial for people prone to cold sores, as it helps ward them off.

- Buckwheat is listed as a hypoallergenic food, meaning that it is low in other allergy-triggering proteins, and therefore, unlikely to cause allergic reactions in most humans. Buckwheat also helps alleviate existing allergies.

- Experts have suggested that due to its relatively low digestibility score, buckwheat protein may have fiber-like effects, including constipation-fighting effects and anti-cancer activity in the colon.

- Buckwheat is supercharged with B complex vitamins including thiamin, riboflavin, niacin, pantothenic acid, pyridoxine, and folate. These vitamins work both synergistically and individually to promote healthy skin and strong hair.

- Due to their high concentration of rutin, buckwheat groats are considered one of the best foods for varicose vein prevention. They also have been credited with fighting inflammatory conditions such as arthritis.

NUTRIENTS
(per 1 cup)

Copper	1.100 mg
Magnesium	231.00 mg
Manganese	1.300 mg
Phosphorus	347.00 mg
Isoleucine	0.498 g
Leucine	0.832 g
Lysine	0.672 g
Niacin	7.020 mg

CACAO

The cacao seed is the dried and fully fermented fatty seed of **THEOBROMA CACAO**, from which cocoa solids and cocoa butter are extracted. They are the basis of chocolate, as well as many Mesoamerican foods such as mole sauce and tejate.

ANCIENT HISTORY

The Olmecs were a prehistoric people comprising one of the first civilizations of Mexico, and the first people known to process and eat cacao beans, which they called *kakaw*. They devised the fermenting, drying, roasting, and grinding process that remain the basis of today's chocolate production, a knowledge they later passed on to the Mayans.

BENEFITS

- In general, cacao is considered to be a rich source of antioxidants such as procyanidins and flavanoids, which may impart anti-aging properties. Cacao contains a high level of flavonoids, specifically epicatechin, which may have beneficial cardiovascular effects on health.

- The stimulant activity of cacao comes from the compound theobromine, which is less diuretic as compared to theophylline found in tea. Prolonged intake of flavanol-rich cacao has been linked to cardiovascular health benefits, though it should be noted that this refers to raw cacao and to a lesser extent, dark chocolate, since flavonoids degrade during cooking and alkalizing processes.

- Polyphenols in cacao beans benefit the cardiovascular system. Research indicates that polyphenols also reduce blood pressure. The magnesium in cocoa also increases heart strength.

- Cocoa beans also contain a substance known as epicatechin, which helps reduce the risks of diabetes, heart disease, cancer, and strokes.

- Cocoa beans reduce anxiety while simultaneously promote alertness. A cup of cacao can provide the same energy as a cup of coffee without the strong crash afterward, as there is after drinking coffee.

NUTRIENTS

(per 1 cup)

Dietary Fiber · · · · · · · · · 28.5 g	Folate · · · · · · · · · · · · 27.5 mcg	Ash · · · · · · · · · · · · · · · · · · 5.0 g
Protein · · · · · · · · · · · · · ·16.9 g	Phosphorus · · · · · · · · · · 631 mg	Caffeine · · · · · · · · · · · · · 198 mg
Total Fat · · · · · · · · · · · · · 11.8 g	Potassium · · · · · · · · · · 1311 mg	

CHIA

SALVIA HISPANICA, commonly known as chia, is a species of flowering plant in the mint family, **LAMIACEAE**, native to central and southern Mexico and Guatemala. The 16th-century **CODEX MENDOZA** provides evidence that chia was cultivated by the Aztecs in pre-Columbian times. Economic historians have suggested it was as important as maize as a food crop.

ANCIENT HISTORY

Pre-Columbian Aztecs and Mayans used chia seeds as a main part of their diet. Aztecs used the seed to stimulate the flow of saliva and to relieve joint pain. Aztec warriors survived on rations of chia seed, which provided them energy and endurance. Native Americans who lived in what is now southwestern United States chewed on chia seeds during forced marches, or on trade missions.

BENEFITS

- A serving of chia seeds has 18% of the recommended daily intake for calcium, which helps maintain bone and oral health, and helps prevent osteoporosis.

- Chia is being studied as a potential natural treatment for type-2 diabetes because of its ability to slow down digestion. The gelatinous coating that develops when exposed to liquids can also prevent blood sugar spikes.

- Chia seeds have been shown to improve blood pressure in diabetic patients. It may also increase healthy cholesterol while lowering total, LDL, and triglyceride cholesterol. Chia seeds are packed with omega-3 fatty acids which are important for brain health.

- A 28 g or 1-ounce serving of chia has 11 grams of dietary fiber, which is about a third of the recommended daily intake for adults. Chia seeds also help maintain healthy bones and teeth. Phosphorus is also used by the body to synthesize protein for cell and tissue growth and repair.

- A 28 g serving of these super seeds has 4.4 grams of protein, nearly 10% of the daily value.

NUTRIENTS
(per 1 cup)

Zinc	1.0 mg
Manganese	0.6 mg
Phosphorus	265 mg
Potassium	44.8 mg
Protein	4.4 g
Calcium	177 mg
Omega-3 (total)	4915 mg
Omega-6 (total)	1620 mg

CHICKPEA

CICER ARIETINUM, is a legume of the family **FABACEAE**, subfamily **FABOIDEAE**. Formerly known as the gram, it is also commonly known as garbanzo or garbanzo bean and sometimes known as ceci, cece, channa, or Bengal gram.

ANCIENT HISTORY

Ancient people associated chickpeas with Venus because they were said to offer medical uses such as boosting male fertility and stimulating the production of breast milk. They were thought to induce menstruation and the production of urine in the treatment of kidney stones. The first record of garbanzo bean consumption dates back to about 7000 BCE in the Mediterranean basin, and subsequently spread to India and Ethiopia.

BENEFITS

- Chickpeas are rich in both soluble and insoluble dietary fiber. Soluble fiber forms a gel-like substance in the digestive tract that snares bile (which contains cholesterol) and ferries it out of the body. Research studies have shown that insoluble fiber not only helps to increase stool bulk and prevent constipation, but also helps prevent digestive disorders.

- Regular intake of chickpeas can lower LDL (bad) and total cholesterol. Garbanzos contain significant amounts of folate and magnesium. Folate lowers the levels of the amino acid homocysteine and strengthens the blood vessels. Studies have found chickpeas lower the risk of heart attack.

- Excellent source of the trace mineral manganese, an important nutrient in energy production and antioxidant defenses. One cup of garbanzo beans supplies 84.5% of the daily value for this mineral.

- Chickpeas contain phytochemicals called saponins, which can act as antioxidants. These nutrients lower the risk of breast cancer, protect against osteoporosis, and minimize hot flashes in post-menopausal women.

- Chickpeas' high iron content is particularly important for menstruating, pregnant, or lactating women, and growing children. Iron is an integral component of hemoglobin, which aids in energy production and metabolism.

NUTRIENTS
(per 1 cup)

Protein · · · · · · · · · · · · · 14.5 g	Phosphorus · · · · · · · · · 276 mg	Manganese · · · · · · · · · · · 1.7 mg
Calcium · · · · · · · · · · · 80.4 mg	Zinc · · · · · · · · · · · · · · · · 2.5 mg	Folate · · · · · · · · · · · · 282 mcg
Iron · · · · · · · · · · · · · · · · 4.7 mg	Copper · · · · · · · · · · · · · 0.6 mg	

FIG

FICUS CARICA, is a species of flowering plant in the genus **FICUS**, from the family **MORACEAE**, known as the common fig.

ANCIENT HISTORY

The fig tree was held sacred in all countries of South-western Asia, and in Egypt, Greece, and Italy, and has been a part of mythology and culture. The fig was mentioned in a Babylonian hymnbook about 2000 BCE, while also figuring prominently in the Genesis story, as well as the New Testament with Jesus' parable of the Fig Tree (Luke 6: 26-40). Figs have also been renowned for centuries as a powerful fertility or sexual supplement, and "prescribed" to correct sexual dysfunction like sterility, endurance, or erectile dysfunction.

BENEFITS

- Figs are often recommended to nourish and tone the intestines and act as a natural laxative because of their high fiber content.

- Figs are rich in minerals including potassium, calcium, magnesium, iron, and copper, and are a good source of antioxidant vitamins A, E, and K. They are also a good fruit source of calcium.

- Their high potassium content may counteract the urinary excretion of calcium caused by high salt diets. This, in turn, helps to keep calcium in bones and lessens the risk of osteoporosis.

- Dried figs contain phenol, omega-3 and omega-6. Fig leaves also have an inhibitory effect on triglycerides, and make the overall number of triglycerides drop.

NUTRIENTS
(per 1 cup)

Iron ·············· 3.0 mg	Potassium ·········· 1013 mg	Manganese ·········· 0.8 mg
Magnesium ·········· 101 mg	Copper ············· 0.4 mg	Vitamin K ·········· 23.2 mcg
	Protein ············· 4.9 g	Calcium ············· 241 mg

FUNGI

A fungus is any member of a large group of eukaryotic organisms that includes microorganisms such as yeasts and molds, as well as the more familiar mushrooms. These organisms are classified as a kingdom, Fungi, which is separate from plants, animals, protists, and bacteria.

ANCIENT HISTORY

Fungi have grown wild since prehistoric times. In traditional Tibetan and Chinese medicine, many varieties of mushroom have been used as the ultimate remedy to treat problems in the lung and kidney systems such as asthma, emphysema, renal failure, backache, fertility and fatigue.

BENEFITS

- About 100 species of mushrooms are being studied for their health-promoting benefits. Of those hundred, about a half dozen really stand out for their ability to deliver a tremendous boost to your immune system. These include portobello, morels, oyster, shiitake, porcini, and button.

- It's important to eat only organically grown mushrooms as they absorb and concentrate whatever they grow in. This is one of the factors that give mushrooms their potency. Mushrooms are known to concentrate heavy metals, as well as air and water pollutants; therefore, healthy growing conditions are a critical factor. As a defense against bacterial invasion, fungi have developed strong antibiotics, which also happen to be effective for humans. Penicillin, streptomycin, and tetracycline all come from fungal extracts.

- Consuming dried white button mushroom extract has been found to be as effective as taking supplemental vitamin D2 or D3 for increasing vitamin D levels (25-hydroxyvitamin D).

- The folate in mushrooms plays an important role in DNA synthesis and repair, thus preventing the formation of cancer cells from mutations in the DNA.

NUTRIENTS

(per 1 cup)

Vitamin D	12.6 IU
Thiamin	0.1 mg
Riboflavin	0.3 mg
Niacin	2.5 mg
Protein	2.2 g
Choline	12.1 mg
Copper	0.2 mg
Selenium	6.5 mcg

GARLIC

ALLIUM SATIVUM, commonly known as garlic, is a species in the onion genus, **ALLIUM**. Its close relatives include the onion, shallot, leek, chive, and rakkyo.

ANCIENT HISTORY

With a history of human use of over 7,000 years, garlic is native to central Asia, and has long been a staple in the Mediterranean region, as well as a frequent seasoning in Asia, Africa, and Europe. Garlic was introduced into various regions throughout the globe by migrating cultural tribes and explorers. By the 6th century BCE, garlic was known in both China and India, the latter country using it for therapeutic purposes. Throughout the millennia, garlic has been a beloved plant in many cultures for both its culinary and medicinal properties.

BENEFITS

- Garlic has been used for treating an enlarged prostate (benign prostatic hyperplasia; BPH), diabetes, osteoarthritis, hay fever (allergic rhinitis), traveler's diarrhea, high blood pressure, cold, and flu. It is also used for building the immune system, preventing tick bites, and preventing and treating bacterial and fungal infections.

- Other uses include treatment of fever, coughs, headache, stomachache, sinus congestion, gout, rheumatism, hemorrhoids, asthma, bronchitis, shortness of breath, low blood pressure, low blood sugar, high blood sugar, and snakebites. It is also used for fighting stress and fatigue, and maintaining healthy liver function.

- Some research indicates that garlic's antibacterial properties might help to prevent food poisoning by killing bacteria like E. coli, Staphylococcus aureus, and Salmonella enteritidis.

- Organo-sulfur compounds found in garlic have been identified effective in destroying the cells in glioblastoma, a type of aggressive brain tumor.

- Diallyl sulfide, a compound in garlic, was 100 times more effective than two popular antibiotics in fighting the bacteria that causes gastroenteritis Campylobacter bacterium, according to the *Journal of Antimicrobial Chemotherapy*.

NUTRIENTS

(per 1 cup)

Protein · · · · · · · · · · · · · · 8.6 g	Calcium · · · · · · · · · · · · 246 mg	Manganese · · · · · · · · · · · 2.3 mg
Vitamin C · · · · · · · · · · · 42.4 mg	Phosphorus · · · · · · · · 208 mg	Selenium · · · · · · · · · · 19.3 mcg
Vitamin B · · · · · · · · · · · 61.7 mg	Copper · · · · · · · · · · · · · · 0.4 mg	

GINGER

Ginger or ginger root is the rhizome of the plant ZINGIBER OFFICINALE, consumed as a delicacy, medicine, or spice. It lends its name to its genus and family, ZINGIBERACEAE. Other notable members of this plant family are turmeric, cardamom, and galangal.

ANCIENT HISTORY

Ginger has been a popular spice and herbal medicine for thousands of years. In China, for example, ginger has been used to help digestion and treat stomach upset, and nausea for more than 2,000 years. Ginger has also been used to help treat arthritis, colic, diarrhea, and heart conditions.

BENEFITS

- Historically, ginger has a long tradition of being very effective in alleviating symptoms of gastrointestinal distress. In herbal medicine, ginger is regarded as an excellent carminative, a substance that promotes the elimination of intestinal gas, and intestinal spasmolytic, a substance that relaxes and soothes the intestinal tract.

- Modern scientific research has revealed that ginger possesses numerous therapeutic properties including antioxidant effects, an ability to inhibit the formation of inflammatory compounds, and direct anti-inflammatory effects. Ginger is widely used for treating loss of appetite, nausea, and vomiting after surgery, nausea resulting from cancer treatment, flatulence, stomach upset, colic, and morning sickness.

- A study found that female athletes taking 3 g of ginger daily had significant decrease in muscle soreness. Ginger can be as effective as ibuprofen in relieving pain from menstrual cramps in women.

- Ginger has antibacterial, antiviral, antioxidant, and anti-parasitic properties. It has been found to reduce the severity of migraine headaches as well as the migraine medication Sumatriptan, with fewer side effects.

NUTRIENTS
(per 1 cup)

Iron · · · · · · · · · · · · · · · · · 3.0 mg	Copper · · · · · · · · · · · · · 0.4 mg	Vitamin K · · · · · · · · · · 23.2 mcg
Magnesium · · · · · · · · · 101 mg	Protein · · · · · · · · · · · · · 4.9 g	Calcium · · · · · · · · · · · · · 241 mg
Potassium · · · · · · · · · · 1013 mg	Manganese · · · · · · · · · · 0.8 mg	

GOJI

LYCIUM BARBARUM and **LYCIUM CHINENSE**, also called wolfberry, are species of boxthorn in the family **SOLANACEAE**. This plant family also includes the potato, tomato, eggplant, deadly nightshade, chili pepper, and tobacco. The two species are native to Asia.

ANCIENT HISTORY

Goji has been used for thousands of years in Tibet and China, both as a culinary ingredient and as a medicine. In Traditional Chinese Medicine, the goji is said to act on the Kidney and Liver meridians to help with lower back pain, dizziness, and eyesight. They are most often consumed raw, made into a tea or extract, or as an ingredient in soups. Native to the Himalayan Mountains of Tibet and Mongolia, the goji berry has only been available in Western countries in recent years.

BENEFITS

- Goji berries are an excellent source of antioxidants such as polyphenols, flavonoids, carotenoids, and vitamins A, C, and E. In fact, the goji berry contains approximately 500 times more vitamin C per weight than an orange and considerably more beta-carotene than carrots. These findings are reinforced by the goji berries' high Oxygen Radical Absorbance Capacity (ORAC) score of 3,290, which shows that they contain much larger concentrations of antioxidants than most other fruits.

- In addition, Goji berries contain complex starches called *Lycium barbarum polysaccharides*, which may benefit the immune function, and may reduce fatigue associated with living at high altitude.

- Goji berries are believed to help maintain a healthy heart and circulation, boost the immune system, protect against cancer, and increase longevity.

- Some researchers suggest that goji berry extracts may improve mood and protect against age-related diseases such as Alzheimer's.

- Goji berries are rich in vitamin A, which may protect against skin damage, help maintain night-vision, and benefit the immune system in a variety of ways.

NUTRIENTS
(per 1 ounce)

Dietary Fiber	4 g
Protein	4 g
Vitamin A	11.0 IU
Vitamin B12	0.1 mcg
Calcium	19.2 mg
Magnesium	57.4 mg
Phosphorus	72.2 mg
Potassium	182 mg

HEMP

Hemp, from Old English hænep, is a commonly used term for high-growing varieties of the **CANNABIS** plant and its products, which include fiber, oil, and seed. Hemp is refined into products such as hempseed foods, hemp oil, wax, resin, rope, cloth, pulp, paper, and fuel.

ANCIENT HISTORY

In Africa, hemp was used for dysentery and fevers. In China, hemp was commonly grown as a seed crop throughout the Spring and Autumn period (770 to 476 BCE), Warring States period (476 to 221 BCE), the Qin dynasty (221 to 207 BCE), and the Han dynasty (206 BCE to 220 AD). The Li Qi places hemp among the "five grains" of ancient China, which included barley, rice, wheat, and soybeans.

BENEFITS

- Hempseeds are a perfect and natural blend of easily digested proteins, essential fats (omega-3 & omega-6), Gamma Linolenic Acid (GLA), antioxidants, amino acids, fiber, iron, zinc, carotene, phospholipids, phytosterols, vitamin B1, vitamin B2, vitamin B6, vitamin D, vitamin E, chlorophyll, calcium, magnesium, sulfur, copper, potassium, phosphorus, and enzymes.

- All amino acids essential to optimum health are found in hempseeds, including the rarely found Gamma Linolenic Acid (GLA). Hempseeds are high in nutritional value and contain 20 different varieties of amino acids and all nine of the essential amino acids. The body can't naturally produce some essential amino acids and these seeds have the capacity to supplement them in their entirety.

- Three tablespoons of hempseeds contain 13 grams of fat (including 3 g of ALA), 1 gram of fiber, and 11 grams of protein. Hempseeds are a complete protein plant food.

- Fiber in food, like hempseeds, improves bowel function by helping prevent constipation.

- Hempseeds are also a rich source of magnesium, phosphorus, iron, and zinc. Three tablespoons meets 50% of the daily value for magnesium and phosphorus, 25% of the daily value for zinc and 15% for iron.

NUTRIENTS
(per ½ cup)

Zinc · · · · · · · · · · · · · · · 17.9 mg

Phosphorus · · · · · · · · 1446 mg

Dietary Fiber · · · · · · · · · · 7.0 g

Protein · · · · · · · · · · · · · 33.0 g

Iron · · · · · · · · · · · · · · · 13.8 mg

Magnesium · · · · · · · · 1071 mg

KALE

BRASSICA OLERACEA is a vegetable with green or purple leaves, in which the central leaves do not form a head. It is considered to be closer to wild cabbage than most domesticated forms of vegetables. The species contains a wide variety of vegetables, including broccoli, cauliflower, collard greens, and Brussels sprouts. The cultivar group **ACEPHALA** also includes spring greens and collard greens, which are similar genetically.

ANCIENT HISTORY

In ancient Greece and Rome, kale was used as a remedy for stomach and intestinal discomfort. It was eaten raw with different kinds of nuts or seeds and also mixed with different vegetables in order to cure diseases.

BENEFITS

- Kale is high in beta-carotenes, vitamin K, and vitamin C, and rich in calcium. Kale, as with broccoli and other brassicas, contains sulforaphane, a chemical with potent anti-cancer properties that is particularly present when the kale is chopped or minced. Boiling decreases the level of sulforaphane; however, steaming, microwaving, or stir-frying does not result in significant loss.

- Along with other brassica vegetables, kale is also a source of indole-3-carbinol, a chemical that boosts DNA repair in cells and appears to block the growth of cancer cells. Kale has been found to contain a group of resins known as bile acid sequestrants, which have been shown to lower cholesterol and decrease absorption of dietary fat. Steaming significantly increases these bile acid-binding properties.

- One cup of kale is filled with 10% of the RDA of omega-3 fatty acids, which help fight against arthritis, asthma, and autoimmune disorders.

- Per calorie, kale has more calcium than milk, which aids in preventing bone loss, preventing osteoporosis, and maintaining a healthy metabolism.

- Kale is filled with fiber and sulfur, both great for detoxifying the body, especially the liver. It is also rich in antioxidants, such as carotenoids and flavonoids, which help protect against various cancers.

NUTRIENTS

(per 1 cup)

Vitamin K · · · · · · · 1062.10 mcg

Vitamin A · · · 885.36 mcg RAE

Vitamin C · · · · · · · · · 53.30 mg

Vitamin E · · · · · 1.11 mg (ATE)

Magnesium · · · · · · · · 23.40 mg

Phosphorus · · · · · · · · 36.40 mg

Folate · · · · · · · · · · · 16.90 mcg

Calcium · · · · · · · · · · 93.60 mg

KELP

Kelps are large seaweeds (algae) belonging to the brown algae, PHAEOPHYCEAE, in the order LAMINARIALES. Kelp grows in underwater "forests" (kelp forests) in shallow oceans, and is thought to have appeared in the Miocene Epoch, 23 to 5 million years ago. The organisms require nutrient-rich water with temperatures between 43°F and 57°F. Known for their high growth rate, the genera MACROCYSTIS and NEREOCYSTIS can grow as fast as 1.5 feet a day, ultimately reaching 100 to 260 feet.

ANCIENT HISTORY

Archaeological evidence suggests that Japanese cultures have been consuming sea vegetables for more than 10,000 years. In ancient Chinese cultures, sea vegetables were a noted delicacy, suitable especially for honored guests and royalty.

BENEFITS

- One of the main benefits of kelp is its high content of iodine, which is a mineral that is essential for the correct functioning of the thyroid gland. If there is not enough iodine in the diet, the thyroid is forced to work harder than it should have to, eventually becoming enlarged.

- An overactive thyroid leads to hormonal imbalances, depression, anxiety, excessive weight loss, ovarian cysts, panic attacks, dry scalp, and hair loss.

- Kelp is a natural and healthy alternative to salt, as it has a salty taste. It is especially important in terms of women's health as it is rich in iron, potassium, and calcium, all beneficial for women of all ages, during menstruation, pregnancy, and for nursing mothers.

- Kelp contains plentiful amounts of chlorophyll, which stimulates red blood cell production, and increases oxygenation in the body.

- Kelp contains many vitamins, especially B, C, and E vitamins, which are essential for cellular metabolism and energy production, as well as antioxidant benefits and blood vessel health.

- Kelp is rich in sodium alginate, an element that protects and removes radiation from the body. Sodium alginate allows calcium to be absorbed through the intestinal wall while binding most of the strontium, which is later excreted from the body.

NUTRIENTS
(per 2 tablespoons)

Calcium ·············· 16.8 mg	Magnesium ············ 12.1 mg	Folate ·············· 18.0 mcg
Iron ················· 0.3 mg	Vitamin K ············· 6.6 mcg	Vitamin C ············ 0.3 mg

LEMON

CITRUS LIMON is a small evergreen tree native to Asia. The tree's ellipsoidal yellow fruit is used for culinary and non-culinary purposes throughout the world, primarily for its juice, though the pulp and rind (zest) are also used in cooking and baking. The juice of the lemon is about 5% to 6% citric acid, which gives lemons a sour taste.

ANCIENT HISTORY

The lemon has Asian origins, specifically from the Far East (India and China), where it was found growing wild. Known in China, India, and in the Mesopotamian civilizations for its antiseptic, anti-rheumatic, and refreshing properties, lemon was considered sacred in Muslim countries, where it was mainly used as an antidote against poisons, as well as to keep the Devil away from homes.

BENEFITS

- While lemons themselves seem acidic, they actually have alkaline properties that help clean the liver and detoxify your body. They also stimulate the digestive tract, making your body better able to absorb other nutrients throughout the day.

- Several fascinating research studies on the healing properties of lemons and limes have shown that cell cycles, including the decision a cell makes about whether to divide (called mitosis) or die (apoptosis), are altered by lemon and lime juice, as are the activities of special immune cells called monocytes.

- In addition to their unique phytonutrient properties, lemons and limes are an excellent source of vitamin C, the primary water-soluble antioxidant, that neutralizes free radicals in the body. Vitamin C has been shown to be helpful in reducing some of the symptoms of osteoarthritis and rheumatoid arthritis, and may even reduce the risk of developing asthma. Consuming lemons, and really any high-in-Vitamin C foods, can help to fight skin damage caused by the sun and pollution, reduce wrinkles, and improve overall skin texture.

NUTRIENTS

Vitamin C ············· 112 mg

Thiamin ············· 0.1 mg

Vitamin B6 ··········· 0.2 mg

Folate ············· 23.3 mcg

Calcium ············· 55.1 mg

Iron ················· 1.3 mg

Potassium ··········· 293 mg

Copper ············· 0.1 mg

LENTIL

LENS CULINARIS is an edible pulse. It is a bushy annual plant of the legume family, grown for its lens-shaped seeds. Lentil colors range from yellow, red-orange, green, brown, and black. Lentils also vary in size, and are sold in many forms, with or without the skins, whole or split.

ANCIENT HISTORY

Lentils have been part of the human diet since the aceramic (before pottery) Neolithic times, being one of the first crops domesticated in the Near East. Archaeological evidence shows they were eaten 9,500 to 13,000 years ago. For millennia, lentils have traditionally been eaten with barley and wheat, three foodstuffs that originated in the same regions and spread throughout Africa and Europe during similar migrations and explorations of cultural tribes.

BENEFITS

- Studies have found that plant lectins, a separate type of plant protein originating from foods like lentils, wheat, peas, and soybeans, have a great influence on cancer cells. Research shows that these lectins cause cytotoxicity and apoptosis, which means that they have a great potential to control cancer growth.

- Lentils are a good source of many vitamins, including vitamin B3, which plays a significant role in boosting the digestive and nervous systems. Vitamin B3 offers many other benefits, including cholesterol control, a decreased risk of diseases like Alzheimer's disease, cataracts, osteoarthritis, and diabetes.

- Lentils also contain high amounts of iron, which is needed by the body for optimum hemoglobin production. Lentils contain 3.3 milligrams of iron in a ½ cup serving. Women age 50 and younger need 18 milligrams of iron a day, and women over the age of 51 and all men need 8 milligrams a day.

- The low levels of Readily Digestible Starch (RDS), 5%, and high levels of Slowly Digested Starch (SDS) 30%, make lentils of great interest to people with diabetes.

- Lentils are an ideal source of protein without adding any extra fat to the body. Lentils also contain magnesium, which helps in relaxing cardiovascular muscles and helping to lower blood pressure.

NUTRIENTS
(per 1 cup)

Protein ··············· 17.9 g	Iron ··············· 6.6 mg	Copper ··············· 0.5 mg
Dietary Fiber ··········· 15.6 g	Phosphorus ·········· 356 mg	Manganese ·········· 1.0 mg
Folate ············· 358 mcg	Zinc ··············· 2.5 mg	

OATS

AVENA SATIVA is a species of cereal grain grown for its seed, which is known by the name "oats" (usually in the plural, unlike other grains). While oats are suitable for human consumption as oatmeal and rolled oats, one of the most common uses is as livestock feed.

ANCIENT HISTORY

The modern oat draws its ancestry from the wild red oat, a plant originating in Asia. Before being consumed as a food, oats were used for medicinal purposes, a use for which they are still honored. In Europe, oats constituted an important commercial crop, since they were a dietary staple for the people of many countries, including Scotland, Great Britain, Germany, and the Scandinavian countries.

BENEFITS

- Oatmeal contains a special type of antioxidant called avenanthramide. Avenanthramides fight off free radicals that attack high-density lipoproteins, or HDL, which is known as the good cholesterol. They also protect LDL cholesterol from oxidizing from copper, which reduces the risk of developing cardiovascular disease.

- Avenanthramides not only protect against heart disease, they also prevent the arteries from hardening. Those antioxidants suppress the production of molecules that allow monocytes to adhere to the walls of the arteries. When paired with vitamin C, the cardiovascular benefits of oatmeal are enhanced; therefore, it is important to include oranges, kiwi, persimmon, or other Vitamin C–rich foods when eating oats.

- Children introduced earlier to oats are less likely to develop persistent asthma.

- Postmenopausal women should eat six servings of oatmeal or other whole grains on a weekly basis. Studies show that men can also reduce their risk of heart failure if they eat one bowl of whole grain cereal or oatmeal per day.

- Oatmeal is a good source of magnesium, which regulates the body's insulin and glucose levels. Oatmeal also contains beta-glucan fiber, which protects against heart disease and revs up the immune system.

NUTRIENTS
(per 1 cup)

Protein · · · · · · · · · · · · · · · 10.6 g

Thiamin · · · · · · · · · · · · 0.4 mg

Iron · · · · · · · · · · · · · · · · · 3.4 mg

Magnesium · · · · · · · · · 112 mg

Phosphorus · · · · · · · · · 332 mg

Zinc · · · · · · · · · · · · · · · · 2.9 mg

Manganese · · · · · · · · · · 2.9 mg

Selenium · · · · · · · · · · 23.4 mcg

PERSIMMON

DIOSPYROS KAKI are the edible fruit of a number of species of trees in the genus **DIOSPYROS** and the **EBENACEAE** family. Although the most popular version of this fruit was originally native to China, it spread around the world over the past few hundred years, and similar species have been found in other parts of the world.

ANCIENT HISTORY

Sweet persimmon fruit has a lot of medicinal properties. In the past, the calyx of the persimmon fruit (the part of the fruit that is connected to the branch of the tree) has been used to make a calyx tea, which was commonly used to stop the hiccups. The fruit itself also has the same effect.

BENEFITS

- Persimmons are one of a few foods associated with killing breast cancer cells without harming normal breast cells, according to one new study. Scientists attributed this to fisetin, a flavonoid that can only be found in persimmons specifically. Fisetin also has been named as a significant contributor in the eradication of colon and prostate cancer cells.

- Persimmons have one of the highest ascorbic acid (vitamin C) contents of any fruit, and a single persimmon has approximately 80% of the daily requirement of that beneficial nutrient. Vitamin C stimulates the immune system and increases the production of white blood cells, which are the primary line of defense for the body against microbial, viral, and fungal infections, as well as foreign bodies or toxins.

- Persimmons have high amounts of manganese, a factor in maintaining healthy mucous membranes and skin, as well as being a known protectant against lung and mouth cancers.

- Persimmons are an excellent source of fiber, which helps keep the body regulated. B-complex vitamins are present to stabilize the metabolic system, along with copper and phosphorus.

- Catechins in persimmon are known to have antibiotic and anti-inflammatory properties, and for protecting small blood vessels from bleeding. They also contain gallocatechins and betulinic acid, which are tumor inhibitors.

NUTRIENTS
(per 1 cup)

Vitamin C · · · · · · · · · · · 16.5 mg

Calcium · · · · · · · · · · · 6.8 mg

Iron · · · · · · · · · · · · · 0.6 mg

Potassium · · · · · · · · · · 77.5 mg

Carotene-β · · · · · · · 253 mcg

Crypto-xanthin-β · · · 1447 mcg

Lutein-zeaxanthin · · · 834 mcg

Lycopene · · · · · · · · · · · 159 mcg

POMEGRANATE

PUNICA GRANATUM is a fruit-bearing deciduous shrub or small tree growing between 16 to 26 ft tall. In the Northern Hemisphere, the fruit is typically in season from September to February, and in the Southern Hemisphere from March to May. As intact arils or juice, pomegranates are used in cooking, baking, meal garnishes, juice blends, smoothies, and alcoholic beverages, such as cocktails and wine.

ANCIENT HISTORY

Pomegranate is mentioned in many ancient texts, notably in Babylonian texts and the Book of Exodus. It was introduced into Latin America and California by Spanish settlers in 1769. In the Indian subcontinent's ancient Ayurveda system of traditional medicine, the pomegranate has been used extensively as a source of traditional remedies.

BENEFITS

- It is a good source of soluble and insoluble dietary fibers, providing about 4 g per 100 g (about 12% of RDA), which aid with smooth digestion.

- Pomegranates help control weight and cholesterol, boost immunity, improve circulation, and contain antioxidant properties against cancer-causing free radicals.

- Pomegranate's antioxidant activity is known to inhibit cell proliferation and invasion, and promote apoptosis (cell death) in various cancer cells.[1]

- The antioxidants in pomegranates may also help to reduce inflammation that contributes to the destruction of cartilage in joints, a key reason for the pain and stiffness felt by many osteoarthritis sufferers.

- Regular consumption of pomegranate has also been found to be effective against prostate cancer, benign prostatic hyperplasia (BPH), diabetes, and lymphoma.[2]

NUTRIENTS

(per 1 cup)

Protein · · · · · · · · · · · · · · 4.7 g

Potassium · · · · · · · · · · · 666 mg

Copper · · · · · · · · · · · · · 0.4 mg

Manganese · · · · · · · · · · 0.3 mg

Vitamin K · · · · · · · · · · 46.2 mcg

Thiamin · · · · · · · · · · · · · 0.2 mg

Folate · · · · · · · · · · · · · 107 mcg

Dietary Fiber · · · · · · · · · · 11.3 g

QUINOA

CHENOPODIUM QUINOA is a grain crop grown primarily for its edible seeds. It is a "pseudocereal" rather than a true cereal, as it is not a member of the grass family. As a chenopod, Quinoa is a member of the same food family that contains spinach, Swiss chard, and beets.

ANCIENT HISTORY

Quinoa (the name is derived from the Spanish spelling of the Quechua name *kinwa*) has been used as a staple in Andean cooking for at least 3,000 years. One of the few plant-based sources of complete protein, the ancient Peruvians called it "the Mother Grain," for they believed it was a gift from the gods.

BENEFITS

- One special amino acid that quinoa contains is called lysine, which is often found in sports supplements by those trying to add lean muscle to their body. Quinoa has also been proven to help raise serotonin levels, which induce calmness and relaxation.

- There are flavonoids in quinoa that are typically only found in other foods like berries, and the levels that it contains are substantial. These flavonoids help prevent cardiovascular disease and inflammatory conditions.

- Quinoa has a high content of manganese, which helps to prevent damage of mitochondria during energy production, as well as to protect red blood cells and other cells from injury by free radicals.

- Quinoa is rich in magnesium, which helps to relax blood vessels and, thereby, to alleviate migraines. Magnesium also may reduce Type 2 diabetes by promoting healthy blood sugar control.

- Quinoa is high in riboflavin (B2). B2 improves energy metabolism within brain and muscle cells and is known to help create proper energy production in cells.

- One cup serving of quinoa contains 15% of the suggested daily allowance of iron. Iron is essential for brain and muscle functioning, as well as for the prevention of cell deficiencies, such as anemia.

NUTRIENTS
(per 1 cup)

Protein · · · · · · · · · · · · · 8.1 g

Iron · · · · · · · · · · · · · · · 2.8 mg

Magnesium · · · · · · · · · 118 mg

Phosphorus · · · · · · · · · 281 mg

Copper · · · · · · · · · · · · · 0.4 mg

Manganese · · · · · · · · · · 1.2 mg

Thiamin · · · · · · · · · · · · 0.2 mg

Folate · · · · · · · · · · · · 77.7 mcg

ROSEMARY

ROSMARINUS OFFICINALIS, commonly known as rosemary, is a woody, perennial herb with fragrant, evergreen, needle-like leaves and white, pink, purple, or blue flowers. It is a member of the mint family **LAMIACEAE**, which includes many other herbs. The name "rosemary" derives from the Latin for "dew" (**ROS**) and "sea" (**MARINUS**), or "dew of the sea."

ANCIENT HISTORY

Several ancient civilizations used rosemary as both medicine and cooking herb, with the earliest written records of the use of rosemary dating from the 5th BCE in Sumerian stone tablets. For Ancient Egyptians, rosemary was believed to have magical powers and was buried with the pharaohs to banish evil spirits. In the Middle Ages, it was burned in sick rooms as a disinfectant and was believed to ward off the plague. The earliest written records of the use of rosemary dates from the 5th BCE by Sumerians, in cuneiform stone tablets.

BENEFITS

- Rosemary has been a popular natural migraine remedy for centuries. Boiling rosemary water and applying it over the head improves mood and helps relieve the pain of migraines. Rosemary oil can also be applied topically as a natural treatment for arthritis, sore muscles, and other joint and muscle pains.

- Rosemary boosts the immune system due to its antioxidant, anti-inflammatory, and anti-carcinogenic properties. It also has antibacterial properties against H. pylori, the bacteria that causes stomach ulcers and staph infections. It is often used to help treat digestive problems, such as upset stomach, constipation, and indigestion, and it helps prevent foodborne illnesses caused from meats or eggs.

- Rosemary contains carnosol, which studies show to be a potent anti-cancer compound against many types of cancer, including cancers of the breast, prostate, skin, and colon, as well as leukemia.

- In 1529, an herbal book recommended rosemary for "weakness of the brain." Today, research has found that rosemary contains carnosic acid, a neuroprotective compound believed to protect against Alzheimer's disease.

- Carnosic acid and carnosol also inhibit COX-2, an enzyme that causes pain and inflammation in the body. They also inhibit the production of excess nitric oxide, which also plays a role in the inflammatory process.

NUTRIENTS
(per 1 ounce)

Calcium · · · · · · · · · · · · 88.8 mg

Iron · · · · · · · · · · · · · · · 1.9 mg

Magnesium · · · · · · · · · 25.5 mg

Potassium · · · · · · · · · · 187 mg

Manganese · · · · · · · · · · 0.3 mg

Vitamin A · · · · · · · · · · · 819 IU

Vitamin C · · · · · · · · · · · 6.1 mg

Folate · · · · · · · · · · · 30.5 mcg

SOURSOP

ANNONA MURICATA is the fruit from a broadleaf, flowering evergreen tree. Soursop is native to Central America, the Caribbean, and northern South America, primarily Colombia, Brazil, Peru, Ecuador, Venezuela, and Puerto Rico. Its flavor has been described as a combination of strawberry and pineapple, with sour citrus notes contrasting with an underlying creamy taste reminiscent of coconut or banana.

ANCIENT HISTORY

In ancient times, people used soursop leaves to prepare tea, which was used in treating liver problems and diabetes. In Africa, this herb is still used as analgesic and efficient cure for fever in children. In Mexico, Colombia, Venezuela, and Harar (Ethiopia), soursop was often used as an *agua fresca* beverage; in Colombia and Venezuela, it was more commonly used as fruit for juices.

BENEFITS

- Soursop is widely promoted (sometimes as "graviola") as an alternative cancer treatment in nutrition. It is believed to be 10,000 times more powerful than classic chemotherapy, as it destroys cancer cells and spares healthy body cells.[3,4]

- Soursop is rich in vitamins and minerals and also in many other nutrients, thus beneficial for overall health. The whole plant has healing powers, including its root and fruit.

- Soursop leaves are used for treating bronchitis, congestion, colic, coughs, diabetes, water retention, gallbladder disorders, flu, heart disease, hypertension, indigestion, and other ailments.

- Soursop is used for disorders of the digestive tract such as mouth sores, diarrhea, colitis, and dysentery. It is also used to treat fevers, asthma, cough, ease childbirth, diabetes, flu, hypertension, parasites, and muscle spasms.

- The soursop plant produces natural substances known as Annonaceous acetogenins in its leaves, bark, and seeds. Numerous in-vitro and clinical studies show that these compounds target various types of cancer cells without damaging healthy cells.[5,6]

NUTRIENTS

(per 1 cup)

Dietary Fiber ·········· 7.4 g	Niacin ··············· 2.0 mg	Potassium ··········· 626 mg
Protein ················ 2.3 g	Calcium ············· 31.5 mg	Copper ··············· 0.2 mg
Vitamin C ··········· 46.4 mg	Magnesium ·········· 47.3 mg	

SPINACH

SPINACIA OLERACEA is an edible flowering plant in the family of **AMARANTHACEAE**. It is native to central and southwestern Asia.

ANCIENT HISTORY

Obscurely referred to for years in England as "the Spanish vegetable," the name of this leafy green veggie was later shortened to the name we call it today. It's thought to originate in ancient Persia. Spinach cultivation spread to Nepal, and by the 7th century, to China, where it's still called "Persian greens." The Moors introduced it to Spain around the 11th century. Spinach was the favorite vegetable of Catherine de Medici, a historical figure from the 16th century who was born in Florence, Italy. Since this time, dishes prepared on a bed of spinach are referred to as "a la Florentine."

BENEFITS

- Spinach is high in niacin and zinc, as well as protein, fiber, vitamins A, C, E, and K, thiamin, vitamin B6, folate, calcium, iron, magnesium, phosphorus, potassium, copper, and manganese.

- Abundant flavonoids in spinach act as antioxidants to keep cholesterol from oxidizing and protect the body from free radicals, particularly in the colon. The folate in spinach is beneficial for the cardiovascular system, and magnesium helps lower high blood pressure.

- Studies also have shown that spinach helps maintain brain function, memory, and mental clarity. The carotenoids found in spinach also protect against eye diseases such as cataracts and macular degeneration.

- One cup of fresh spinach, or 1/6 cup of cooked spinach, contains twice the daily vitamin K requirement. This, along with the calcium and magnesium in spinach, is essential to maintain healthy bones.

- The dark green color of spinach leaves indicates they contain high levels of chlorophyll and health-promoting carotenoids such as beta-carotene, lutein, and zeaxanthin.

- Spinach contains high contents of dietary magnesium, which is necessary for energy metabolism, maintaining muscle and nerve function, and maintaining blood pressure.

NUTRIENTS
(per 1 cup)

Vitamin A	2813 IU	Folate	58.2 mcg	Magnesium	23.7 mg
Vitamin C	8.4 mg	Protein	0.9 g	Manganese	0.3 mg
Vitamin K	145 mcg	Calcium	29.7 mg		

SWEET POTATO

IPOMOEA BATATAS is a dicotyledonous plant that belongs to the family **CONVOL-VULACEAE.** Its large, starchy, sweet-tasting, tuberous roots are a root vegetable. The young leaves and shoots are sometimes eaten as greens. The sweet potato is only distantly related to the potato (**SOLANUM TUBEROSUM**) and does not belong to the nightshade family.

ANCIENT HISTORY

Sweet potatoes are native to Central and South America, and are one of the oldest vegetables known to humans. They have been consumed since prehistoric times as evidenced by sweet potato relics dating back 10,000 years that have been discovered in Peruvian caves. Christopher Columbus brought sweet potatoes to Europe after his first voyage to the New World in 1492.

BENEFITS

- Considering fiber content, complex carbohydrates, protein, vitamin A, and potassium, the sweet potato ranked highest in nutritional value, according to the Center for Science in the Public Interest.

- Sweet potatoes are considered low on the glycemic index scale, and recent research suggests they may reduce episodes of low blood sugar and insulin resistance in people with diabetes.

- Among younger men, diets rich in beta-carotene may play a protective role against prostate cancer. Beta-carotene has also been shown to have an inverse association with the development of colon cancer.

- For women of childbearing age, consuming iron from plant sources promotes fertility. The vitamin A in sweet potatoes is also essential during pregnancy and lactation for hormone synthesis.

NUTRIENTS
(per 1 cup)

Protein · · · · · · · · · · · · · · · 4.0 g	Vitamin B6 · · · · · · · · · · 0.6 mg	Copper · · · · · · · · · · · · · 0.3 mg
Vitamin A · · · · · · · · · · 38433 IU	Pantothenic Acid · · · · · 1.8 mg	Manganese · · · · · · · · · · · · 1.0 mg
Vitamin C · · · · · · · · · · · 39.2 mg	Potassium · · · · · · · · · · · · 950 mg	

TOMATO

SOLANUM LYCOPERSICUM, commonly known as a tomato plant, is the edible, often red fruit or berry of the nightshade family, **SOLANACEAE**. Its many varieties are now widely grown, sometimes in greenhouses in cooler climates.

ANCIENT HISTORY

The species originated in Central America and the South American Andes. Its use as a food originated in Mexico and spread throughout the world following the Spanish colonization of the Americas. A member of the deadly nightshade family, tomatoes were erroneously thought to be poisonous (although the leaves can be) by Europeans who were suspicious of the bright, shiny fruit. Native versions were small, like cherry tomatoes, and most likely yellow rather than red.

BENEFITS

- Tomatoes contain the carotene lycopene, one of the most powerful natural antioxidants known. Cooked tomatoes have higher concentrations of lycopene than raw.

- Lycopene has also been shown to improve the skin's ability to protect against harmful UV rays. A study done by researchers at Manchester and Newcastle universities revealed that tomato can protect against sunburn and help keep the skin looking youthful.

- Tomatoes contain all four major carotenoids: alpha- and beta-carotene, lutein, and lycopene. These carotenoids may have individual benefits, but also have synergy as a group.

- When tomatoes are eaten along with healthy fats, like avocado or olives, the body's absorption of the carotenoid phytochemicals in tomatoes can increase by 2 to 15 times, according to a study from Ohio State University.[7]

NUTRIENTS
(per 1 cup)

Protein · · · · · · · · · · · · · · · · 1.3 g

Vitamin A · · · · · · · · · · · · 1241 IU

Vitamin C · · · · · · · · · · · 18.9 mg

Vitamin K · · · · · · · · · · 11.8 mcg

Magnesium · · · · · · · · · 16.4 mg

Phosphorus · · · · · · · · 35.8 mg

Potassium · · · · · · · · · · 353 mg

Manganese · · · · · · · · · 0.2 mg

TURMERIC

CURCUMA LONGA is a rhizomatous herbaceous perennial plant of the ginger family, **ZINGIBERACEAE**. When not used fresh, the rhizomes are boiled for about 30 to 45 minutes and then dried in hot ovens, after which they are ground into a deep orange-yellow powder commonly used as a spice in Indian cuisine and curries, for dyeing, and to impart color to mustard condiments. One active ingredient in it is curcumin. It has a distinctly earthy, slightly bitter, slightly hot peppery flavor and a mustardy smell.

ANCIENT HISTORY

In India, turmeric has been used traditionally for thousands of years as a remedy for stomach and liver ailments, as well as topically to heal sores, mainly for its antimicrobial properties.

BENEFITS

- While studies in humans are still in very early stages, lab and animal studies have shown promising effects of curcumin in the fight against cancer. Curcumin "interferes with several important molecular pathways involved in cancer development, growth and spread," according to the American Cancer Society, even killing cancer cells in the lab setting and shrinking tumors and boosting the effects of chemotherapy in animals.

- Curcumin has been deemed to carry anti-inflammatory powers, which have led to a number of studies examining the benefits of turmeric to people with joint pain or arthritis. One of the most promising found that turmeric extract supplements worked just as well as ibuprofen in patients with knee osteoarthritis.

- Turmeric helps prevent prostate cancer, stop the growth of existing prostate cancer, and even helps destroy cancer cells. Active components in turmeric protect against radiation-induced tumors.

- Turmeric can be used in the treatment of diabetes by moderating insulin levels. It also improves glucose control and increases the effect of medications used to treat diabetes.

- Turmeric contains a substance known as lipopolysaccharide, which helps stimulate the body's immune system. Its antibacterial, antiviral, and antifungal agents also help strengthen it.

NUTRIENTS

(per 1 ounce)

Niacin	1.4 mg	Potassium	707 mg	Iron	11.6 mg
Vitamin C	7.3 mg	Calcium	51.2 mg	Magnesium	34 mg
Vitamin K	3.8 mg	Copper	0.2 mg		

WHEATGRASS

Wheatgrass is a food prepared from the cotyledons of the common wheat plant, *Triticum* AESTIVUM (subspecies of the family POACEAE). Wheatgrass differs from wheat malt in that it is served freeze-dried or fresh, while wheat malt is convectively dried. Since wheatgrass juice is extracted from wheatgrass sprouts, it is gluten-free.

ANCIENT HISTORY

Ancient Egyptians purportedly found these young leafy blades of wheat sacred and prized them for their positive effect on health and vitality. The consumption in modern times began in the 1930s as a result of experiments by Charles F. Schnabel. The agricultural chemist conducted his first experiments using fresh cut grass in an attempt to nurse dying chickens back to health.

BENEFITS

- Wheatgrass contains vitamin A, vitamin C, and vitamin E, iron, calcium, magnesium, and amino acids. Wheatgrass is used for increasing production of hemoglobin, the chemical in red blood cells that carries oxygen; improving blood sugar disorders, such as diabetes; preventing tooth decay; improving wound healing; and preventing bacterial infections. It is also used for removing deposits of drugs, heavy metals, and cancer-causing agents from the body, and for removing toxins from the liver and blood.

- Wheatgrass is also used to treat various disorders of the urinary tract, including infection of the bladder, urethra, and prostate; benign prostatic hypertrophy (BPH); kidney stones; and in "irrigation therapy," the use of a mild diuretic, along with lots of fluids, to increase urine flow.

- Wheatgrass is a complete source of protein. This protein is in the form of polypeptides, simpler and shorter chains of amino acids that the body uses more efficiently in the bloodstream and tissues.

- In addition to flooding the body with therapeutic dosages of vitamins, minerals, antioxidants, enzymes, and phytonutrients, wheatgrass is also a powerful detoxifier, especially of the liver and blood.

- Wheatgrass contains beneficial enzymes, including Superoxide Dismutase (SOD), also found in every cell of the human body. These enzymes help protect from carcinogens by lessening the effects of radiation. SOD also break down superoxide radicals (toxic to living cells) and turn DNA mutations, into harmless components consisting of oxygen and hydrogen peroxide.

NUTRIENTS

(per 1 cup)

Riboflavin · · · · · · · · 7429 mg	Vitamin B12 · · · · · · · · 1.4 mcg	Copper · · · · · · · · · · · 48.6 mg
Niacin · · · · · · · · · · · 7200 mg	Potassium · · · · · · · · 2943 mg	Manganese · · · · · · · 4000 mg
Vitamin B6 · · · · · · · · 1114 mg	Zinc · · · · · · · · · · · · · · 1771 mg	

THE MASTER PLANT RECIPES

IT IS INTERESTING TO NOTE THAT THE FIRST USE OF THE WORD RECIPE IN THE MIDDLE AGES REFERRED TO A "MEDICAL PRESCRIPTION," WHICH CAME FROM THE LATIN WORD MEANING "TO TAKE," AND WAS REPRESENTED BY THE ABBREVIATION RX. IT WASN'T UNTIL 1700'S THAT THE USE OF THE WORD EVOLVED TO REFER TO THE PREPARATION OF FOOD.

THE MASTER PLANTS RECIPES EMPLOY BOTH THE OLD AND MODERN USE OF THE WORD, FOR THESE RECIPES ARE MORE THAN MERE LISTS OF INGREDIENTS AND PREPARATION DIRECTIONS; THEY ARE TRULY A PRESCRIPTION FOR OPTIMUM HEALTH. USING THE MASTER PLANTS, THE CREATIVE RECIPES THAT FOLLOW ARE A COMPILATION OF MEALS SO DELICIOUS, SO SATISFYING, THAT IT MAY BE EASY TO FORGET THAT THEY CAN BE USED TO HELP PREVENT CHRONIC DISEASE.

SO DON YOUR APRON, BRING THIS BOOK INTO THE KITCHEN, AND GET READY TO WHIP UP A DOSE OF DELICIOUSNESS!

apulia rucola salad

Apulia is an ancient and picturesque region, making up the "heel" of Italy's "boot." Rucola—arugula—is prominent in Italian cooking, adding its peppery flavor and many nutritional benefits to pastas, pizzas, sandwiches, and—yes—fresh salads.

YIELD: 2 SERVINGS

ingredients

- 2 organic cabbage leaves
- 1 handful arugula (about 1 cup)
- Juice of 1 lemon, divided
- Freshly ground black pepper to taste
- 1 cup chickpeas, cooked
- 3 button mushrooms, chopped
- 5 cherry tomatoes
- 1 organic carrot, chopped
- Shoyu or tamari
- Pinch of kelp powder
- ½ avocado, pitted, scooped, and mashed (optional, see page 273)

method

Wash the cabbage leaves, pat dry, and place on a serving plate. Add arugula and any other greens, if desired. Sprinkle the leaves with juice from half of the lemon. Add a pinch of the ground pepper and add the chickpeas, mushrooms, tomatoes, and carrot.

Add the remaining lemon juice, a few drops of the shoyu or tamari, a pinch of the kelp powder, and a scoop of the mashed avocado, if desired.

mediterranean green lasagna

Lasagna is known as the ultimate Italian "comfort food"—zesty, creamy, and rich. This fresh, raw, plant-based version substitutes zucchini for the traditional pasta, but is just as zesty, creamy, rich, and comforting as the traditional version.

ingredients

FOR THE MARINARA SAUCE:

- 5 organic Roma tomatoes with skins
- 1 fresh sage leaf
- 1 teaspoon shoyu or tamari
- Pinch of paprika

FOR THE "RICOTTA" CHEESE CREAM:

- 1 cup raw cashews, quick-soaked in hot water for 10 minutes or soaked in water overnight
- 2 tablespoons organic, non-GMO silken tofu
- 1/2 teaspoon fresh or 1/8 teaspoon dried thyme
- 1/2 teaspoon fresh or 1/8 teaspoon dried bay leaves
- 1/2 teaspoon fresh or 1/8 teaspoon dried basil
- 1 tablespoon nutritional yeast
- 1 teaspoon shoyu or tamari

FOR THE CRUMBLE LAYER:

- 1 garlic clove or 1/8 teaspoon garlic powder
- 6 fresh sage leaves
- 1 cup walnuts

FOR THE LASAGNA:

- 1 extra-large or two medium organic, non-GMO zucchini
- 1 handful organic arugula (about 1 cup)
- 15 organic basil leaves, chopped (plus some whole leaves for garnish)

method

In a food processor, combine the marinara sauce ingredients until liquid. Transfer to a small container and set aside.

In a food processor, combine the "ricotta" cheese ingredients for about 30 seconds or until mixture is creamy. Transfer to a small container and set aside.

In a food processor, combine the crumble layer ingredients for about 10 seconds. Transfer to a small container and set aside.

Lastly, using a mandoline in the 0.5 mm setting, slice zucchini lengthwise, creating long, thin pieces. Set aside, lying flat. (You will not be using the first, short slices; therefore, keep them in an airtight container and use later in a soup, stew, whole grain dish, smoothie, or salad, such as the Persepolis Kale Salad, page 199.)

TO ASSEMBLE THE LASAGNA:

Place a couple of the zucchini slices on a serving dish. Place the slices halfway on the center of the plate. You will be building up the lasagna from this half.

Start by adding a layer of the arugula, one thick layer of the ricotta cheese and one layer of the chopped basil. Add two more zucchini slices, and continue adding one layer of cheese, one layer of crumbles, and one layer of marinara. Fold in the bottom slices of zucchini.

Continue adding another layer each of arugula and basil. Fold in the second layer of zucchini and top with cheese cream and marinara sauce. Repeat the process with the rest of the ingredients.

Garnish with whole basil leaves.

damascus-crusted asparagus

Asparagus, from the Greek language for "sprout" or "shoot" is a member of the lily family and is native to eastern Mediterranean and Asia Minor regions, where it is prized for its unique flavor.

YIELD: 4 SERVINGS

ingredients

- 1 bunch asparagus (about 12 spears)
- 2 tablespoons walnuts, Brazil nuts, or almonds
- ¼ cup nutritional yeast
- ½ teaspoon ground pepper
- Pinch of paprika
- ¼ cup whole wheat breadcrumbs
- Juice of ½ lemon

method

Preheat the oven to 350°F.

To remove the white bottom end of the asparagus, hold each asparagus spear with both hands and bend it near the white end. The white end will snap off.

In a food processor, blend the nuts for about 5 seconds or until crumbled. Transfer to a small bowl and mix in the nutritional yeast, pepper, paprika, and breadcrumbs.

Arrange the asparagus spears side by side in a baking dish, and sprinkle with the nut crumb mixture. Bake for 20 minutes. Sprinkle with some lemon juice and serve.

Chef's Note: For softer asparagus, bake for another 10 minutes.

Ishtar's Asparagus

In ancient Mesopotamia, the cradle of civilization, Ishtar was worshipped as a goddess of love and sexuality. Asparagus and almonds, with their high vitamin E content, are considered by many to be aphrodisiacs. With its rich, creamy sauce, this is a dish fit for a god or goddess!

YIELD: 2 TO 4 SERVINGS

ingredients

- 12 to 15 spears fresh asparagus
- 1 small onion, peeled and quartered (about ½ cup)
- 8 garlic cloves
- 1 tablespoon organic, non-GMO white miso
- 1 tablespoon nutritional yeast
- 1½ tablespoon gluten-free flour, such as quinoa, buckwheat, or chickpea flour
- ¼ cup almonds
- ½ cup non-dairy milk
- Freshly ground black pepper to taste or kelp sprinkles for garnish

method

To remove the white bottom end of the asparagus, hold each spear with both hands and bend it near the white end. The white tip will snap off. Set aside.

In a food processor, chop the onion and the garlic with one cup of filtered water. Transfer the mixture to a saucepan and add the miso. Sauté for about 8 minutes, or until aromatic.

In the food processor, blend the nutritional yeast, flour, almonds, and milk until creamy.

Add the asparagus spears to the saucepan, arranging side by side, and allow them to cook for about 5 minutes. Turn the asparagus over. Cook an extra 5 minutes or until slightly brown.

Place the asparagus in a serving dish, and pour the cream mixture over the middle of the vegetables. Sprinkle with a pinch of pepper or kelp sprinkles.

aztec avocado boats

The Aztec people grew a wide variety of fruits and vegetables; among the most prominent were tomatoes, onions, and avocados, in addition to various seeds. These Aztec avocado boats are a colorful, fresh, and delicious modern interpretation of an ancient civilization's favorite foods.

ingredients

- ○ Juice of 1 lemon (about 3 tablespoons)
- ○ ½ organic apple with skin, diced (about ¾ cup)
- ○ 4 to 6 organic cherry tomatoes, halved (about ¼ cup)
- ○ 1 cup peas, lentils, or chickpeas, cooked
- ○ ½ onion or 1 shallot, minced
- ○ 1 handful leafy greens (arugula, spinach, kale, or chard) (about 1 cup)
- ○ 2 sprigs fresh cilantro, chopped
- ○ Freshly ground black pepper to taste
- ○ 3 ripe Hass avocados,* halved and pitted (see page 273)
- ○ Sesame seeds or sunflower seeds, for garnish

method

Combine all the ingredients up to the avocados in a mixing bowl, reserving a teaspoon or two of the lemon juice. Stir until well combined and sprinkle with the reserved lemon juice. Fill the avocado boats with veggie-apple mixture and garnish with the sesame or sunflower seeds.

*Chef's Note: When an avocado is ripe and ready to be eaten, its outside is tender to the touch, and the small stem or "belly" is easily removed. To accelerate ripening, place the avocado in a paper bag for a day or two.

{AVOCADO}

cashew e pepe

Cacio e Pepe (Cheese and Pepper) is a classic Italian pasta dish. This plant-based version replaces dairy cheese with a healthful yet rich and creamy cashew-avocado sauce.

YIELD: 2 SERVINGS

ingredients

- ½ avocado, pitted (see page 273)
- 1 cup raw cashews
- 2 tablespoons nutritional yeast
- 3 tablespoons shoyu soy sauce or tamari, divided
- ¼ cup non-dairy milk
- Juice of ½ lemon, divided
- 7 ounces (about ⅓ of a standard package) whole grain or plant-based spaghetti*
- 3 garlic cloves, chopped (optional)
- 4 fresh parsley sprigs, chopped, divided
- 1 tablespoon organic, non-GMO miso paste
- ½ teaspoon freshly ground pepper, plus more for garnish

method

Fill a large pot one-third of the way with filtered water. Bring to a boil.

Carve out the avocado pulp with a spoon. Add it to a food processor, along with the cashews, the nutritional yeast, 1 tablespoon of the shoyu or tamari, and the non-dairy milk. Blend for about 20 to 30 seconds or until mixture is creamy. Add half of the lemon juice, cover slightly, and set aside.

Place the uncooked spaghetti into the pot of boiling water. If desired, hold the spaghetti together and break the bundle in half before adding it to the boiling water. Some Italian chefs use this approach to boil the pasta homogeneously in the water and to avoid dealing with extra-long strands of spaghetti when eating. Depending on the type of spaghetti you choose, the cooking times may vary. Follow the package's cooking instructions for best results.

Add the garlic, two sprigs of the parsley, the miso, and ½ cup water to a large saucepan. Sauté over medium heat for about 8 to 10 minutes, or until the garlic browns a little. Add ½ cup of extra water in 1-tablespoon increments in case it evaporates too quickly.

Remove the cooked spaghetti from the pot and add it to the saucepan, reserving the cooking water. Add the avocado cream and a little of the pasta water as necessary to help the pasta and cream merge together, and stir all ingredients well. Add pepper and remaining 2 tablespoons of the shoyu or tamari. Stir again and serve immediately.

For garnish, sprinkle with lemon juice, the remaining two sprigs of parsley, and additional pepper to taste.

Chef's Note: To ensure the whole grain or plant-based pasta is made without eggs, dairy, and gluten, be sure to read the ingredient list on the package. There are many 100% plant-based options available today, such as buckwheat, quinoa, bean, whole grain, or rice pasta.

cinque terre stuffed ravioli

Cinque Terre—"five lands"—refers to a picturesque spot on the Italian Riviera consisting of five small towns known for their lush vineyards, pristine water, and bountiful farmers' markets. This fresh ravioli dish is nearly as beautiful as the land for which it is named.

YIELD: 2 SERVINGS

ingredients

FOR THE RAVIOLI:

○ **2 medium organic red beets**
○ **A few leaves of fresh basil**

FOR THE RELISH:

○ **1 cup fresh organic raspberries**
○ **2 tablespoons 100% pure maple syrup or ½ banana**
○ **2 dates, pitted**

FOR THE CHEESE:

○ **1 cup cashews**
○ **1 teaspoon shoyu or tamari**
○ **1 tablespoon nutritional yeast**
○ **¼ cup non-dairy milk**

method

Peel the beets. Using an adjustable ceramic or BPA-free mandoline, slice raw beets on the 0.5 mm setting. Pat dry or place on paper towel. Set aside.

In a food processor, blend the raspberries, maple syrup or banana, and dates until puréed. Pour into a small container and set aside.

Rinse the food processor. Blend the remaining ingredients (except for the basil) for about 20 seconds or until the mixture reaches a creamy consistency.

Arrange half the beet slices on a serving plate. Add a layer of the cream mixture to each slice and top with a second beet slice. Garnish with chopped basil. Pour some of the raspberry relish over beets and enjoy together.

Chef's Note: For an alternative presentation, the raspberry relish can be drizzled or pooled on the serving plate before the ravioli.

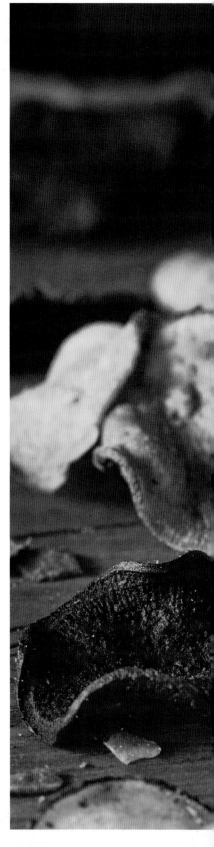

{ B E E T }

marrakesh beet chips

Yucca, beets, and potatoes are dietary staples in many countries, including Morocco. While they are usually eaten boiled or steamed, this recipe is a playful and colorful (not to mention flavorful) take on these delicious and healthful vegetables.

YIELD: 4 TO 6 SERVINGS

ingredients

- ½ medium yucca root (also called cassava)
- 1 medium organic sweet potato
- 3 medium organic beets
- 2 teaspoons fresh turmeric, minced or 2 tablespoons organic turmeric powder

- 3 tablespoons organic onion, minced or 3 tablespoons organic onion powder
- 3 teaspoons dried bay leaves
- 3 teaspoons garlic powder
- ½ teaspoon paprika (optional) Freshly ground black pepper, to taste

method

To prepare the yucca, beets, and sweet potato, use a vegetable peeler to remove their skins. Rinse and set aside.

Using an adjustable ceramic or BPA-free mandoline, slice the vegetables on the 0.5 mm setting to make paper-thin slices. Place the slices in a large bowl. Add all of the spices and gently mix well with your hands.

Dehydrate the chips in a food dehydrator set to at least 115°F for 24 to 48 hours or until crispy. This makes about two dehydrator trays of chips. They start to get soggy soon after they are taken out of

the dehydrator, so place them in an airtight container and consume them within a few days. For crispier chips, leave in the dehydrator for another 2 hours.

Chef's Note: Regular potatoes (not the sweet potato kind) are part of the nightshade family and contain natural toxins when consumed raw. Therefore we don't recommend dehydrating regular potatoes.

andean pepper boats

Bell peppers are a staple in South and Central American cuisine, making an appearance in nearly every meal. Their various colors and shapes make for beautiful presentations.

ingredients

○ **2 medium bell peppers, any color**

○ **6 large porcini or cremini mushrooms, diced (about one cup)**

○ **1 medium organic pear with skin, diced**

○ **¼ cup dried fruit (raisins, goji berries, dried dates, or figs)**

○ **1 sprig fresh parsley, chopped**

○ **1 sprig fresh or ⅛ teaspoon dried oregano**

○ **1 sprig fresh or ⅛ teaspoon dried thyme**

○ **1 teaspoon sesame seeds**

○ **Freshly ground black pepper to taste**

method

Preheat the oven at 350°F.

Cut each pepper in half and discard seeds and stems. Place the pepper halves cut-side up in a glass or silicone baking dish.

In a small bowl, combine the mushrooms, pear, dried fruit of choice, and herbs. Stuff the peppers with the mushroom mixture.

Place the stuffed peppers in the oven and bake for 30 minutes or until lightly browned, rotating the tray after 15 minutes.

Sprinkle with the sesame seeds and freshly ground pepper, and serve immediately.

columbus's favorite goulash

Although peppers—both hot and sweet—were cultivated in Central and South America for thousands of years, it was Christopher Columbus who introduced peppers to Europe. This was a sort of "happy accident," as Columbus had mistaken the pepper plants for the plants that produce peppercorns. This recipe pays homage to the pepper dishes the indigenous people offered Columbus.

YIELD: 3 TO 4 SERVINGS

ingredients

- 1 medium organic red bell pepper
- 1 medium organic yellow bell pepper
- 4 to 7 ounces of organic, non-GMO firm tofu
- ½ medium white onion
- 1 fresh sprig parsley or ½ teaspoon dried
- 1 cup vegetable broth (optional)
- ½ teaspoon dried rosemary
- 1 fresh bay leaf or ½ teaspoon dried bay leaf (or one whole dried bay leaf)
- Pinch of dried oregano
- 6 organic Roma tomatoes
- 1 teaspoon black sesame seeds
- 1 fresh sage leaf or ½ teaspoon dried sage

method

Slice each pepper in half and remove seeds and stem. Slice each pepper half into long, thin strips. Lastly, cut the strips in half and set aside.

Slice the tofu into long strips, and the slice strips in half.

In a food processor, chop the onion and parsley together until minced. Transfer to a saucepan with one cup of water or vegetable broth, and sauté for 3 to 5 minutes or until the onions are translucent.

Add the pepper and tofu slices to the saucepan and add one cup of water. Add the rosemary, bay, and oregano, and sauté on medium heat for 5 minutes, stirring frequently.

Chop the tomatoes in a food processor for about 10 seconds until puréed and add to saucepan. Add the sesame seeds and sage, and let simmer for 12 to 15 minutes, covered, over low to medium heat. Serve immediately.

{BLUEBERRY}

apache cheesecake

The cheesecake of the Standard American Diet is an artery-clogging amalgam of cheese, butter, eggs, and sugar. This raw, plant-based version boasts all of the flavor but only a fraction of the fat and none of the cholesterol of the traditional original. What's more, it provides dietary fiber, healthy omega-3s, and antioxidants.

YIELD: 10 TO 12 SMALL SERVINGS

ingredients

FOR THE CRUST:

- ½ cup dates, pitted
- ½ cup walnuts

FOR THE CHEESECAKE:

- Juice of ½ lemon
- 1½ cup raw cashews, quick-soaked in hot water for 10 minutes or soaked in water overnight
- 3 dates, pitted
- 2 tablespoons organic, non-GMO silken tofu

FOR TOPPING:

- 1 cup organic blueberries

method

In a food processor, combine the crust ingredients until the mixture forms a ball. Drop the mixture in 1 tablespoon amounts into 10 to 12 silicone muffin cups. Press to fill out the bottom of each muffin cup. Set aside.

In a food processor, combine all the cheesecake ingredients for about 30 seconds or until the mixture is thick and creamy. Add 2 to 3 tablespoons of the mixture to each of the muffin cups, or until each cup is filled to the top.

Top with a few blueberries and freeze the cups for about 4 hours.

Allow the cheesecake to thaw for 5 to 10 minutes before serving. Enjoy immediately.

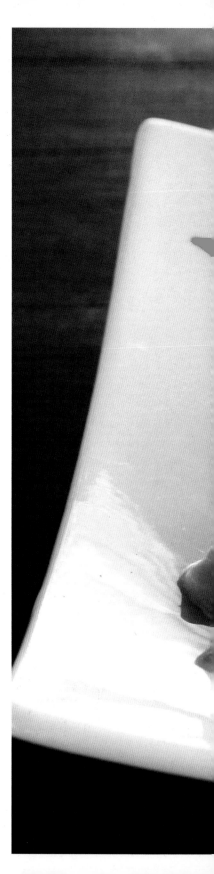

{ BLUEBERRY }

blueberry hopi parfait

The ancient Hopi people were expert farmers, but they were also adept at foraging, eating many fruits, nuts, and seeds. This colorful parfait is rich in protein, vitamins, and antioxidants. The addition of seeds and nuts supplies a healthful dose of omega-3 fatty acids, which can help lower triglyceride levels and reduce or prevent inflammation in the body.

YIELD: 2 REGULAR / 4 SMALL SERVINGS

ingredients

- 5 tablespoons organic, non-GMO silken tofu
- 1½ bananas, peeled (1 whole, ½ sliced)
- 1 cup fresh organic blueberries, divided
- 1 cup gluten-free rolled oats
- 2 tablespoons chia seeds
- ¼ cup sunflower seeds
- ½ cup fresh organic raspberries
- 1 tablespoon nuts, any type (optional)
- ½ tablespoon shredded coconut (optional)
- 2 tablespoons almond butter, unsweetened

method

In a food processor, blend the tofu and 1 whole banana. Pour into a small container and set aside.

Rinse the food processor and purée ½ cup of the blueberries. Set the purée aside.

To assemble the parfait, you will split the following ingredients between two dishes for regular servings or split between four dishes for smaller servings. Spoon a layer of fresh, whole blueberries in the serving dishes. Add a layer of the tofu-banana cream, one

layer of rolled oats, one thin layer of chia seeds, and one layer of sunflower seeds.

Add a layer of the raspberries, a second layer of the tofu-banana cream, and some banana slices. Top with the blueberry purée, nuts (optional), and shredded coconut (optional), a dollop of almond butter, and any leftover fruit.

Chef's Note: Although the tofu-banana cream will naturally darken, the parfait will keep in the refrigerator covered for a day or two.

amazon nutty steaks

These savory tofu steaks are packed with protein and make for a hearty entrée.

YIELD: 2 SERVINGS

ingredients

- 3 dates, pitted
- ½ cup Brazil nuts
- 2 tablespoons almond butter, unsweetened
- 1 teaspoon shoyu or tamari
- 2 pieces of organic, non-GMO firm tofu (about 3 ounces each), drained

- 2 tablespoons vegetable broth (optional)
- 1 cup mushrooms, any variety, chopped
- Sprinkle of fresh or dried thyme
- Sprinkle of fresh or dried oregano

- 1 teaspoon organic, non-GMO miso paste
- ½ cup non-dairy milk
- Sprouts (any organic, non-GMO variety)
- ¼ cup pomegranate seeds, dried cranberries, or fresh figs

method

Soak the dates in a small container with water. Set aside.

In a food processor, chop the Brazil nuts, pulsing for a few seconds at a time. The nuts will be chopped very quickly; take care not to over-blend. Transfer into a small container and set aside.

Remove the dates from the container, reserving the soaking water. In the food processor, blend the almond butter, dates, shoyu or tamari, and 2 tablespoons of the date water until creamy and smooth. Transfer to a container and set aside.

Add the tofu pieces to a saucepan with 2 tablespoons of water or vegetable broth and sauté for 2 to 3 minutes, flipping once through. Let the tofu brown a bit, and add extra tablespoons of the date water if saucepan dries.

In a separate saucepan, add the mushrooms, thyme, oregano, and miso. Sauté for 3 minutes and add the non-dairy milk. Simmer over low heat for 4 to 5 minutes until sauce thickens. Stir frequently.

Remove the tofu from heat and place on a serving dish. With a knife or small spatula, spread the almond butter mixture over the tofu and cover all sides. Sprinkle the tofu steaks abundantly with the Brazil nut crumble mixture, covering all sides as well.

Remove the mushrooms from heat, and pour over the tofu steaks. Top with your favorite sprouts, pomegranate seeds, dry cranberries, or fresh figs.

{ B R A Z I L   N U T }

carioca pear crumble

The locals of Rio de Janeiro, Brazil, refer to themselves as
cariocas. This delicious raw dessert featuring Brazil nuts features a
beautiful presentation sure to impress.

YIELD: 4 SERVINGS

ingredients

FOR THE CRUMBLES:

- ¼ cup almonds
- ¼ cup Brazil nuts

FOR THE MINT CREAM:

- 5 tablespoons organic, non-GMO silken tofu
- 1 dried or fresh fig
- 10 fresh mint leaves
- ¼ cup non-dairy milk
- Juice of ½ lemon

FOR THE TOWERS:

- 1 large or 2 medium organic pears with skin
- Juice of ½ lemon
- Pomegranate seeds or fresh berries, for garnish

method

In a food processor, mix the almonds and the Brazil nuts slightly by pulsing for 3 seconds, twice. The nuts' consistency should be crumbly but not mushy. Pour crumbles in a separate container and set aside.

In the food processor, blend all the cream ingredients for 20 seconds or until a smooth consistency is reached.

Slice the pears thinly using a mandoline or vegetable slicer. Spread the pear slices on a flat dish and sprinkle them with the remaining lemon juice. This will help prevent the pears from turning brown.

Place a pear slice on an individual serving dish. Add a teaspoon of the mint cream, add a small sprinkle of the nut crumble, and add a second pear slice. Add another teaspoon of the mint cream, another sprinkle of nuts, and top with a third pear slice.

Repeat the process adding another 5 slices of pear with the mint cream and nuts in between.

Create the rest of the towers and top with fresh pomegranate seeds or berries. Serve immediately.

{BROCCOLI}

emperor's broccoli soup

With a full day's supply of vitamins A and C in every bowl, this is truly a super-powered soup! The addition of turmeric adds an anti-inflammatory boost as well.

YIELD: 3 SERVINGS

ingredients

- 1 medium organic red onion, minced
- ½ medium bell pepper, seeds and stem removed
- 2 fresh or dried bay leaves
- ½ head organic broccoli with stem, cut into chunks (about 2 cups)
- 1 handful organic kale, chopped (about 1 cup)
- Small handful of raw cashews (about ¼ cup), divided
- 2 cups low-sodium, organic vegetable broth
- 1 tablespoon organic, non-GMO light miso paste
- ½ teaspoon turmeric
- 1 to 2 teaspoons tamari or shoyu
- ¼ teaspoon paprika
- Freshly ground black pepper to taste

method

In a food processor, chop the onion, bell pepper, and bay leaves until minced. Transfer to a medium or large pot and cook over medium heat with ½ cup water. Let simmer for about 6 minutes, stirring frequently.

In a high-powered blender or food processor, blend the broccoli chunks, kale, cashews (reserving a few broccoli florets for garnish), and vegetable broth. Blend for 30 seconds or until the mixture becomes a thick liquid. Pour into the pot with the simmering onion and bell pepper and mix well. Add miso, turmeric, tamari or shoyu, and paprika, and cook for another 6 to 8 minutes over medium heat.

Remove the bay leaves and serve. Add freshly ground black pepper to taste and garnish with leftover broccoli bits and a few cashews.

satay broccoli wings

Satay is a Malaysian and Indonesian dish traditionally made of seasoned meat—such as chicken wings—served with a sauce. This recipe features more healthful broccoli "wings" with a very flavorful sauce.

YIELD: 2 TO 3 SERVINGS

ingredients

FOR THE WINGS:

- ○ ½ bunch broccoli with stem (about 12 to 16 ounces)
- ○ 6 garlic cloves
- ○ 1 cup filtered water or vegetable broth
- ○ 1½ tablespoons sesame seeds

FOR THE SATAY SAUCE:

- ○ 3 tablespoons shoyu or tamari
- ○ 2 to 3 tablespoons lemon juice (about 1 lemon)
- ○ 4 tablespoons organic almond butter, unsweetened
- ○ ½ cup filtered water

method

Slice the broccoli florets off the main bunch starting from the outer florets. Slice vertically, leaving at least 1 to 2 inches of stem. This will create the wings. Set aside.

Chop the garlic in a food processor or mince with a knife. Transfer to a saucepan. Sauté with the water or vegetable broth for about 3 to 5 minutes or until the garlic browns a bit.

Add the broccoli to the saucepan and cook for about 6 minutes, covered. For softer broccoli, cook 3 to 5 minutes longer, adding additional water if needed.

In a medium-size container, combine all satay sauce ingredients and stir with a fork. Set aside.

Serve the florets and pour the sauce over the vegetables. Sprinkle with the sesame seeds and enjoy immediately.

nepal's buckwheat wraps

Nearly every household in Nepal grows buckwheat, a plant cultivated for its seeds. Because of the seeds' resemblance to grain (and because it is rich in complex carbohydrates), buckwheat is often called a "pseudo cereal," as is often cooked as a sort of porridge for breakfast. Here, however, the naturally gluten-free buckwheat makes an appearance for lunch or dinner, incorporated into hearty, tasty wraps.

ingredients

- ½ medium organic onion, diced (about ½ cup)
- 3¼ cups filtered water, divided
- 1 tablespoon organic, non-GMO miso paste
- ⅛ teaspoon dry or 1 fresh bay leaf
- ⅛ teaspoon dry or 1 fresh sage leaf
- 1¼ cups buckwheat, uncooked
- 1 tablespoon nutritional yeast
- 1 large organic celery stalk, sliced (about ½ cup)
- 1 organic carrot, peeled and shredded (½ cup)
- Pinch of paprika
- Freshly ground black pepper to taste
- 6 large organic chard or cabbage leaves, deveined, washed, and patted dry

method

Sauté the onions for about 3 minutes with a ¼ cup of the water. Add the miso, bay, sage, and the remaining 3 cups of water and bring to a boil. Add the buckwheat and cook over medium heat, covered, for about 15 minutes or until buckwheat is soft.

Remove from heat and fluff. Transfer to a mixing bowl and add the yeast, celery, carrot, paprika, and pepper. Stir and mix well.

Stuff the leaves by adding about 3 tablespoons of the buckwheat mixture toward the wide end of the leaf. Fold the sides of the leaf over filling, and starting with the stem end, roll the leaf up, compressing the mixture a bit, like when wrapping a burrito or a sushi roll. Use a bamboo toothpick or skewer if necessary to keep the wrap together.

Serve and enjoy with hummus, avocado, peas, chickpeas, or tomatoes.

{BUCKWHEAT}

the monk's cacao porridge

Each morning, the monks in Myanmar (formerly Burma) leave their monastery to gather ingredients for their morning meal. Since they are not allowed to work for money, they open their bowls to citizens on the street, who contribute grains and other ingredients from which porridge is made. This hearty, nutty porridge features buckwheat. It contains many antioxidants and, despite its name, is naturally gluten-free. Combined with antioxidant-rich raw cacao powder and almonds, this is the perfect meal to fuel the start of your day.

YIELD: 2 SERVINGS

ingredients

○ ½ cup buckwheat

○ 1 banana, peeled

○ 2 teaspoons raw cacao powder

○ ½ cup non-dairy milk

○ 1 tablespoon almond butter, unsweetened

○ ¼ almonds

○ ½ cup fresh fruit, any type

method

To cook the buckwheat, bring 2 cups of water to a boil. Stir in the buckwheat, and bring back to a boil. Reduce the heat and simmer, covered, until just about all of the liquid has been absorbed, about 10 to 12 minutes. Let cool down or refrigerate if room-temperature or chilled porridge is desired.

In a food processor or blender, combine the banana, cacao, non-dairy milk, and almond butter and process until smooth.

Divide the buckwheat into 2 serving dishes. Pour the cacao mixture over the buckwheat and sprinkle with the almonds and fruit. Serve immediately.

Chef's Note: This porridge also can be enjoyed chilled. Buckwheat also makes a great substitute for oats and breakfast cereals, and as a side dish substitute for rice.

caribbean cacao pancakes

Yes, it is possible to enjoy a sweet breakfast standard—pancakes—on a whole foods, plant-based diet. This recipe uses omega-3 rich flax "eggs" (ground flaxseeds mixed with water) and dates to sweeten the batter naturally. The dates and the cacao powder create a sunny Caribbean flavor to this breakfast favorite.

YIELD: 7 PANCAKES

ingredients

- 2 tablespoons ground flaxseeds
- 6 tablespoons filtered water
- ¼ cup walnuts
- 4 medjool dates, pitted
- 1¼ cups non-dairy milk
- 1 cup quinoa flour or buckwheat flour (or all-purpose whole wheat flour)
- 2 tablespoons cacao powder
- Fresh fruit of your choice for topping
- 1 recipe Date Sauce (page 275)

method

In a food processor, blend the ground flaxseeds with the water for about 10 seconds until mixture is well blended and thick. Transfer to a mixing bowl and set aside.

In the food processor, chop the walnuts by pulsing for 2 to 3 seconds only. You want the walnuts to be chunky. Add to the mixing bowl.

In the food processor, combine the dates and non-dairy milk until thoroughly blended. Add to the mixing bowl.

Add the flour and cacao to the mixing bowl. Whisk to combine all ingredients thoroughly.

Heat up a non-stick pan or skillet. (To ensure pan is hot enough, drop a sprinkle of water into the empty pan; it will evaporate and disappear very quickly when ready.)

Pour a ladleful (about ¼ cup) of the pancake batter into the pan or skillet, forming round, flat shapes. When holes cover most of the pancake surface, flip over and cook for another minute or two. Repeat process with the remaining pancake batter.

Serve and top with the creamy date sauce (this is your replacement for maple syrup), and some fresh fruit of your choice, such as berries, currants, chopped bananas, mango, or persimmon.

olmec fudge brownies

The Olmec were prehistoric people comprising one of the first civilizations of Mexico. This dense, chocolaty fudge is a sweet tribute to knowledge handed down by this ancient civilization.

ingredients

FOR THE FUDGE:

○ **4 tablespoons cacao powder**

○ **6 large prunes, pitted**

○ **6 large medjool dates, pitted
1 cup nuts, any variety
(almonds, walnuts, Brazil nuts,
pecans, or mixed)**

FOR THE CHOCOLATE ICING:

○ **1 recipe Chocolate Spread
(page 275)**

FOR GARNISH:

○ **5 pecans, chopped or whole**

method

In the food processor, combine
the fudge ingredients until mixture
is compact and well combined.
Transfer to a 8 x 8-inch square
cake pan, and press the mixture
against the dish with a spatula.
Spread evenly through the dish.

Lay a thick layer of chocolate
icing over the fudge. Garnish with
whole or chopped pecans, slice,
and serve.

chichén-itzá blackberry mousse

Chichén Itzá was a large pre-Columbian city built by the Maya people of the Terminal Classic period. This mousse is a rendition of the powerful chia seed with an equally healing berry blended into one for a sweet tribute to Mayan cooking.

YIELD: 2 TO 3 SERVINGS

ingredients

○ 2 tablespoons chia seeds

○ 6 tablespoons filtered water

○ 9 medjool dates, pitted

○ 1 cup organic blackberries

method

In a food processor, combine the chia seeds and the water. Blend continuously for about 30 seconds or until the mixture is completely blended and the seeds are pulverized. Transfer to a mixing bowl and set aside.

In the food processor, combine the dates and blackberries until creamy. Transfer to the mixing bowl and combine well with the chia mixture until blended.

Place mixture in small serving bowls or in a medium-size serving bowl. Refrigerate for 20 minutes and serve.

Chef's Note: The mousse will last a couple of days refrigerated in a medium-size airtight container.

{ C H I A }

incan mango pudding

The ancient Incans, Mayans, and Aztecs consumed chia seeds for sustainable energy when they had to travel long distances on foot. It is easy to see why: a single ounce of chia seeds contains 11 grams of fiber, 4 grams of protein, and 5 grams of omega-3 healthy fat, as well as antioxidants. Chia seeds readily absorb liquid, becoming gelatinous and soft. This not only makes them easier to digest, but makes for an easy and quick-to-make pudding, with a texture similar to tapioca.

YIELD: 4 SMALL / 2 REGULAR SERVINGS

ingredients

- 1 whole mango, peeled, pitted, and chopped (about one cup), divided
- 2 medjool dates, pitted
- ¾ cup filtered water, divided
- 4 tablespoons chia seeds
- ¼ cup prunes, kiwi, or other tropical fruit, chopped or sliced

method

Blend half of the mango in the food processor with the dates and ½ cup of the water. Transfer to a medium-size container, add chia seeds, and stir. Let the pudding sit for about 20 minutes, stirring occasionally.

Pour chia mixture into two or four serving bowls.

In a food processor, combine the remaining mango chunks with the remaining ¼ cup of water. Pour mango liquid over chia puddings and top with the chopped tropical fruits.

{CHICKPEA}

lebanese chickpea stew

Chickpeas—also known as garbanzo beans—are a staple in Lebanese cuisine. This lively, flavorful stew is the ultimate comfort food.

YIELD: 2 SERVINGS

ingredients

- 8 garlic cloves
- ½ cup water or vegetable broth
- 3 medium organic tomatoes
- ⅛ teaspoon dried or ½ teaspoon fresh thyme
- ⅛ teaspoon dried or ½ teaspoon fresh bay leaf
- ⅛ teaspoon dried rosemary
- 2 cups filtered water
- 1 tablespoon organic, non-GMO miso paste
- 1 cup chickpeas, cooked
- 1 handful fresh spinach (about 1 cup)
- Freshly ground black pepper to taste

method

In a food processor, chop the garlic cloves until minced.

In a medium saucepan, sauté the garlic with the ½ cup of water or vegetable broth over medium heat. Sauté for 3 to 5 minutes.

In the food processor, blend tomatoes until puréed and add to saucepan. Add herbs, water, and miso paste. Stir. Cook for about 10 minutes, or until sauce bubbles. Add the chickpeas and cook for another 6 minutes.

Serve on a bed of fresh spinach and sprinkle with fresh pepper. Enjoy with rice or quinoa, potatoes, corn, or avocado.

{CHICKPEA}

jordanian roasted chickpeas

The chickpea (or garbanzo bean) is one of the major food legume crops in Jordan, since they are a prominent part of the Jordanian diet. Although appearing in a variety of entrées and side dishes such as stews or hummus, in this recipe, chickpeas are seasoned and roasted to eat as a fun snack.

YIELD: 3 SERVINGS

ingredients

- ½ tablespoon organic garlic powder
- ½ tablespoon organic onion powder
- ⅛ teaspoon freshly ground black pepper
- ⅛ teaspoon turmeric powder
- Pinch of paprika
- 1½ cups chickpeas, cooked

method

Preheat the oven to 400°F.

Add all ingredients except for chickpeas to a mixing bowl. Mix the spices well.

Place chickpeas in a single layer on a baking tray. Use a silicone baking dish or an oven tray lined with a parchment or silicone sheet.

Sprinkle half of the spice mixture over the chickpeas, reserving the rest to sprinkle over when turning the chickpeas. Bake for 25 minutes or until chickpeas are lightly browned.

Shake the tray a bit to carefully to turn the chickpeas over. Sprinkle with the rest of the spice mixture and continue baking for another 15 minutes. Serve.

{ F I G }

babel fig pie

At once sweet, chewy, smooth, and crunchy, fresh figs add a unique flavor and texture to any dish. This raw pie combines fresh figs with other antioxidant powerhouses such as flax seeds, nuts, and fresh berries to make a very healthful dessert.

YIELD: ONE 8-INCH PIE (4 TO 5 SERVINGS)

ingredients

FOR PIE CRUST:

- ¼ cup flaxseeds
- 8 dates, pitted
- ½ cup walnuts
- ½ cup almonds
- ½ cup pumpkin seeds

FOR FILLING:

- 1 banana (optional), peeled and thinly sliced
- 5 to 6 medium fresh figs, thinly sliced
- 10 fresh blackberries
- Currants, for garnish

method

In a food processor, process the flaxseeds, pulsing for about 10 seconds or until they disintegrate into a powder. Transfer into a mixing bowl and set aside.

In a food processor, combine the rest of the pie crust ingredients until mixture is compact. Transfer to the mixing bowl and blend together with flaxseeds. If you have a small food processor, combine the nut and seed ingredients with one date each. This will allow the date to mix well with each of the other ingredients.

Using a spatula or bare hands, mold the mixture into an 8- or 9-inch pie dish. (See Chef's Note, below.) Press flat onto bottom of pie dish, pressing some of the mixture ½ inch up the sides.

If adding a banana, add the thin slices covering the crust. Arrange fig slices in a second layer covering the banana. Lastly, add blackberries along the crust edge of the pie and some currants for garnish.

Chef's Note: We recommend using a silicone, ceramic, or glass dish.

{ F I G }

goddess's baked onion tarts

High in beneficial sulphur compounds, the allium vegetables—which include onions and garlic—should be an essential part of your daily diet. Roasting the onions mellows their flavor, bringing out a bit of sweetness, and with the fig paste and black sesame seeds, they make a beautiful presentation on your dinner table.

YIELD: 8 SERVINGS

ingredients

- **4 whole organic onions**
- **5 dried or fresh figs**
- **4 tablespoons organic, non-GMO silken tofu**
- **1½ teaspoons black sesame seeds, divided**
- **½ cup nuts, any kind**

method

Preheat the oven to 350°F.

Slice the onions in half. Slice just enough from the end of each onion half so both halves can stand upright without toppling over.

Bake for 25 to 30 minutes or until the onions look brown and crispy. As an option, you can loosen the rings of each onion and bake them separately.

In a food processor, combine the figs, tofu, and 1 teaspoon of the sesame seeds, and blend until creamy.

Place the baked onions on a serving dish and spread about 1 tablespoon of fig paste on each onion half. Sprinkle with the reserved sesame seeds and enjoy.

Chef's Note: Use a piece parchment paper or a silicone baking sheet when silicone trays are not available.

{FUNGI}

kyoto fungi risotto

Traditional risotto is a delicious dish of Arborio rice—a refined white rice—and often contains butter, cream, and/or cheese to achieve its decadent richness. It is also notoriously time-consuming and challenging to make. This Naked recipe, however, contains fiber- and nutrient-rich brown rice and heart-healthy plant milk. What's more, preparation is a breeze.

YIELD: 2 TO 3 SERVINGS

ingredients

- ○ ¾ cup white button or cremini mushrooms
- ○ 2½ cups filtered water
- ○ 1 cup organic brown rice, uncooked
- ○ 1 tablespoon organic, non-GMO miso paste
- ○ 2-inch long piece fresh bell pepper, chopped
- ○ 1 cup non-dairy milk
- ○ Two or three sprigs of fresh parsley or cilantro, and a slice of orange for garnish

method

In a food processor, slice or chop the mushrooms, pulsing for 3 seconds.

Boil the water in a medium saucepan. Add the rice, miso, and bell pepper. Return to a boil and cook for 5 minutes. Reduce to medium-low heat, cover, and cook for 35 to 40 minutes or until most of the liquid is absorbed. (See Chef's Note, below.)

Add the non-dairy milk and the mushrooms. Stir. Cook for about 10 more minutes, uncovered, until liquid is creamy.

Turn off the heat and let sit for a couple of minutes. Serve and garnish with fresh parsley or cilantro.

Chef's Note: Short- and long-grain brown rice have different cooking times. For long-grain brown rice, use 2¼ cups water to 1 cup rice. For short-grain, use 2½ cups water.

tibetan creamy caps

In traditional Tibetan and Chinese medicine, many varieties of mushrooms have been used as the ultimate remedy to treat problems in the lung and kidney systems, such as asthma, emphysema, renal failure, backache, fertility, and fatigue. This recipe, savory but with the surprise tang of pineapple, is a fine tribute to the delicious and healthful mushroom.

ingredients

- 2 cups fresh pineapple chunks
- ½ teaspoon fresh or ⅛ teaspoon dried oregano
- ½ teaspoon fresh or ⅛ teaspoon dried bay leaves
- 1 tablespoon shoyu or tamari
- 8 button or cremini mushrooms
- Fresh sprouts, any kind
- 3 fresh cherry tomatoes

method

Preheat the oven to 350°F.

Chop the pineapple chunks into small pieces and place in a small bowl. Add the oregano, bay leaves, and shoyu or tamari. Mix well.

Holding the mushrooms caps gently, carefully twist off the stems. Reserve the stems to use in the filling, if desired. Rinse the caps lightly to remove excess dirt, trying not to allow the water inside the cap.

If using the reserved mushroom stems, wash and slice off the bottoms. Chop the stems into small pieces and combine with the chopped pineapple mixture.

Place the mushroom caps on a silicone, ceramic, or glass baking dish, and stuff each cap with the chopped pineapple mixture.

Bake the stuffed caps for 25 minutes or until lightly browned. Top with fresh sprouts and cherry tomato slices and serve.

{ G A R L I C }

agrodolce fig bruschetta

Agrodolce ("agro"=sour; "dolce"=sweet) is a flavorful sauce used in Italian cooking. In this recipe, figs lend their sweet flavor to the traditionally savory bruschetta for a delicious appetizer.

YIELD: 10 SMALL BRUSCHETTA (3 TO 4 SERVINGS)

ingredients

- ○ 10 slices sprouted, whole wheat, or other plant-based, gluten-free bread
- ○ 2 to 3 fresh garlic cloves
- ○ Freshly ground black pepper to taste

FOR THE FIG PÂTÉ:

- ○ 5 dried or fresh figs
- ○ 4 tablespoons organic, non-GMO silken tofu
- ○ 1 tablespoon black sesame seeds
- ○ ½ cup nuts, any kind

FOR THE TOPPING:

- ○ 5 cherry tomatoes, sliced
- ○ ½ cup mushrooms, any type, sliced
- ○ ½ cup arugula, chopped

method

Preheat the oven to 300°F.

Bake the bread for about 10 minutes or until toasted and crispy. Cut fresh garlic cloves in half and rub onto the toasted bread, or mince it and add a bit to each piece of bread.

In a food processor, combine all the fig pâté ingredients until smooth and creamy. Spread a thick layer of the pâté over the garlic bread.

Top with the tomatoes, mushrooms, and arugula. Sprinkle with the ground black pepper and serve.

{GARLIC}

kazakh sautéed veggies

Sautéing vegetables in a bit of water, instead of oil, retains vegetables' nutritional properties without adding unhealthful fats. Turmeric adds an antioxidant boost to this flavorful—and colorful—dish.

YIELD: 2 TO 4 SERVINGS

ingredients

- 1 large organic tomato
- 1 organic zucchini
- 2 organic carrots
- 1 medium organic bell pepper
- 1 medium organic eggplant
- 1 cup filtered water, divided, plus more if needed
- 6 garlic cloves, chopped or whole
- 2 bay leaves, chopped
- ½ teaspoon turmeric powder
- 1 tablespoon shoyu or tamari
- 2 teaspoon organic, non-GMO miso paste
- 1 sprig fresh fennel greens
- Freshly ground black pepper to taste

method

Slice the tomato, zucchini, carrots, and bell pepper. Set aside.

Remove the eggplant stem, and cut the eggplant in half and then in quarters. Cut into smaller pieces if desired.

Place a saucepan over medium heat. Add ½ cup water, garlic, bay leaves, and turmeric. Sautè for 3 minutes, then add the carrots. Simmer for another 5 minutes covered.

Add the zucchini and eggplant to the saucepan and stir. Add the remaining ½ cup water and more if needed. Simmer over low heat, covered, for 20 to 25 minutes.

Add the shoyu or tamari, miso, and bell pepper. Stir and simmer for about 5 minutes (or longer if softer peppers are desired).

Serve garnished with fresh tomato slices, fresh fennel greens, and ground pepper.

ming's roasted cauliflower

Ginger root (Zingiber officinale) has been used in China for over 2,000 years to treat indigestion, upset stomach, diarrhea, and nausea. Today, health care professionals worldwide commonly recommend ginger to help prevent or treat nausea and vomiting associated with motion sickness, pregnancy, and cancer chemotherapy. It is also used as a treatment for minor stomach upset, as a supplement for arthritis, and may even help prevent heart disease and cancer.

YIELD: 4 SERVINGS

ingredients

- 1 large cauliflower
- 2 teaspoons finely grated fresh ginger
- 1 tablespoon tahini
- 1 tablespoon organic, non-GMO miso paste
- 3 tablespoons vegetable broth
- 3 dried prunes or dates, pitted
- ½ teaspoon ground turmeric
- Green onions, sliced, for garnish (optional)
- Freshly ground black pepper to taste
- White and black sesame seeds, for garnish

method

Preheat the oven to 425°F. Cut the leaves and stem off the bottom of the cauliflower head so that it sits flat.

In a food processor, mix the ginger, tahini, miso paste, broth, prunes or dates, and turmeric. Using your hands, rub the mixture over the cauliflower, making sure you get it everywhere, even on the bottom.

Roast the cauliflower in the oven for 45 minutes, or until it is soft and brown. Remove the cauliflower from the oven and top with a sprinkle of the green onions (optional), a pinch of the ground black pepper, and sesame seeds before serving.

{ GINGER }

holy anti-inflammatory tea

This tea is a triple powerhouse of anti-inflammatory compounds: the protease in the ginger, the curcumin in the turmeric, and the anethole in the fennel seeds all fight to reduce inflammation in the body. A little date paste adds some essential sweetness as well as additional antioxidants.

YIELD: 2 CUPS

ingredients

- ○ 3 cups filtered water
- ○ 1-inch piece fresh ginger, peeled
- ○ 1-inch piece fresh turmeric, peeled
- ○ 1 tablespoon fennel seeds
- ○ 2 teaspoons date sauce (page 275)

method

Add all ingredients to a pot, and bring to a boil. Continue to simmer for about 8 to 10 minutes. Serve and sweeten with a teaspoon of date paste.

{ G O J I }

himalayan goji rice

Goji berries grow on perennial woody shrubs in the sheltered valleys of the Himalayan regions of Tibet and Mongolia. Most goji berries sold outside of this growing region are sold dried, since fresh goji berries are very delicate and are easily damaged. Fortunately, dried goji berries retain all the antioxidant and nutrient qualities of their fresh counterparts. This Naked recipe is a nutritious take on a traditional rice dish.

YIELD: 4 TO 5 SERVINGS

ingredients

- 2½ cups filtered water
- 2-inch stalk Ceylon cinnamon or ½ teaspoon powdered Ceylon cinnamon
- 1 cup non-dairy milk
- 1 cup brown rice
- 1 teaspoon 100% pure maple syrup
- ½ cup coconut flakes (plus more for garnish)
- 2 tablespoons organic, non-GMO white miso paste
- ½ cup goji berries
- ¼ cup whole or sliced almonds

method

In a medium pot, bring water, cinnamon, and non-dairy milk to a boil. Add rice, syrup, coconut, and miso. Bring back to a boil and cook on high for 5 minutes.

Reduce to medium heat and cook for another 35 minutes or until water is absorbed.

Mix in the goji berries and serve. Top with almonds and a sprinkle of coconut flakes.

{ G O J I }

ningxia goji macaroons

Goji berries, also known as wolfberries, are cultivated primarily in an autonomous region of north central China called Ningxia (pronounced neeng-SHAH). Goji berries contain Vitamins A, B2, and C, as well as antioxidants. They have long been touted as a "superfood" that may boost the immune system, protect against heart disease and cancer, and may also improve life expectancy. All which makes these cute little cookies taste all the sweeter!

YIELD: 5 MACAROONS

ingredients

- ○ ½ cup unsweetened coconut flakes
- ○ ½ cup dried goji berries
- ○ ½ cup sunflower seeds or almonds
- ○ 3 tablespoons almond butter, unsweetened
- ○ 2 tablespoons dark chocolate bits

method

Pour coconut flakes on a small dish. Set aside.

In a food processor, combine remaining ingredients and blend for about 10 to 12 seconds or until mixture is homogeneous and sticky. Scoop about 1 tablespoon of the mixture to make five 1-inch balls.

Roll goji balls in the coconut flakes to coat. Serve.

qi carrot wraps

Qi is a concept unique and fundamental to Chinese medicine. Translating to "vital energy," these Qi Carrot Wraps are sure to energize you any time of day with their combination of different nuts, seeds, and veggies.

YIELD: 12 TO 16 WRAPS (ABOUT 4 SERVINGS)

ingredients

FOR THE HUMMUS:

- 1 cup chickpeas, cooked
- ¼ cup hempseeds
- ¼ cup non-dairy milk
- 1 teaspoon tahini
- 1 teaspoon organic, non-GMO light miso paste
- Juice of ½ lemon
- Freshly ground black pepper to taste

FOR THE WRAPS:

- 2 large organic carrots
- 2 tablespoons pine nuts
- ½ cup fresh organic sprouts
- Pinch of paprika

method

MAKING THE HUMMUS:

Add all of the hummus ingredients to a food processor and blend until smooth.

MAKING THE WRAPS:

Using an adjustable ceramic or BPA-free mandoline, slice the carrots on the 0.5 mm setting lengthwise.

Place carrot slices on a flat surface and spread hummus and sprouts on the slices to about ½ inch from the edges. Roll carrots to form a cylinder. Top with extra sprouts, pine nuts, a pinch of paprika, and ground pepper.

steps to heaven hemp bars

These fabulous treats are a great source of energy, stamina, and flavor, as well as a nutritious snack for everyone in the family. Shedding extra weight is easy when eating fiber-full foods like oats and fruits, and with the touch of coconut, chia, and dates, you will definitely taste sweet heavenly bliss!

YIELD: 4 SERVINGS

ingredients

- ½ cup organic hempseeds
- ½ banana, peeled
- 2 tablespoons chia seeds
- ½ cup gluten-free rolled oats
- ¼ cup pumpkin seeds
- ¼ cup nuts, any kind
- 1 tablespoon coconut flakes, unsweetened
- 3 medjool dates, pitted

method

In a mixing bowl combine the hempseeds, banana, and chia seeds.

Add the oats, pumpkin seeds, nuts, coconut, and dates to a food processor and blend until smooth. Transfer to the mixing bowl and combine with the rest of the ingredients until mixture is well blended.

Transfer mixture into a small glass or silicone baking dish (use an 8 x 8-inch pan for thin bars; a smaller pan for thicker bars). Press the mixture evenly and firmly over the bottom of the dish. Cut into four evenly sized bars and refrigerate. Keep in the refrigerator until ready to serve.

mesopotamian kale pesto

YIELD: 1 ¼ CUPS (6 TO 10 SERVINGS, DEPENDING ON USE. SEE CHEF'S NOTE, BELOW.)

ingredients

- 2 handfuls organic kale, deveined and chopped (about 2 cups)
- 2 small garlic cloves, peeled
- ⅓ cup raw pistachios, shelled
- ⅛ teaspoon red or black pepper
- 1 tablespoon tamari
- Juice of ½ lemon

method

In a food processor, process all ingredients slowly until smooth and creamy. Store the pesto in the refrigerator for up to 2 weeks.

Chef's Note: Use this pesto as a dip, a spread for bruschetta, or toss with spiralized raw zucchini "noodles."

{ K A L E }

persepolis kale salad

Persepolis—"the City of Persians"—was the ceremonial capitol of the ancient Achaemenid Empire. The people ate a wide variety of local fruits and vegetables, including leafy greens, pomegranate seeds, and herbs. This fresh and colorful salad is a veritable rainbow of vitamins and nutrition.

YIELD: 2 SERVINGS

ingredients

- 4 organic kale leaves (green, red, or black)
- Juice of 1 lemon
- 4 organic radishes, sliced
- 2 large organic carrots, sliced
- 1½ cups fresh pineapple, diced small, divided
- 1 large organic, non-GMO zucchini
- 2 medium tomatoes, halved
- 1 avocado, pitted, scooped, and sliced (see page 273)
- ½ cup pomegranate seeds
- Freshly ground black pepper to taste

method

To devein the kale, simply hold the leaf's stem with one hand, and run your other hand along the stem tightly. The entire leaf will come off the vein. Chop the kale leaves in small pieces and transfer to a large bowl.

Sprinkle the kale leaves with the lemon juice and massage leaves a bit.

Add the radishes, carrots, and a cup of the pineapple chunks to the mixing bowl. Stir.

Using a mandoline on the 0.5 mm setting, slice the zucchini length wise, creating long, thin pieces. Set aside, lying flat. Place 2 of the largest zucchini slices sideways (on their edges) in the center of a plate, creating a ring. Place two tomato halves where the ends of both of the zucchini pieces meet. The tomatoes will help keep the zucchini ring in place.

Carefully add the kale salad mixture inside the zucchini ring you've created. Repeat the process with the rest of the ingredients.

Top with some of the avocado slices, the remaining pineapple chunks, and some pomegranate seeds. Sprinkle with some ground black pepper and serve.

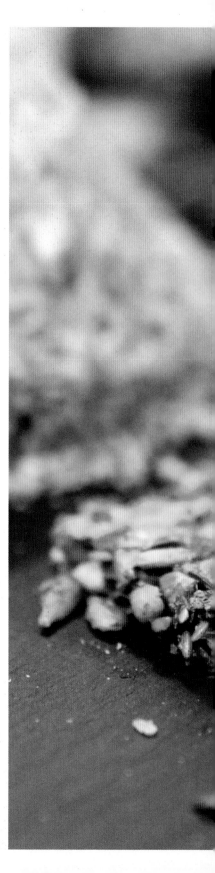

{ K E L P }

keobab kelp pâté

A bit of kelp powder adds a bit of savory, "fishy" flavor to this pâté. Enjoy this with sprouted or whole wheat bread, celery, carrot, zucchini, or cucumber sticks, or Crackers (page 268) as pictured.

YIELD: 1½ CUPS

ingredients

- ○ 1 cup beans, cooked, any kind
- ○ 1½ tablespoons kelp powder
- ○ 1 tablespoon shoyu or tamari
- ○ Juice of ½ lemon
- ○ ¼ cup walnuts
- ○ 3 tablespoons pumpkin or hempseeds, or a mix of both

method

Add the beans, kelp, shoyu or tamari, and lemon to a mixing bowl. Mash all ingredients together until mixture is well combined.

In a food processor, blend walnuts by pulsing for about 3 seconds once. The walnuts should be chunky, not pulverized. Add to the mixing bowl and mix.

In the food processor, chop the pumpkin or hempseeds, and place in a small container. Set aside.

With wet hands, mold the bean mixture into a patty or ball. Sprinkle or cover with the seeds or seed mixture and serve.

{ K E L P }

madagascar "tuna" salad

This is a very versatile salad. The eggplant can be replaced with other base ingredients like whole wheat bread, whole pita bread, or raw cabbage leaves. The salad can also be enjoyed on its own as a side dish, in a sandwich, or as a stuffing mixture for whole tomatoes, apples, baked squash, or potatoes.

YIELD: 16 BITES (ABOUT 4 SERVINGS)

ingredients

- ○ 1 Machiaw eggplant (long type)
- ○ 1 cup chickpeas, cooked
- ○ 2 sprigs fresh parsley
- ○ ½ organic apple, with skin
- ○ 2 teaspoons organic kelp powder
- ○ Juice of ½ lemon
- ○ 1 teaspoon shoyu or tamari
- ○ Sunflower seeds, for garnish
- ○ Sprinkle of nutritional yeast or freshly ground black pepper

method

Preheat the oven to 400°F.

Slice the eggplant into ¼-inch slices and place the slices flat on a silicone, glass, or ceramic baking dish. Bake for 15 minutes or until lightly brown. Turn slices over and bake for another 10 minutes. Remove from the oven.

In a food processor, pulse all remaining ingredients until chopped. Scoop a tablespoon of mixture onto each eggplant slice. Top with sunflower seeds and a sprinkle of nutritional yeast or freshly ground black pepper to taste.

{ L E M O N }

bhutan lemon smoothie

This recipe offers a unique way to enjoy lemons: in a creamy, delicious morning shake.

YIELD: 2 SERVINGS

ingredients

- Juice of 1 lemon
- 1 banana, peeled
- 1 cup non-dairy milk
- ½ cup oats
- ¼ cup walnuts
- 1 to 2 dates, pitted
- 1 cup filtered ice cubes

method

Combine ingredients in a high-powered blender and serve.

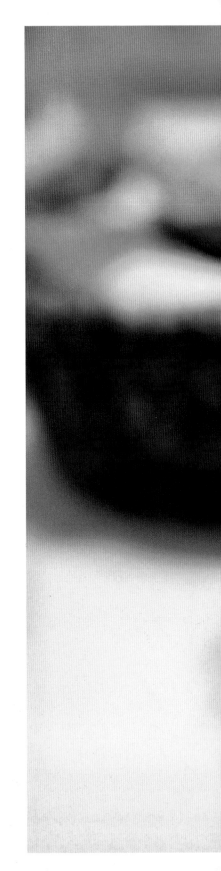

{ L E M O N }

tantric lemon bliss tarts

These colorful, fresh, raw tarts are as beautiful to look at as they are delicious to taste.

YIELD: 6 TO 8 TARTS

ingredients

FOR THE LEMON CREAM:

○ **Juice of 1 orange (about ⅓ cup)**

○ **Juice of ½ lemon**

○ **½ cup cashews**

○ **2 tablespoons silken tofu**

FOR THE TARTS:

○ **2 whole organic carrots**

○ **8 dried prunes, pitted**

○ **½ cup hempseeds**

FOR TOPPING:

○ **3 organic strawberries**

○ **Fresh mint leaves**

method

MAKING THE CREAM:

In a food processor, blend the orange juice, lemon juice, cashews, and silken tofu until creamy and smooth. Set aside. Rinse the food processor.

MAKING THE TARTS:

Rinse each carrot and chop off the stem ends. Slice the carrots and transfer the pieces to the food processor. Process for a few seconds until chopped. Do not over-chop because the carrots will become mushy. Add to a large mixing bowl.

Repeat process with prunes and hempseeds, and add to the carrots

in the mixing bowl. Using a spatula, mix the ingredients well until fully combined.

Scoop the mixture in 1 tablespoon amounts into small silicone muffin cups. Press the mixture lightly against each cup to form a small tart, creating a thick bottom and slightly up the sides of each cup. Fill the tarts with the lemon cream. Slice the strawberries in quarters and add to the tarts, along with a mint leaf for garnish. Serve.

Chef's Note: We recommend using silicone cups. These are chemical- and metal-free and non-stick, allowing the food to be removed easily.

{ L E N T I L }

demeter's harvest burgers

The ancient Greeks worshipped Demeter as the goddess of the harvest, believing she made the crops grow each year. These delicious burgers, with their variety of vegetables and grains, are a fitting tribute to the goddess of agriculture.

YIELD: 2 SERVINGS

ingredients

- 1 cup lentils, cooked
- 1 tablespoon shoyu or tamari
- 1/8 teaspoon dried bay leaves
- 1 small organic carrot
- 2 medium or 1 large potato, peeled and cooked
- 1/2 medium onion
- 1 sprig organic parsley or cilantro
- 3 tablespoons flaxseeds
- 9 tablespoons filtered water
- 2 tablespoons nutritional yeast
- 2 tablespoons sprouted grain, gluten-free bread crumbs

method

Preheat the oven to 350°F. In a mixing bowl, combine the lentils, shoyu or tamari, and bay leaves.

In a food processor, blend the carrot, potato, onion, and parsley or cilantro. Add to the mixing bowl.

In the food processor, blend the flaxseeds and the 9 tablespoons of water for 20 seconds or until smooth. Add to the mixing bowl. Mix thoroughly.

Mix the breadcrumbs and nutritional yeast together in a small bowl.

With wet hands, make 1-inch patties from the lentil mixture and transfer to the breadcrumb bowl. Cover patty completely with breadcrumbs, then remove and transfer to a silicone, glass, or ceramic baking dish. Repeat with remaining lentil mixture.

Bake for 15 to 20 minutes or until patties are crisp and browned. Serve with Naked Mayo (page 272).

{LENTIL}

plato's lentil risotto

Plato, the ancient Greek philosopher and mathematician, was a very wise man, widely considered to be the father of modern philosophy. The classic "comfort food" risotto gets an imaginative and healthful twist with this recipe, in which the Arborio rice is swapped out for protein- and fiber-packed lentils, and the creaminess comes from mashed potatoes instead of cheese. Very wise, indeed!

YIELD: 4 SERVINGS

ingredients

- 1 cup brown lentils
- 4 medium organic yellow potatoes with skin, sliced
- 1 medium carrot, sliced
- 2 bay leaves, whole
- 1 sage leaf, whole
- ⅛ teaspoon dried or ½ teaspoon fresh oregano
- 2 fresh sprigs parsley or cilantro, divided
- 5 cups filtered water
- 1 cup millet

method

In a large pot, add the lentils, potatoes, carrot, bay leaves, sage, oregano, one sprig of parsley or cilantro, and the water. Bring to a boil and reduce to medium heat. Cook for about 25 to 30 minutes, with the lid covering 90 percent of the pot.

Remove some of the potatoes from the pot and mash them with a fork or potato masher. Return the mashed potatoes to the pot and stir. Add the millet, stir, and cook for another 5 minutes.

Serve and garnish with the remaining chopped parsley or cilantro.

nile's pan-seared oatmeal

The oldest known oat grains were found among Egyptian ruins dating back to about 2000 BCE. This unique and playful take on traditional oatmeal pan-sears the batter into a small cake or snack bar.

YIELD: 3 SERVINGS

ingredients

- 1 tablespoon flaxseeds
- 3 tablespoons filtered water
- 2 dried prunes or dates, pitted
- 2 small dried or fresh figs
- ¼ cup sunflower seeds
- 2 cups gluten-free oats
- ½ banana, peeled
- 4 tablespoons non-dairy milk
- ½ cup fresh fruit or berries, sliced

method

In a food processor, combine the flaxseeds and water until smooth. Transfer to a large mixing bowl.

In the food processor, blend the prunes or dates, figs, and sunflower seeds until mixture is compact. Add it to the mixing bowl.

Add the oats, banana, and milk, and combine all ingredients with your hands or a spatula until mixture is well blended.

Place a large silicone cookie or egg mold in a non-stick saucepan. Add enough of the oat mixture to fill up the shape of the mold. Remove mold carefully and cook for about 1 to 2 minutes over medium heat. Carefully flip over and cook the other side for about a minute.

Repeat the process for the rest of the mixture and serve, topped with the fresh fruit or berries.

Chef's Note: This oat pancake can be a bit dry for some palates, though it can also be used as a snack bar. To make it moist and enjoy it for breakfast, add a banana cream sauce over the oatmeal (combining 1 banana and 1 cup of non-dairy milk in a high-powered blender), and a bit of Date Sauce (page 275).

{OATS}

pharaoh's holy bites

These may be the fastest cookies you will ever make. A raw recipe with minimal preparation, these cute little cookies provide a great source of energy and nutrition in every bite.

YIELD: 9 COOKIES (ABOUT 4 SERVINGS)

ingredients

FOR THE COATING:

○ **2 tablespoons flaxseeds**

○ **2 tablespoons chia seeds**

○ **2 tablespoons pistachios**

FOR THE COOKIES:

○ **½ cup gluten-free rolled oats**

○ **½ cup walnuts**

○ **¼ cup pumpkin seeds**

○ **4 medjool dates, pitted**

○ **1 tablespoon unsweetened coconut flakes**

○ **1 banana, peeled**

method

In a food processor, chop each coating ingredient separately and set each aside in a small bowl or container.

In the food processor, combine the cookie ingredients and blend for about 10 to 12 seconds or until mixture is well blended and sticky. With wet hands, scoop cookie mixture by the tablespoon and form into nine 1¼-inch balls.

Roll 3 of the balls in the chopped flaxseeds, 3 in the chia seeds, and 3 in the chopped pistachios to coat. Serve.

Chef's Note: Cookies will keep for a couple days at room temperature or refrigerated.

{ PERSIMMON }

ming's raw crumble cream

Combined with chia seeds and goji berries, this crumble makes a very healthful treat.

YIELD: 6 SERVINGS

ingredients

- ○ **1 persimmon, chopped**
- ○ **2 bananas, peeled**
- ○ **2 tablespoons chia seeds**

FOR TOPPING:

- ○ **¼ cup goji berries**
- ○ **Dark chocolate shavings, for garnish (optional)**

method

Blend the persimmon in a food processor for 20 seconds or until creamy. Slice the bananas and divide among six small serving bowls. For each serving, sprinkle with the chia seeds and a dollop of the persimmon cream. Top each serving with the goji berries and dark chocolate, if desired.

zen persimmon pico de gallo

The soft and sweet flavor of persimmon is a delicious addition this savory pico de gallo. It is great on chips, toasted bread, or as topping for rice, beans, or potatoes.

YIELD: 1 BOWL (4 SERVINGS)

ingredients

- 1 avocado, pitted, scooped, and mashed (see page 273)
- 1 medium organic Fuyu persimmon, diced (Hachiya persimmon may be used, but it is softer and sweeter)
- ½ white onion, minced (about ½ cup)
- 2 medium organic tomatoes, diced (about 1½ cups)
- 1 organic cucumber, diced
- ¼ teaspoon fresh or ⅛ teaspoon dried cayenne pepper, chopped, (optional)
- 2 sprigs fresh cilantro, chopped
- Juice of ½ orange
- Freshly ground black pepper to taste

method

Combine all the ingredients in a bowl and serve.

fabulous mediterranean pkhali

In the Eurasian country of Georgia, pkhali (the "kh" is pronounced as a guttural "h") is a whole category of vegetable dishes that range from salad to pâté to side dish. One thing they have in common, however, is a base of spinach, beets, beans, nuts, and herbs. This spinach dish is so delicious and versatile that can be enjoyed as a pâté, dip, sandwich stuffing, or side dish.

ingredients

○ **2 handfuls fresh spinach (about 2 cups)**

○ **½ medium beet**

○ **1 shallot**

○ **1 cup walnuts**

○ **1 cup red, kidney, black, or white beans, cooked or canned**

○ **⅛ teaspoon fresh or dried bay leaf**

○ **⅛ teaspoon fresh or dried thyme**

○ **Pinch of freshly ground black pepper**

○ **3 tablespoons pomegranate seeds**

method

Wash the spinach thoroughly, and drain. Squeeze to remove excess moisture and pat dry with a towel.

In a food processor, pulse the beet for a few seconds until minced. Transfer to a small bowl and set aside.

Separately process the shallot, walnuts, spinach, and beans in the food processor and transfer to a single large bowl. (Because they are of different textures, processing these ingredients individually will prevent any one item from being over-processed.) Add the herbs and the pepper to the mixture and stir together.

Take ⅓ of the mixture and blend it with the chopped beet. Scoop out 2 tablespoons of the mixture and mold a patty in your hands. Make a small nook in the middle of the patty with your finger and place on a serving dish, nook-side up.

Repeat the process with the remaining (non-beet) mixture to create the rest of the patties. Fill the nooks with pomegranate seeds and enjoy immediately.

{POMEGRANATE}

shiva's antioxidant pudding

The beautiful pomegranate has long been a Hindu symbol of prosperity and well-being and appears often in ancient Indian art. Pomegranate seeds are like little jewels packed with antioxidant power.

YIELD: 2 SERVINGS

ingredients

- 1 banana, peeled
- 1 cup non-dairy milk
- 1 cup fresh pineapple, chopped
- 2 tablespoons chia seeds, divided
- 1 organic kiwi with skin, thinly sliced
- ½ cup pomegranate seeds
- Fresh mint leaves, for garnish

method

Mix the banana, milk, and pineapple in a high-powered blender. Transfer liquid into a medium bowl and add the 2 tablespoons of chia seeds. Stir and let sit for 20 minutes.

Line the sides of two small glass or ceramic serving cups with a layer of kiwi slices by pressing them lightly against the sides of the cups. Fill each cup with the chia pudding and top with the pomegranate seeds. Garnish with mint leaves and enjoy immediately.

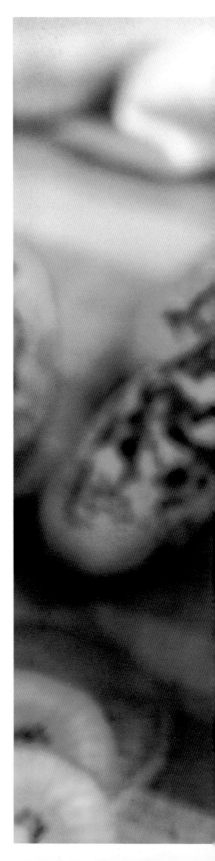

machu picchu's quinoa cookies

Quinoa makes a unique appearance in these flavorful little cookies.

YIELD: 8 OR 9 COOKIES (ABOUT 4 SERVINGS)

ingredients

- 2½ cups filtered water
- 1 cup quinoa, any color or mixed colors
- ½ cup walnuts
- ¼ cup cacao powder, divided
- 1 banana, peeled
- Dried or fresh berries, for garnish
- Fresh mint, for garnish

method

Add water to a small pot and bring to a boil. Add the quinoa and cook, uncovered, for about 15 minutes or until the small white tails of the seeds appear. Fluff and set aside. Let cool for 10 minutes.

In a food processor, blend the walnuts for about 10 seconds or until relatively smooth. Add to a mixing bowl. Add 1 tablespoon of the cacao powder, the banana, and 1 cup of the cooked quinoa. (You will have leftover quinoa for another batch of cookies or another recipe.) Mash the banana and blend all ingredients together.

Transfer the remaining cacao powder to a small round container.

With wet hands, scoop of the quinoa mixture by the tablespoon to make nine 1-inch balls. Wash and dry your hands. Roll each ball in the cacao powder to coat them completely.

Serve with fresh mint and fresh or dried berries.

Chef's Note: Cookies will keep for a day or two refrigerated in an airtight container.

{QUINOA}

quechua quinoa bowl

Quinoa was popular among the Inca and Quechuan people because of its adaptability to be grown under a wide variety of conditions. Although eaten like a grain, quinoa is actually a seed.

YIELD: 4 SERVINGS

ingredients

- 2½ cups filtered water
- 1 cup quinoa, any color, or mixed colors
- 1 teaspoon organic, non-GMO miso paste
- 1 bay leaf
- 6 button mushrooms
- 12 organic cherry tomatoes
- ½ organic yellow bell pepper
- ½ red organic onion
- 1 sprig fresh parsley, for garnish
- Pinch of freshly ground black pepper

method

Add the water to a small pot and bring to a boil. Add the quinoa, miso, and bay leaf, and cook, uncovered, for about 15 minutes or until the small white tails of the seeds appear. Fluff and set aside. Let cool for 10 minutes.

Thinly slice the mushrooms and transfer to a mixing bowl. Slice the cherry tomatoes in half and add to mixing bowl.

Dice the bell peppers, the onion, and the mushrooms and add to the bowl. Add the cooked quinoa and mix well.

Garnish with fresh parsley and ground pepper and serve.

Chef's Note: This bowl can be enjoyed warm during winter days or cold during the summer. Other ingredients can also be added, such as cooked legumes, or vegetables such as carrots, zucchini, radish, or garlic.

valle d'itria's roasted onions

The picturesque Valle d'Itria is situated in Puglia, located in the "heel" of Italy's "boot." The unique geology of Valle d'Itria consists of beautiful caves and rolling hills. It also has many vineyards, some of which produce the grapes to make various wines and vinegars, including some of the finest Italian balsamic vinegars. For this recipe, baking mellows the onions, while the balsamic vinegar and rosemary add a delightfully piquant flavor.

ingredients

○ **2 cups filtered water**

○ **2 teaspoons miso paste**

○ **1 tablespoon shoyu or tamari**

○ **6 medium white onions**

○ **2 teaspoons dried or 2 tablespoons fresh oregano, chopped**

○ **2 teaspoons dried or 2 tablespoons fresh rosemary, chopped (plus additional fresh rosemary for garnish)**

○ **6 teaspoons gluten-free balsamic vinaigrette, any flavor**

method

Preheat the oven to 350°F.

In a food processor or blender, combine the water with the miso and the shoyu or tamari. Set aside.

Remove the outer layer of each onion. Slice the bottoms off so the onions can stand on their own without tipping. Make two cuts on the top of each onion, forming an X.

Transfer the onions to a silicone or glass baking tray. Sprinkle the oregano and rosemary over the onions. Add ½ cup of the miso-shoyu/tamari water to the bottom of the tray and bake for 30 to 40 minutes or until the onions are soft. Add ½ cup of additional mixed water every 10 minutes if needed to avoid the tray from drying out.

Remove the tray from the oven. Spoon a teaspoon of the balsamic vinaigrette over each onion. Garnish with the remaining rosemary and serve. Enjoy as a side or appetizer, or with your favorite whole grain or legume dish.

{ ROSEMARY }

sumerian rosemary roast

Sumer was the southernmost region of the cradle of civilization: Mesopotamia—what is now modern-day Iraq and Kuwait. The Sumerian people used a wide variety of herbs and spices in their cooking, including the rosemary, which are the leaves of an evergreen shrub. Rosemary pairs particularly well with roasted potatoes, making for a fragrant, hearty dish.

YIELD: 2 TO 3 SERVINGS

ingredients

- **12 medium potatoes, any kind (purple, yellow, or red), quartered**
- **6 garlic cloves**
- **3 tablespoons fresh rosemary (about 3 sprigs), chopped**
- **3 tablespoons fresh thyme (about 2 sprigs), chopped**
- **½ teaspoon freshly ground black pepper**

method

Preheat the oven to 400°F.

Bring a large pot of water to a boil. Once boiling, add the potatoes and boil for 8 minutes. Drain the potatoes in a colander, then transfer to a baking tray, spread in an even, single layer. In a small bowl, combine the garlic, rosemary, thyme, and pepper. Sprinkle the spices over the potatoes, turning the potatoes so they are evenly covered with the spices. Cook for about 45 minutes, flipping once halfway through the cooking time, until the edges are perfectly browned and crisp. Serve immediately.

Chef's Note: Adding oil is not necessary. We recommend using a silicone tray, silicone sheet, or a sheet of baking parchment paper to avoid burning and sticking to the pot.

el dorado's golden ice cream

Soursop (also called graviola) is a large, spiny fruit with sweet white flesh native to Mexico and Central and South America. While it is often used in beverages, ice creams, and other sweet foods, it is also known for its anti-inflammatory properties, and currently is being studied for its potential to prevent or slow the growth of certain cancers.

YIELD: 4 SERVINGS

ingredients

○ **2 cups soursop pulp or 2 whole soursops, pits and seeds removed**

○ **½ cup non-dairy milk**

○ **4 medjool dates, pitted**

○ **10 fresh mint leaves**

method

In a high-powered blender, mix all ingredients until creamy and smooth. Add water as needed to keep the mixture circulating through the blender.

Pour mixture in an airtight container or silicone molds and freeze for at least 4 to 6 hours.

{ S O U R S O P }

tayrona's secret smoothie

Tayrona National Natural Park is one of the most popular destinations in the Caribbean region of Colombia, and is home to many species of flora and fauna. This refreshing smoothie boasts a flavor as lush as this beautiful site.

YIELD: 2 SERVINGS

ingredients

- ○ 1 cup soursop, pitted
- ○ 1 banana, peeled
- ○ 1 handful organic kale or spinach (about 1 cup)
- ○ 1 tablespoon maca powder
- ○ 2 cups filtered water
- ○ 1 cup filtered ice cubes

method

Blend all ingredients in a high-powered blender for 30 seconds and serve.

{SPINACH}

armenian spinach rice

Traditional Armenian cuisine utilizes quality fresh ingredients. One dish—dzhash—is a brothy stew, with the vegetarian version consisting of vegetables and spices served over rice. This recipe highlights spinach, both cooked and raw, with other colorful, flavorful vegetables and herbs to create a satisfying, delicious dish.

YIELD: 4 SERVINGS

ingredients

- 1 cup organic brown rice, uncooked
- 2¼ cups filtered water for short-grain rice or 2½ cups for long-grain
- 1 tablespoon organic, non-GMO miso paste, shoyu, or tamari
- 3 garlic cloves
- 2-inch piece bell pepper
- 1 bay leaf
- ⅛ teaspoon dried or ½ teaspoon fresh thyme
- ⅛ teaspoon paprika
- Pinch of freshly ground black pepper
- 2 sprigs fresh parsley or cilantro, plus more for garnish
- 2 handfuls fresh spinach (about 2 cups), divided
- 8 to 10 organic cherry tomatoes
- Black sesame, chia, or poppy seeds, for garnish (optional)

method

In a medium pot, bring the water to a boil. Add all ingredients up to the spinach and bring back to a boil.

Lower heat to medium-low, and cook for about 30 to 35 minutes, covered, or until most of the water is absorbed. Remove the lid and fluff. Remove from heat. Add 1 handful of the spinach and combine together. Let sit for 5 minutes, covered.

Place the rest of the spinach on a serving dish and serve the rice on top. Add the tomatoes (whole or sliced) and some parsley or cilantro, plus black sesame or poppy seeds (optional) for garnish.

{ S P I N A C H }

persian green antioxidant smoothie

Packed with naturally occurring antioxidants, vitamins, and phytonutrients, this refreshing smoothie may help prevent or slow cell damage in the body.

YIELD: 2 TO 3 SERVINGS

ingredients

- 1 handful fresh organic spinach (about 1 cup)
- 1 handful fresh organic kale (about 1 cup), stems removed
- 1 medium organic pear with skin
- 1 medium organic carrot
- 1 tablespoon maca powder
- 1 tablespoon chia seeds
- 1 medium banana, peeled
- 2 cups filtered water
- 1 cup filtered ice cubes

method

Blend all ingredients in a high-powered blender for 30 seconds and serve.

{ S W E E T   P O T A T O }

polynesian layered bake

While European explorers are often credited with introducing different foods around the world, recent DNA evidence suggests that sweet potatoes made their way to Polynesia from South America nearly 400 years before Christopher Columbus set sail. As a result, sweet potatoes and yams have long been a staple food of the Polynesian people.

YIELD: 4 SERVINGS

ingredients

- 6 dried figs
- ½ cup dried cranberries
- ½ cup walnuts
- 3 tablespoons hempseeds
- 1 large organic sweet potato, peeled
- ½ cup filtered water
- 4 sprigs fresh mint or tarragon, for garnish

method

Preheat the oven to 300°F.

In a food processor, chop the figs, cranberries, walnuts, and hempseeds until a paste is formed.

Using an adjustable ceramic or BPA-free mandoline, thinly slice the raw sweet potato on the 0.5 mm setting. Arrange a layer of the potato slices in a 9 x 9-inch or similar-size silicone or glass baking dish. Add a second layer of potatoes in the opposite direction to create balance. Add a ¼-inch-thick layer of the fig paste over the potato layer. Repeat the process with the remaining sweet potato slices and fig paste. Pour the water

evenly over the dish to provide moisture while it cooks.

Bake for 25 minutes or until the potatoes are cooked thoroughly. If necessary, add extra water while baking if the dish dries out.

Garnish with the fresh mint or tarragon leaves and serve.

Chef's Note: This dish can be served as side dish or dessert.

{ S W E E T   P O T A T O }

samoa sacred potatoes

Sweet potatoes have long been a staple of the Polynesian people. This Naked recipe, with its inclusion of berries and coconut, brings a taste of the tropics to your table, and with it, all the amazing power of beta-carotene, antioxidants, and healthy omega-3s.

YIELD: 4 SERVINGS

ingredients

- **4 jewel sweet potatoes**
- **4 tablespoons almond butter, unsweetened**
- **¼ cup whole walnuts**
- **¼ cup berries of your choice (goji, blueberries, raspberries, blackberries)**
- **¼ cup raisins**
- **Sprinkle of shredded, unsweetened coconut**

method

Preheat the oven to 400°F.

Slice potatoes partially open lengthwise. Add a tablespoon of almond butter to each potato. Continue adding the rest of ingredients, dividing them equally among the potatoes.

Bake for 30 minutes or until potatoes are soft inside. To test if they are ready, pierce a potato with a sharp knife in one of the sides. If the knife goes in easily, the potatoes are done.

Serve and sprinkle with the coconut shreds.

Chef's Note: As an option, you can partially bake potatoes first for 25 minutes to make them soft and easier to fill. After filling, return to the oven and bake for an additional 5 to 8 minutes.

{ T O M A T O }

mayan stuffed tomatoes

Tomatoes and avocados featured prominently in Mayan cuisine. This delicious, colorful dish is plated with beautiful presentation sure to impress.

YIELD: 4 SERVINGS

ingredients

- ○ 4 large organic tomatoes
- ○ 2 avocados, pitted and scooped (see page 273)
- ○ Juice of ½ lemon
- ○ 1½ cups chickpeas, cooked
- ○ 1½ cups quinoa, cooked
- ○ 1 tablespoon shoyu or tamari

- ○ 1 handful organic leafy greens (arugula, spinach, or chard), chopped (about 1 cup)
- ○ Freshly ground black pepper to taste
- ○ 2 sprigs fresh organic cilantro, chopped, for garnish

method

PREPARING THE TOMATO:

Slice off the tomato stem. Remove the tomato pulp carefully and set aside.

PREPARING THE AVOCADOS:

Slice avocado halves in two, and place each piece in a serving dish.

Sprinkle with fresh lemon juice and set aside.

BUILDING THE DISH:

In a mixing bowl, combine the chickpeas, quinoa, shoyu or tamari, pepper, and leafy greens. Mix well. Stuff the tomatoes with the mixture and press down to ensure the tomatoes are completely stuffed. Serve garnished with cilantro.

To enjoy the tomatoes, simply cut and chop all ingredients and eat together.

{ T O M A T O }

sunday's italian ragù

In Italian cuisine, a ragù is typically a hearty, meat-based tomato sauce. But this plant-based version, with spinach, kale, and flavorful spice, is just as hearty (and much more healthful) than the traditional sauce. Enjoy with your favorite vegetable, rice, soba, whole grain, or quinoa noodles.

YIELD: 4 SERVINGS

ingredients

- 8 organic garlic cloves, chopped
- ¼ white onion, chopped (about ¼ cup)
- ½ cup filtered water, or more if needed
- 5 large organic tomatoes, divided
- 1 handful organic kale (about 1 cup)
- 1 handful organic spinach (about 1 cup)
- 1 handful fresh basil (about ¼ cup)
- ½ organic red bell pepper
- ½ teaspoon paprika
- 1 cup low-sodium vegetable broth
- ½ teaspoon salt-free seasoning

method

In a large saucepan, add the garlic, onion, and water. Sauté for 3 to 5 minutes until browned a bit.

In a food processor, purée four of the tomatoes and add to the saucepan. Dice the remaining tomato and add it to the saucepan.

In the food processor, chop the kale, spinach, basil, and pepper, and add to the saucepan. Add the paprika, broth, and salt-free seasoning. Cover and simmer for about 20 to 25 minutes or until the sauce thickens. For a thinner sauce, add 1 cup or more of filtered water. Stir frequently.

mumbai curcuma healing smoothie

This delicious, Indian-inspired smoothie incorporates curcuma—turmeric—with fresh pineapple for a bright, refreshing drink. Their combined nutrients make this smoothie a powerful cleanser, digestive aid, immune booster, and disease fighter.

YIELD: 2 SERVINGS

ingredients

- 1½ cups fresh pineapple chunks
- 1–inch piece turmeric root, peeled, or 1 teaspoon turmeric powder
- ½ banana, peeled
- 1 cup filtered ice cubes
- 2 cups filtered water
- 1 teaspoon chia seeds

method

In a high-powered blender, mix the pineapple, turmeric, banana, ice, and water until smooth. Pour into two glasses and sprinkle with chia seeds. Enjoy immediately.

Chef's Note: We recommend this smoothie daily with a meal or first thing in the morning. Pineapple and turmeric may be added to any other smoothie as well.

{ T U R M E R I C }

vedic turmeric croquettes

Vedic recipes (also known as ayurvedic) combine specific foods and flavors that have a detoxifying effect on the body. These crispy croquettes are especially delicious when served with Naked Mayo (page 272).

YIELD: 6 CROQUETTES

ingredients

- 3 teaspoons of ground flaxseeds, 9 teaspoons of filtered water
- 1 cup chickpeas, cooked
- ½ medium organic white onion
- 1 teaspoon turmeric powder or 1-inchpiece turmeric root, peeled
- 3 tablespoons quinoa flour or all-purpose flour
- 1 sprig fresh parsley
- ½ teaspoon dried bay leaves
- ½ teaspoon fresh or ⅛ teaspoon dried thyme
- ½ teaspoon fresh or ⅛ teaspoon dried oregano
- 2 teaspoons organic, non-GMO miso paste
- ¼ cup nutritional yeast

method

Preheat the oven to 380°F.

In a food processor, blend the flaxseeds and water for about 10 seconds or until mixture is smooth. Transfer to a mixing bowl.

Blend the rest of the ingredients (except for the miso and nutritional yeast) and add to the mixing bowl, along with the miso paste. Stir all ingredients together until well combined.

Place nutritional yeast separately in a small container and set aside.

With wet hands, scoop out a small amount of the chickpea mixture, and create spheres of about 1½ inches. Transfer each sphere to the container with the nutritional yeast and gently roll it, making sure all sides are covered with the yeast. Repeat the process for all spheres and place in a silicone baking tray.

Bake for about 30 minutes or until crust is crispy, rotating the tray once halfway through.

Serve on a bed of fresh spinach and enjoy with a one or two tablespoons of Naked Mayo (page 272), if desired.

{WHEATGRASS}

manna quinoa breakfast bowl

Originally, manna was a biblical reference to a substance that miraculously supplied food to the Israelites in the wilderness. In modern times, it refers either to something giving substantial nourishment or something received as a welcome benefit. In the case of this Naked recipe, it is both!

YIELD: 2 SERVINGS

ingredients

FOR THE SMOOTHIE:

○ **1 handful organic wheatgrass, chopped (about ½ cup)**

○ **2 organic kale or chard leaves**

○ **1 organic kiwi with skin**

○ **1 cup non-dairy milk**

○ **1 banana, peeled**

FOR THE BOWL:

○ **½ cup quinoa, cooked**

○ **½ organic apple, any kind, chopped**

○ **¼ cup pomegranate seeds or berries**

○ **2 tablespoons seeds (pumpkin, chia, or sunflower)**

method

In a high-powered blender, combine all smoothie ingredients and blend for about 20 seconds. Divide smoothie between two bowls. Divide the quinoa among the bowls, and top with apple, pomegranate or berries, and seeds of your choice.

{WHEATGRASS}

the essenes gazpacho

The Essenes were members of an ancient Jewish sect who were credited with developing the technique of making sprouted bread prepared at a low temperature. They also made many raw dishes including soups. This refreshing, raw, chilled soup is perfect for the summer months, but delicious and nutritious all year round. Enjoy it with your favorite sprouted bread.

YIELD: 2 SERVINGS

ingredients

FOR THE SOUP:

- 1 handful organic wheatgrass, chopped (about ½ cup)
- 1 handful organic spinach (about 1 cup)
- 1 cup pineapple chunks
- 1 cup almond or coconut milk

FOR TOPPING:

- ¼ medium organic red or white onion, diced (about ¼ cup)
- 3 organic cherry tomatoes, sliced
- ½ cup raw cashews
- Fresh tarragon, chopped

method

In a high-powered blender, process the soup ingredients until smooth. Refrigerate for 20 to 30 minutes.

Stir with a spoon for a few seconds and pour into two soup bowls. Garnish with topping ingredients and enjoy immediately.

ESSENTIAL RECIPES

HERE ARE SOME OF OUR FAVORITE ESSENTIAL RECIPES! THESE OF COURSE CAN COMPLEMENT ANY OF THE MASTER PLANTS RECIPES, BUT WE LIKE TO THINK THEY ARE THE ARSENAL OF "CLASSICS" YOU CAN BE COMFORTABLE MAKING ANYTIME. RANGING FROM SMOOTHIES AND SIDES, TO CONDIMENTS AND SNACKS, THEY ARE ALL QUICK, EASY, AND OF COURSE, USEFUL. DON'T WORRY, WE DIDN'T FORGET TO INCLUDE A FEW COOKIE RECIPES TOO!

lemon dressing

YIELD: ABOUT ¾ CUP

ingredients

- Juice of ½ lemon
- 1 garlic clove
- 2 tablespoons tahini
- ¼ cup non-dairy milk
- 1 medjool date, pitted
- Pinch of freshly ground black pepper

method

In a food processor, chop the garlic clove until minced. Add the rest of the ingredients and process until smooth.

ranch dressing

YIELD: ABOUT 1¼ CUPS

ingredients

- 6 organic fresh basil leaves
- 1 sprig organic fresh dill
- 3 tablespoons silken tofu
- 1 cup non-dairy milk
- ½ cup sunflower seeds
- 1 tablespoon lemon juice
- 2 tablespoons nutritional yeast
- 1 teaspoon shoyu or tamari

method

Combine all the ingredients in high-powered blender or food processor. Pour into a glass container and refrigerate for a few hours in order to allow the flavors to meld. Use within a week.

turmeric date dressing

YIELD: ABOUT 1 CUP

ingredients

- 2 medjool dates, pitted
- ½ tablespoon turmeric powder
- 1 tablespoon organic, non-GMO silken tofu
- ¾ cup non-dairy milk

method

Add all ingredients to a high-powered blender or food processor and blend well. Serve with your favorite salad.

DRINKS

all-star pregnancy smoothie

YIELD: 2 SERVINGS

ingredients

- 1 cup fresh organic spinach
- ¼ cup fresh or 1 shot liquid wheatgrass
- 1 mango, peeled, or with skin if organic
- ½ avocado, pitted and scooped (see page 273)
- 1 kiwi, peeled
- 1 tablespoon pumpkin seeds
- 2 cups filtered water
- 1 cup filtered ice cubes

method

Combine all the ingredients in a high-powered blender for 20 to 30 seconds or until liquid and smooth. Serve and drink immediately.

cancer fighter smoothie

YIELD: 2 SERVINGS

ingredients

- 2 organic kale leaves, deveined
- ¼ cup fresh or 1 shot liquid wheatgrass
- 1 garlic clove
- 1 cup fresh pineapple chunks
- 1 inch fresh organic turmeric, peeled
- 1 banana, peeled
- 2 cups filtered water
- 1 cup filtered ice cubes

method

Combine in a high-powered blender for 20 to 30 seconds or until liquid and smooth. Serve and drink immediately.

classic almond milk

YIELD: ABOUT 4 CUPS

ingredients

- 1 cup raw almonds, quick-soaked in hot water for 10 minutes or soaked overnight (8 to 10 hours)
- 4 cups filtered water
- 3 medjool dates, pitted

method

Drain the almonds from their soaking water and rinse them thoroughly under cool running water. In a high-powered blender, combine the almonds, water, and dates. Pulse the blender a few times to break up the almonds, and then blend continuously for 2 minutes.

Pour the milk through a nut-milk bag by placing over a bowl and gently squeezing the bottom of the bag to release the milk. Alternatively, use a teapot filter and squeeze the liquid through the filter.

Transfer the milk into an airtight container or jar and refrigerate.

Chef's Note: Milk will last for about 2 to 3 days. Shake before using.

classic hemp milk

YIELD: ABOUT 3 CUPS

ingredients

- 1 cup raw shelled hempseeds
- 3 cups filtered water
- 4 pitted dates, soaked

method

In a high-powered blender, combine the hempseeds, water, and dates, and blend continuously for one minute. Consume unstrained.

If smoother milk is preferred, pour the milk through a nut-milk bag, by placing the bag over a bowl and gently squeezing the bottom of the bag to release the milk.

Alternatively, use a teapot filter and squeeze the liquid through the filter.

Transfer the milk into an airtight container or jar and refrigerate.

Chef's Note: Milk will last for about 2 to 3 days. Shake before using.

digestion booster smoothie

YIELD: 2 SERVINGS

ingredients

- 1 cup organic kale leaves, chopped and deveined
- 1 orange, peeled
- 1 organic carrot
- 1 cup fresh pineapple chunks
- 1 tablespoon flaxseeds, chopped
- 2 cups filtered water
- 1 cup filtered ice cubes

method

Combine in a high-powered blender for 20 to 30 seconds or until liquid and smooth. Serve and drink immediately.

green protein smoothie

YIELD: 2 SERVINGS

ingredients

- 1 handful fresh organic spinach (about 1 cup)
- 3 organic broccoli florets
- 1 banana, peeled
- 1 handful pumpkin seeds (about 1 ounce)
- 1 teaspoon chia seeds
- 1 tablespoon hempseeds
- 2 cups filtered water
- 1 cup filtered ice cubes

method

Combine in a high-powered blender for 20 to 30 seconds or until liquid and smooth. Serve and drink immediately.

heart-thriving smoothie

YIELD: 2 SERVINGS

ingredients

- 1 cup organic kale leaves, chopped and deveined
- ¼ cup fresh or 1 shot liquid wheatgrass
- ¼ cup pomegranate seeds
- 1 banana, peeled
- ¼ cup rolled oats
- 1 apple with skin
- 1 tablespoon flaxseeds, chopped
- 2 cups filtered water
- 1 cup filtered ice cubes

method

Combine in a high-powered blender for 20 to 30 seconds or until liquid and smooth. Serve and drink immediately.

kidney and liver cleansing smoothie

YIELD: 2 SERVINGS

ingredients

- 3 spears organic asparagus
- 1 handful fresh organic spinach (about 1 cup)
- ¼ cup fresh or 1 shot liquid wheatgrass
- ½ organic beet, peeled
- 1 organic apple with skin
- 1 handful walnuts (about 1 ounce)
- 1 banana, peeled
- 2 cups filtered water
- 1 cup filtered ice cubes

method

To remove the white bottom end of the asparagus, hold each spear with both hands and bend it near the white end. The white end will snap off. Add to a high-powered blender and combine all ingredients for 20 to 30 seconds or until liquid and smooth. Serve and drink immediately.

man-power smoothie

YIELD: 2 SERVINGS

ingredients

- 1 handful fresh organic spinach (about 1 cup)
- ¼ cup fresh or 1 shot liquid wheatgrass
- ½ organic red beet
- 1 banana, peeled
- 1 handful Brazil nuts
- 1 handful organic blueberries
- 1 tablespoon maca powder
- 2 cups filtered water
- 1 cup filtered ice cubes

method

Combine in a high-powered blender for 20 to 30 seconds or until liquid and smooth. Serve and drink immediately.

brown rice

YIELD: 4 SERVINGS

ingredients

- 1 cup organic brown rice
- 2¼ cups filtered water for short grain rice or 2½ for long grain
- 1 tablespoon organic, non-GMO miso paste, shoyu, or tamari
- 2-inch piece bell pepper
- 3 garlic cloves

method

In a medium pot bring the water to a boil. Add the rice, miso, shoyu, or tamari, bell pepper, and garlic. Return to a boil.

Lower heat to medium-low and cook for about 30 to 35 minutes, covered, or until water is absorbed. Remove the lid and stir to make sure there is no water in the bottom of the pot. Remove garlic and pepper if desired. Serve and enjoy with legumes, vegetables, tubers, or in salads.

buckwheat

YIELD: 4 SERVINGS

ingredients

- 1 cup organic buckwheat
- 2 cups filtered water
- 1 tablespoon shoyu or tamari

method

Bring the water to a boil. Add the buckwheat and cook uncovered for about 8 minutes, or until the water is almost absorbed. Lower the heat and cook over low heat for another 10 minutes or until the remaining water is absorbed. Add shoyu or tamari.

Because of buckwheat's versatility, it can be enjoyed warm or chilled. Serve and enjoy with legumes, salads, soups, and breakfast bowls.

millet

ingredients

- ○ 2 cups filtered water
- ○ 1 cup millet
- ○ 1 teaspoon shoyu or tamari
- ○ 1 garlic clove
- ○ 1 bay leaf

method

Bring the water to a boil. Add the millet and return to a boil.

Bring down to low heat. Add the rest of the ingredients and cover. Cook for 10 to 15 minutes, or until all water is absorbed.

Chef's Note: Millet is great on its own, but also pairs well with almost any soup or stew.

beans

YIELD: 4 TO 6 SERVINGS

ingredients

- ○ 2 cups beans (red, black, white, kidney, or pinto)
- ○ 5 cups filtered water
- ○ 2 bay leaves
- ○ 1 sage leaf
- ○ 1/8 teaspoon dried or 1/2 teaspoon fresh thyme
- ○ 1 sprig fresh cilantro
- ○ 2 garlic cloves
- ○ 1/2 medium onion, any kind
- ○ 3 medium organic tomatoes
- ○ 1 tablespoon organic, non-GMO miso paste
- ○ Freshly ground black pepper to taste

method

Soak the beans overnight. Discard the soaking water and rinse three or four times under running water.

Transfer the beans into a large pot with water. Make sure there is at least 2 inches of water over the beans. Add bay and sage leaves, thyme, and cilantro, and cook for 45 minutes over medium heat, or until beans are soft. Check the packaging cooking instructions for best results.

In a food processor, chop the garlic and onion until minced. Add to a saucepan and sauté for 3 to 5 minutes.

Chop the tomatoes in the food processor until liquid and add to the saucepan.

Add the miso and let simmer over low heat until sauce thickens, for about 8 to 10 minutes. Transfer the sauce to bean pot and stir. Serve and sprinkle with the freshly ground black pepper.

Serve hot or cold with buckwheat, rice, quinoa, or millet, with tubers such as potatoes or yucca, or with avocado, plantains, or salad.

quinoa

YIELD: 4 SERVINGS

ingredients

- 1 cup quinoa
- 1½ cups filtered cold water
- 1 teaspoon organic, non-GMO miso paste (optional)

method

Place the quinoa in a fine mesh strainer and rinse under cold running water to remove any residual bitter saponins. Bring the rinsed quinoa and the water to a boil in a medium pot. Add miso paste and cover. Bring down to low-medium heat and simmer for about 12 minutes or until the white tails of the quinoa appear. Remove from heat and fluff with a fork.

Because of quinoa's versatility, it can be served warm or chilled, and can be added to soups, desserts, salads, entrées, or even smoothies.

chickpeas

YIELD: 4 TO 6 SERVINGS

ingredients

- 2 cups chickpeas, uncooked
- 5 cups filtered water
- 2-inch piece fresh bell pepper
- 2 bay leaves
- 1 sage leaf
- ⅛ teaspoon dried or ½ teaspoon fresh thyme
- 1 tablespoon organic, non-GMO miso paste
- ½ onion, any kind (about ½ cup)
- 3 to 5 garlic cloves
- 3 medium organic tomatoes
- Freshly ground black pepper to taste

method

Bring the chickpeas and water into a boil. Add the remaining ingredients (except onion, garlic, and tomatoes) and cook for 45 minutes over medium heat or until the chickpeas are soft.

Chop the onions, garlic, and tomatoes in a food processor until liquid and add to pot. Stir and simmer for 10 more minutes.

Serve and sprinkle with freshly ground black pepper.

Serve hot or cold with buckwheat, rice, quinoa, millet, with tubers such as potatoes or yucca, or with avocado, plantains, or salad.

lentils

ingredients

- ○ 2 cups brown lentils, uncooked
- ○ 5 cups filtered water
- ○ 2-inch piece fresh bell pepper
- ○ 2 bay leaves
- ○ 1 sage leaf
- ○ 1/8 teaspoon dried or 1/2 teaspoon fresh thyme
- ○ 1 sprig fresh cilantro
- ○ 1 tablespoon organic, non-GMO miso paste
- ○ 3 medium organic tomatoes
- ○ Freshly ground black pepper, for serving

method

Bring the lentils and water to a boil. Add the remaining ingredients (except tomatoes) and cook for 35 minutes over medium heat or until lentils are soft.

Chop tomatoes in a food processor until liquid and add to pot. Stir and simmer for 5 more minutes.

Serve and sprinkle with freshly ground black pepper.

Serve hot or cold with buckwheat, rice, quinoa, or millet, with tubers such as potatoes or yucca, or with avocado, plantains, or salad.

SIDES AND SOUPS

spicy baked plantain chips

Plantains are a sweeter and equally hearty alternative to homemade potato chips.

YIELD: 2 SERVINGS

ingredients

- ⅛ teaspoon paprika
- ⅛ teaspoon ground cumin
- ⅛ teaspoon dried thyme
- ⅛ teaspoon black pepper
- ⅛ teaspoon cayenne pepper
- 1 large green plantain
- Pink Himalayan salt to taste

method

Preheat the oven to 400°F.

Combine all the spices together in a mixing bowl.

To peel the plantain, cut off the ends. Then, using the tip of the knife, slice the peel lengthwise from top to bottom, just enough to cut through the peel, but not enough to slice into the plantain. Then use your hands to remove the peel from the plantain.

Using a mandoline on the 0.5 mm setting or a chef's knife, slice the plantain into thin slices. Add slices to the spices in the mixing bowl and combine the ingredients with your hands.

Line a baking tray with parchment or a silicone sheet. Lie the slices out flat onto the lined tray, making sure none of them are stuck together or on top of one other.

Bake for about 10 minutes. Remove the sheet from the oven and carefully flip the chips over one at a time. Place back in the oven and bake for another 8 minutes, taking care not to burn the chips.

Remove from the oven and transfer to a serving bowl. Sprinkle with a bit of pink Himalayan salt and serve.

Chef's Note: Enjoy as a side, appetizer, or snack. To make plantains chips that are not spicy, skip the paprika and cayenne pepper, and replace with equivalent amounts of garlic powder and onion powder.

crackers

ingredients

- 2 medjool dates
- 1 cup filtered water
- 1 tablespoon salt-free seasoning or Herbamare®
- 1 cup flaxseeds
- 3 teaspoons chia seeds
- 3 teaspoons sunflower seeds
- 3 teaspoons pumpkin seeds

method

Preheat the oven to 250°F. In a food processor, combine the dates and water until completely blended. Transfer to a large bowl and add the salt-free seasoning or Herbamare®, flaxseeds and chia seeds. Soak for 20 minutes.

Line a large baking sheet with parchment paper or use a silicone baking tray or sheet.

Add the rest of the ingredients to the mixing bowl and combine until mixture is well combined. Spread the mixture evenly on the lined baking sheet or silicone dish. Score the dough into the desired shape (squares, rectangles, circles, or free-form).

Bake for 45 minutes. Flip mixture over by placing a second parchment sheet over the mixture. Turn over and use the new sheet to bake for another 30 minutes. Cracker dough will be hard and crispy when done.

Remove from the oven and let it cool off. Enjoy with Keobab Kelp Pâté (page 200), Sweet Potato Hummus (page 270), Zen Persimmon Pico de Gallo (page 218), or Naked Guacamole (page 273).

kale chips

ingredients

- 5 fresh organic kale leaves
- ½ cup hempseeds
- ½ cup nutritional yeast
- 2 tablespoons garlic powder
- 2 tablespoons onion powder

method

To devein the kale, simply hold the leaf's stem with one hand, and run your other hand along the stem tightly. The entire leaf will come off the vein.

Chop the kale leaves in small pieces and rinse them thoroughly in water. Transfer to a large baking sheet or dehydrator tray and spread them out.

Combine the rest of the ingredients in a small bowl and mix well. Cover the wet kale leaves with the mixture.

Dehydrate for 12 to 24 hours or until crispy. As a second option, bake at 180°F for about an hour, or until kale is crispy, checking every 20 minutes to avoid burning the chips.

potato salad

ingredients

- ○ 6 red organic potatoes with skin, quartered
- ○ 1 cup organic celery, sliced
- ○ ½ cup onion, chopped
- ○ ½ cup fresh organic parsley, chopped
- ○ 2 tablespoons fresh organic dill, chopped
- ○ Freshly ground black pepper to taste

FOR THE DRESSING:

- ○ 1 cup cashews, soaked overnight or quick-soaked in hot water for 10 minutes, then drained and rinsed
- ○ 2 medjool dates, pitted
- ○ 2 garlic cloves, chopped
- ○ 1 tablespoon Dijon mustard
- ○ 2 tablespoons nutritional yeast
- ○ 2 tablespoons apple cider vinegar
- ○ 1 teaspoon shoyu
- ○ 1 cup non-dairy milk

method

MAKING THE POTATOES:

Add the quartered potatoes to a large pot and cover them with water by 1 or 2 inches. Cover slightly and bring to a boil. Cook for 10 minutes or until you can pierce them with a fork. Drain the potatoes.

Slice the potatoes further into bite-size pieces and transfer them to a mixing bowl. Add the celery, onion, parsley, and dill.

MAKING THE DRESSING:

In a blender, combine the cashews with the remaining dressing ingredients until the mixture is smooth and creamy. Combine the dressing gently with the potatoes and serve.

Enjoy it warm or cold.

sweet potato hummus

YIELD: ABOUT 4 CUPS

ingredients

- 1 pound organic sweet potatoes, peeled and cut into 1-inch pieces
- 1 cup chickpeas, cooked
- Juice of ½ lemon
- 3 tablespoons tahini
- 1 teaspoon ground cumin
- 1 garlic clove, chopped
- Freshly ground black pepper

method

Set a steamer basket in a large pot. Fill with water to just below the basket. Bring to a boil.

Add the potatoes and reduce to a simmer, cover, and cook until tender, 10 to 12 minutes.

Add the potatoes to a food processor and blend until mashed. Transfer to a large container and set aside.

In the food processor, combine the chickpeas, lemon juice, tahini, cumin, and garlic. Purée for about

1 minute, adding filtered water 1 tablespoon at a time if necessary to thin the mixture to desired consistency.

Season with the pepper and let cool. Serve immediately or refrigerate in an airtight container for up to 5 days.

Serve with whole or sprouted pita bread, raw vegetables such as celery and carrots, or as dip for Crackers (page 268).

traditional-style yucca

YIELD: ABOUT 5 TO 6 SERVINGS

ingredients

- 2 pounds yucca, peeled and sliced lengthwise
- 1 cup filtered water
- 1 tablespoon of organic, non-GMO miso paste
- 4 garlic cloves
- ½ onion, any kind, chopped (about ½ cup)
- 2 Roma tomatoes
- A few drops of lemon juice

method

Add the yucca to a large pot and add enough water to cover the yucca by an inch or two. Stir in the miso. Bring to a boil over medium-high heat, cover, and cook until tender, about 15 minutes. Drain, and place the yucca on a serving plate.

In a food processor, chop the garlic and transfer to a saucepan. Combine onion and sauté for 3 minutes. Chop the tomato and add

to the saucepan. Sauté for another 5 minutes, covered. Pour the hot tomato mixture over the yucca and sprinkle with lemon juice drops. Serve immediately.

chilled watermelon soup

YIELD: 8 SERVINGS

ingredients

- 1 yellow or red seedless watermelon, diced (about 9 cups)
- 3 medjool dates, pitted
- 2 tablespoons fresh lemon juice
- 1 cup slightly sweet white wine (such as Riesling) or ¾ cup filtered water
- 1 teaspoon ginger, chopped
- ½ cup sparkling water
- 2 tablespoons fresh mint, chopped

method

Combine all the ingredients (except for sparkling water and mint) in a blender until smooth. Let sit ½ hour, refrigerated.

Strain the soup. Add the sparkling water and stir. Divide among 8 bowls and serve. Garnish with mint.

classic potato soup

YIELD: 4 SERVINGS

ingredients

- 6 medium potatoes, peeled and chopped
- 5 cups filtered water
- 1 bay leaf
- 1 sage leaf
- ⅛ teaspoon dried or ½ teaspoon fresh thyme
- 1 tablespoon organic, non-GMO miso paste
- 1 sprig fresh cilantro
- 2 cups non-dairy milk
- Freshly ground black pepper

method

Place the potatoes and water in a large pot. Add the bay leaf, sage, thyme, miso, and cilantro and bring to a boil. Reduce heat to medium-low. Cover and simmer until the potatoes have softened, about 30 minutes.

Remove the potatoes from the pot and purée in a food processor until smooth, or place potatoes in a bowl and mash with a potato masher or a hand blender until smooth.

Return the potatoes to pot. Stir in the non-dairy milk and ground pepper. Simmer for another 8 minutes and serve.

cashew cheese

YIELD: ½ CUP

ingredients

- 2/3 cup raw cashews, soaked overnight or quick-soaked in hot water for 10 minutes
- 2 garlic cloves, peeled
- 1 tablespoon fresh lemon juice
- 1 to 2 teaspoons dried rosemary
- 3 teaspoons nutritional yeast
- Filtered water, as needed

method

Combine all ingredients in a high-powered blender or food processor. Add water in 1-tablespoon increments as needed to achieve the desired consistency.

fig pâté

YIELD: ABOUT 1 CUP

ingredients

- 5 dried or fresh figs
- 4 tablespoons organic, non-GMO silken tofu
- 1 tablespoon black sesame seeds
- ½ cup nuts, any kind

method

In a food processor, mix all ingredients until creamy. Serve as dip, spread, or topping for bruschetta.

naked mayo

YIELD: ABOUT ¾ CUP (ABOUT 12 1-TABLESPOON SERVINGS)

ingredients

- ½ cup silken tofu
- Juice of ½ lemon
- 1 teaspoon apple cider vinegar
- 1 tablespoon applesauce
- ½ teaspoon pink Himalayan salt
- ¼ teaspoon dry mustard

method

In a small container, whisk ingredients together until well combined. Refrigerate in an airtight container. Mayo will last for about a week.

naked guacamole

YIELD: ABOUT 2 CUPS

ingredients

- 2 ripe avocados
- 1 organic Roma tomato
- ¼ white onion
- 1 sprig cilantro
- 1 jalapeño pepper (optional)
- Juice of ½ lemon
- ⅛ teaspoon ground pepper

method

TO PIT AN AVOCADO:
Using a chef's knife, carefully cut the avocado in half lengthwise, from stem to bottom. Do not try to slice through the pit. Instead, guide the knife around it so the avocado is separated into two halves, each still stuck to the pit. Twist the two halves apart, and the pit will stick to one half. To remove the pit, hold the half with the pit in the palm of your hand and carefully thwack the knife down onto the pit just hard enough so that the blade edge sticks in the pit. Twist the knife to loosen the pit, which will detach cleanly from the flesh when you lift the knife. Be careful not to cut your hand! A sharp, heavy chef's knife works best because you will have to strike the pit much harder with a light, dull knife. Remove the pit from the knife with a kitchen towel. This will protect your fingers and give you a grip on the slippery pit.

Scoop the avocado pulp into a mixing bowl. Smash with a fork. Dice the tomato, onion, cilantro, and jalapeño (optional) and add to the bowl. Add the lemon juice and pepper. Stir well and serve.

pico de gallo

YIELD: 2 SERVINGS

ingredients

- 2 firm Roma tomatoes
- 2 tablespoons diced bell pepper
- ¼ red onion, diced
- 2 garlic cloves, diced
- Juice of 1 lemon
- 1 jalapeño pepper (optional)
- 2 sprigs fresh cilantro, chopped

method

Cut tomatoes in half. Over a mixing bowl, squeeze out extra juice and seeds. Dice the tomatoes and add to a serving bowl. Add the bell pepper, onion, and garlic to the bowl. Add the lemon juice. Finely dice the jalapeño, removing the seeds if you would like it less hot. Add to the bowl, and season with the chopped cilantro. Stir and serve.

sofrito

ingredients

- 1 pound plum tomatoes
- 1 medium red bell pepper
- 1 medium yellow onion
- 5 garlic cloves, smashed and peeled
- 1 bunch fresh cilantro, large stems trimmed
- ½ cup vegetable broth
- 1 teaspoon shoyu or tamari
- 1 tablespoon organic, non-GMO miso paste
- Pinch of paprika
- Pinch of freshly ground black pepper

method

In a food processor, combine the tomatoes, peppers, onion, garlic, and cilantro. In batches, pulse the mixture until finely chopped.

Transfer the mixture to a large pot and add the remaining ingredients. Cook for about 25 minutes, stirring occasionally, over medium heat. Use with your favorite meal as a topping, such as for potatoes, yucca, legumes, buckwheat, etc.

To store, let it cool completely and transfer to an airtight container. Sauce will keep refrigerated for about 10 days, or frozen for up to 4 months.

chocolate spread

YIELD: ABOUT ¾ CUP (ABOUT 12 1-TABLESPOON SERVINGS)

ingredients

- 1 ripe avocado, pitted and scooped (see page 273)
- 1 banana, peeled
- 2 teaspoons cacao powder

method

Combine all ingredients in a food processor until smooth and creamy. Spread will keep for a day or two refrigerated.

carrot cookies

YIELD: 10 COOKIES

ingredients

- 2 medjool dates
- 1 organic carrot
- 1 banana, peeled
- 1 cup gluten-free rolled oats
- 1 tablespoon almond butter, unsweetened

method

In a food processor, blend the dates and the carrot. Add to a mixing bowl. Add the banana and the oats. Blend together until mixture is uniform. With wet hands, shape the mixture into 1-inch round bites.

Chef's Note: Suggested toppings for the cookie bites are raw cacao powder, chocolate bits, shredded coconut, goji berries, or chia, pumpkin, or flaxseeds.

date sauce

YIELD: ABOUT ¾ CUP (ABOUT 12 1-TABLESPOON SERVINGS)

ingredients

- 1 cup filtered water
- 4 medjool dates, pitted

method

In a food processor, combine both ingredients until the mixture is creamy. Refrigerate and use as liquid sweetener.

chia pudding

YIELD: 2 SERVINGS

ingredients

- 1 cup non-dairy milk
- 2 dates, pitted
- 3 tablespoons chia seeds

method

Combine the milk and the dates in a food processor until well combined. Transfer to a small container and whisk with the chia seeds. Let sit for at least 20 minutes or overnight.

Options: To flavor the pudding, you can add ingredients to the milk mixture such as cacao (1 tablespoon cacao powder) or ½ cup fruit (any kind).

Top with fruit, nuts, or granola.

naked pie crust

YIELD: 1 (8-INCH) PIE CRUST

ingredients

- 1 cup nuts, any kind, or a mixture of nuts
- 2 dried figs
- 4 medjool dates, pitted

method

Place all ingredients in a food processor and blend until mixture is well combined. Pat mixture into the bottom and sides of pie dish and fill with the desired ingredients.

three-ingredient oat cookies

YIELD: 10 COOKIES

ingredients

- ½ cup nuts, any kind
- 1 cup gluten-free rolled oats
- 1 banana, peeled

method

In a food processor, blend the nuts and add to a mixing bowl. Add the banana and the oats. Blend together until mixture is uniform. With wet hands, shape mixture into 1-inch, round bites.

Chef's Note: Suggested toppings for the cookie bites are raw cacao powder, chocolate bits, shredded coconut, goji berries, or chia, pumpkin, or flaxseeds.

Thank You,

To Luigi Lastella, my dad, for his sacrifice, hard work, and love for the land. He taught me the value of real food and agriculture in the traditional and beloved Mediterranean way.

To Dr. John McDougall, and Dr. T. Colin Campbell for helping us understand how important it is to eat sustainably; for ourselves and our planet.

To Margarita Restrepo, whose vision and tireless work continues to spread awareness of plant-based nutrition around the world.

To Coleen O'Shea, Jennifer Kasius, and Running Press, for believing in our work.

—MICHELE

To Michele, for being an archangel of light. Thank you for inspiring the idea of *Master Plants* and allowing me to be part of it.

To my parents, for being my structure and support, and without whom I would not be here.

To Denise DeSerio, for lending her amazing talent and unconditional love, work, and support to *Master Plants* and *Naked Food Magazine*. Without you, none of it would have been possible.

To my little London, through whom I am a constant witness of the magnificence of nature and the purity of the heart.

To the now, for helping me understand the true meaning of life.

—MARGARITA

GLOSSARY

Adzuki: Adzuki, from Japanese: red bean. A leguminous plant, *Phaseolus angularis*, with yellow flowers and pods containing edible brown seeds that is widely cultivated as a food crop in China and Japan.

Alfalfa: A plant, *Medicago sativa*, of the legume family, usually having bluish-purple flowers, originating in the near east and widely cultivated as a forage crop. First documented between 1835–45.

Allspice: The dried, unripe berries of an aromatic tropical American tree, *Pimenta dioica*, used whole or ground as a spice. First documented between 1615–25.

Amaranth: Any plant of the genus *Amaranthus*, some species of which are cultivated as food and some for their showy flower clusters or foliage.

Barley: A plant cultivated since prehistoric times, grown for forage and grain. Barley is the fourth-largest crop grown in the world. It is used to feed grazing livestock, eaten as a whole grain, milled into flour for baking, and dried to make malt. It is also an ingredient in both beer and whisky. The old English root of barley is bærlic, most likely from a proto-Indo-European source that means "bristle, point, or projection."

Bilberry: The fruit of several shrubby species of the genus *Vaccinium*. First documented between 1570–80.

Breadfruit: A large, round, starchy fruit borne by a tree, *Artocarpus altilis*, of the mulberry family, native to the pacific islands, used, baked or roasted, for food. First documented between 1690–1700.

Buckwheat: An Asian plant of the dock family that produces starchy seeds. The seeds are used for fodder and are also milled into flour that is widely used in the United States. Buckwheat is an alternative source of complex carbohydrates for breakfast or any other meal or snack. First documented in the mid-16th century.

Bulgur: A form of wheat that has been parboiled, cracked, and dried. First documented between 1925–30.

Cantaloupe: A variety of melon, *Cucumis melo* var. *cantalupensis*, of the gourd family, having a hard scaly or warty rind, grown in Europe, Asia, and the United States. First documented between 1730–40.

Capsicum: Any plant of the genus *Capsicum*, of the nightshade family, as *C. annuum*, the common pepper of the garden, occurring in many varieties. First documented between 1655–65.

Caraway: A plant, *Carum carvi*, of the parsley family, native to Europe, characterized for its finely divided leaves and umbels of white or pinkish flowers. First documented between 1325–75.

Cherimoya: A tropical American tree, *Annona cherimola*, characterized by leaves with velvety, hairy undersides and yellow-to-brown fragrant flowers. It is also notable by its leathery, scalelike skin, and soft pulp. First documented between 1730–40.

Chia: Either of two aromatic annual plant species (*Salvia columbariae* or *S. hispanica*) in the mint family, native to Mexico and the southwest United States and having clusters of blue or violet flowers and edible seedlike fruits. Chia is common throughout California and the great basin.

Chives: A small bulbous plant, *Allium schoenoprasum*, related to the leek and onion, having long, slender leaves that are used as a seasoning. First documented between 1350–1400.

Chlorella: Any freshwater, unicellular green alga of the genus chlorella. First documented in 1890.

Currant: The small, edible, acid round fruit or berry of certain wild or cultivated shrubs of the genus *Ribes*. First documented between 1300–50.

Damson: Also called damson plum. The small, dark-blue or purple fruit of a plum, *Prunus insititia*, of the rose family, introduced into Europe from Asia Minor. First documented between 1350–1400.

Dill: A plant, *Anethum graveolens*, of the parsley family, having aromatic seeds and finely divided leaves, both of which are used for flavoring food. First documented in the year 900.

Dragonfruit: Is the fruit of several cactus species. "Pitaya" usually refers to fruit of the genus *Stenocereus*, while "Pitahaya" or "Dragonfruit" always refers to fruit of the genus *Hylocereus*. First documented between 1750–60.

Dulse: A coarse, edible, red seaweed, *Rhodymenia palmata*. First documented between 1540–50.

Durian: The edible fruit of a tree, *Durio zibethinus*, of the Bombax family, of southeastern Asia. It is characterized for having a hard, prickly rind, a highly flavored, pulpy flesh, and an unpleasant odor. First documented between 1580–90.

Elderberry: The berrylike fruit of the elder, used in making wine and jelly. First documented between 1400–50.

Feijoa: A shrub, *Feijoa sellowiana*, of the Myrtle family, native to South America, bearing edible, greenish, plum-like fruit. First documented in 1858.

Frisée: A variety of endive (*Cichorium endivia* var. *crispum*) having curly, finely dissected leaves. Also called curly endive.

Genip: Either of two tropical American trees that yield the genip fruit. The genip fruit can be sweet or sour. The sour variety is often eaten with chili powder, salt, and lime, while the sweet variety is often eaten plain.

Goji: Goji berry or wolfberry is the fruit of *Lycium barbarum* and *Lycium chinense*, two very closely related species of boxthorn in the family Solanaceae (which also includes the potato, tomato, eggplant, deadly nightshade, chili pepper, and tobacco). The two species are native to southeastern Europe and Asia.

Gooseberry: The edible, acid, globular, sometimes spiny fruit of certain prickly shrubs belonging to the genus *Ribes*, of the Saxifrage family, first documented between 1525–35.

Goosefoot: A plant of temperate regions with divided leaves that resemble to foot of a goose. Some varieties, like quinoa, are edible, while many are common weeds.

Guacamole: A dip made of mashed avocado mixed with chopped onions and other seasonings. Guacamole dates from at least the 1500s, when it was made by the Aztecs in Mexico. Guacamole is a Spanish word that's based on the Aztec language Nahuatl's *Ahuaca-Molli*, a combination of Ahuacatl, "avocado," and Molli, "sauce." in the United States, guacamole has surged in popularity over the last several decades, with avocados especially in demand right before Super Bowl Sunday and Cinco De Mayo.

Guava: Any of the numerous tropical and subtropical American trees or shrubs belonging to the genus *Psidium*, of the Myrtle family, especially *P. guajava*, bearing large, yellow, round or pear-shaped fruit; and *P. littorale*, bearing smaller, yellowish to deep-red, oval fruit. First documented between 1545–55.

Hemp: Any plant of the genus *Cannabis*; a coarse bushy annual with palmate leaves and clusters of small green flowers; yields tough fibers and narcotic drugs. Similar in taste to sunflower seeds, these nuts are derived from hempseeds, which are also used to grow cannabis.

Hijiki: A dark brown seaweed that grows in treelike fronds, used dried and shredded in Japanese cookery. First documented in 1867, where the word "Hijiki" first appeared in an English-language publication.

Honeydew melon: A variety of the winter melon, *Cucumis melo* (Inodorus group), having a smooth, pale green rind and sweet, juicy, light green flesh. First documented between 1915–20.

Huckleberry: The dark blue or black edible berry of any of various shrubs belonging to the genus *Gaylussacia* of the Heath family. First documented between 1660–70.

Jackfruit: A large, tropical, milky-juiced tree, *Artocarpus heterophyllus*, of the Mulberry family, having stiff and glossy green leaves, cultivated for its very large, edible fruit and seeds. Also refers to the fruit of this tree, which may weigh up to 70 pounds. First documented between 1810–20.

Jicama: The large, edible, tuberous root of a tropical American plant, *Pachyrhizus erosus*, of the Legume family, eaten as a vegetable either raw or boiled. First documented between 1900–05.

Kamut: A trademark for an ancient variety of durum wheat.

Kelp: Any large, brown, cold-water seaweed of the family Laminariaceae, used as food and in various manufacturing processes. First documented between 1350–1400.

Kombu; A brown Japanese seaweed, sun-dried before use in sushi, stocks, etc.

Kumquat: A small, round or oblong citrus fruit having a sweet rind and acid pulp, used chiefly for preserves. First documented between 1865–70.

Leek: A plant, *Allium ampeloprasum*, of the Amaryllis family, related to the onion, having a cylindrical bulb and leaves used in cookery. First documented before the year 1000.

Legume: Legumes come from the family Leguminosae, and a trait all legumes share is that they grow in a type of pod such as peas, peanuts, lentils, soy, and clover. Legumes are high in protein, fiber, and other essential nutrients.

Lichee: The fruit of a Chinese tree, *Litchi chinensis*, of the Soapberry family, consisting of a thin, brittle shell enclosing a sweet, jellylike pulp and a single seed. First documented between 1580–90.

Maca: Also referred to as the "Peruvian gingseng" or the "Peruvian miracle," Maca root is a hardy perennial that belongs to the radish family. It is native to the slopes of the Andean mountains of Peru and Bolivia, where it has long been used as both a root vegetable and a medicinal herb. After more than 2,000 years of being cultivated in Peru, it continues to be used widely in the region.

Macadamia: The edible, hard-shelled seed of this tree. First documented between 1900–05.

Mamoncillo: The genip, *Melicoccus bijugatus*.

Mangosteen: The juicy, edible fruit of an East Indian tree, *Garcinia mangostana*. First documented between 1590–1600.

Millet: Any of various small-grained annual cereal and forage grasses of the genera *Panicum*, *Echinochloa*, *Setaria*, *Sorghum*, and *Eleusine*.

Milo: A grain sorghum having white, yellow, or pinkish seeds, grown chiefly in Africa, Asia, and the United States. First documented between 1880–85.

Miso: A fermented seasoning paste of soybeans, often with rice or barley added, used to flavor soups and sauces. First documented between 1720–30.

Nectarine: A variety or mutation of peach having a smooth, fuzz-less skin. First documented between 1610–20.

Nori: A seaweed having a mildly sweet, salty taste, usually dried, used in Japanese cookery mainly as a wrap for sushi. One of the oldest descriptions of nori is dated to around the 8th century.

Nutritional Yeast: Not to be confused with brewer's yeast or baking yeast, nutritional yeast is an essential part of a plant-based diet, both for its nutrients and for its cheesy, nutty flavor. Nutritional yeast is true to its name, as it is an excellent source of B vitamins, folic acid, selenium, zinc, and protein. On average, a 2-tablespoon serving provides 9 g of protein and is a complete protein, providing all nine amino acids the human body cannot produce. In addition, it is low in fat and gluten-free. Yeasts are members of the fungi family, and nutritional yeast is made from a single-celled organism, *Saccharomyces cerevisiae*, which is grown on molasses and then harvested, washed, and dried with heat to kill or "deactivate" it. Because it's inactive, it doesn't froth or grow like baking yeast, so it has no leavening ability. Nutritional yeast is available in both flaked and powdered form. If you are using the powdered yeast, you will need only about half as much as the flakes.

Oat: Annual grass of Europe and North Africa used as food and fodder (referred to primarily in the plural: "oats"). Oats are grown for both animal feed and human consumption. The old English root is "grain of the wild oat plant." The source of this word isn't known for sure, though it may come from the old *norse eitill*, "nodule" or "single grain."

Okra: A shrub, *Abelmoschus esculentus*, of the Mallow family, bearing beaked pods. First documented between 1670–80; said to be of West African origin, though precise source unknown.

Parsnip: A plant, *Pastinaca sativa*, cultivated varieties of which have a large, whitish, edible root. First documented between 1350–1400.

Physalis: The small, edible, tomato-like fruit of the plant *Physalis pruinosa*, of the nightshade family. First documented between 1840–50.

Pitaya: Any of several cacti of the genus *Lemaireocereus* and related genera, of the southwestern United States and Mexico, bearing edible fruit. First documented between 1750–60.

Plantain: A banana tree bearing hanging clusters of edible angular greenish starchy fruits in the tropics and subtropics. Any of numerous plants of the genus *Plantago*.

Potato: An edible tuber native to South America; a staple food of Ireland. Potato, which comes from the Spanish word *patata*, originally meant "sweet potato."

Protein: Any of a large group of nitrogenous organic compounds that are essential constituents of living cells; consist of polymers of amino acids; essential in the diet of animals for growth and for repair of tissues. The linguistic origins of protein are from the Greek *proteios*, means "first place" or "primary."

Quinoa: A goosefoot found in the Andes, where it was widely cultivated for its edible starchy seeds before the introduction of old world grains. The grain-like seeds of the quinoa, used as food and in the production of alcoholic drinks.

Rambutan: The bright red, oval fruit of a Malayan sapindaceous tree, *Nephelium lappaceum*, covered with soft spines, or hairs, and having a slightly tart taste. First documented between 1700–10.

Rhubarb: Any of several plants belonging to the genus *Rheum*, of the Buckwheat family, as *R. officinale*, having a medicinal rhizome, and *R. rhabarbarum*, having edible leafstalks. First documented between 1350–1400.

Rye: A widely cultivated cereal grass, *Secale cereale*, having one-nerved glumes and two- or three-flowered spikelets. First documented between before the year 900.

Scallion: Any onion that does not form a large bulb; a green onion. First documented between 1300–50.

Shallot: A plant, *Allium cepa aggregatum* (or *A. ascalonicum*), related to the onion, having a divided bulb used for flavoring in cookery. First documented between 1655–65.

Shoyu: A Japanese variety of soy sauce made from soya beans that have undergone a fermentation process. Natural shoyu employs the use of a centuries-old method of fermentation involving a special koji (*Aspergillus oryzae*), which converts hard-to-digest soy proteins, starches, and fats into easily absorbed amino acids, simple sugars, and fatty acids. First documented between 1725–30.

Sorghum: A cereal grass, *Sorghum bicolor* (or *S. vulgare*), having broad, corn-like leaves and a tall, pithy stem bearing the grain in a dense terminal cluster. First documented between 1590–1600.

Spelt: A wheat, *Triticum aestivum spelta*, native to southern Europe and western Asia, used for livestock feed and as a grain for human consumption. First documented before 1000.

Spirulina: Any of the blue-green algae of the genus *Spirulina*, sometimes added to food for its nutritional value.

Tahini: A paste made from ground, hulled sesame seeds used in North African, Greek, Turkish, and Middle Eastern cuisine. East Asian sesame paste is typically made of unhulled seeds. Tahini is served as a dip on its own or as a major component of hummus, baba ghanoush, and halva. The oldest mention of sesame is in a cuneiform document written 4,000 years ago that describes the custom of serving the gods sesame wine.

Tamari: A rich, naturally fermented soybean sauce containing little or no wheat and thicker than soy sauce.

Taro: A stemless plant, *Colocasia esculenta*, of the Arum family, cultivated in tropical regions, in the Pacific Islands and elsewhere, for the edible tuber.

Tarragon: An old world plant, *Artemisia dracunculus*, having aromatic leaves used for seasoning. First documented between 1530–40.

Teff: A grass, *Eragrostis tef*, native to Northern Africa, where it is cultivated for its edible seeds. First documented between 1780–90.

Tofu: A soft, bland, white cheese-like food, high in protein content, made from curdled soybean milk; used originally in Oriental cooking but now in a wide variety of soups and other dishes. First documented between 1875–80.

Tomatillo: *Physalis ixocarpa*, a plant of the nightshade family, native to Mexico, having yellow flowers with five blackish spots in the throat and bluish, sticky berries in a purple-veined calyx. First documented between 1910–15.

Turnip: *Brassica napobrassica*, a plant of the Brassicaceae family, having a yellow- or white-fleshed, edible tuber. First documented between 1790–1800.

Vitamin A: Any of several fat-soluble vitamins essential for normal vision; prevents night blindness or inflammation or dryness of the eyes.

Vitamin B: Originally thought to be a single vitamin but now separated into several B vitamins.

Vitamin B1: A B vitamin that prevents beriberi and maintains appetite and growth.

Vitamin B2: A B vitamin that prevents skin lesions and weight loss.

Vitamin B3: A B vitamin used to treat and prevent high cholesterol. It is also used for circulation problems, migraine headaches, dizziness, and diarrhea.

Vitamin B6: A B vitamin that is essential for metabolism of amino acids and starch.

Vitamin B12: Vitamin B12 (*Cobalamin*) plays a role in making DNA, and also helps keep nerve cells and red blood cells healthy.

Vitamin C: A vitamin found in fresh fruits (especially citrus fruits) and vegetables; prevents scurvy.

Vitamin D: A fat-soluble vitamin that prevents rickets.

Vitamin E: A fat-soluble vitamin that is essential for normal reproduction; an important antioxidant that neutralizes free radicals in the body.

Vitamin K: A fat-soluble vitamin that aids in the clotting of blood.

Wakame: A brown seaweed, *Undaria pinnatifida*, of coastal Japan and Korea, growing in coarse, stringy clumps and usually dried for use in Asian soups, salads, and side dishes. In 1867 the word "*wakame*" appeared in an English-language publication.

Watercress: A cress, *Nasturtium officinale*, of the mustard family, usually growing in clear, running streams and having pungent leaves. First documented between 1300–50.

Yam: The starchy, tuberous root of any of various climbing vines of the genus *Dioscorea*, cultivated for food in warm regions. First documented between 1580–90.

Yucca: Any of several evergreen plants of the genus *Yucca*, having usually tall stout stems and a terminal cluster of white flowers. Found in the warmer regions of North America.

REFERENCES

The Modern Paradigm

GENES VS. LIFESTYLE

1. Ford, ES. Bergmann, MM. Kröger, J. Schienkiewitz, A. Weikert, C. Boeing, H. "Healthy Living Is the Best Revenge: Findings from the European Prospective Investigation Into Cancer and Nutrition-Potsdam Study." *US National Library of Medicine National Institutes of Health. National Center for Biotechnology Information.* U.S. National Library of Medicine. (2009)

EMBRACING ANCIENT WISDOM

1. Touzeau A, et al., "Diet of ancient Egyptians inferred from stable isotope systematics." *Journal of Archaeological Science*" (2014): 114-124.

THE HARD FACTS

1. Ward, BW. Schiller, JS. Goodman, RA. "Multiple chronic conditions among US adults: a 2012 update," Prev Chronic Dis. 2014;11:130389. DOI: http://dx.doi.org/10.5888/pcd11.130389.

2. Centers for Disease Control and Prevention. "Death and Mortality," NCHS FastStats Web site. http://www.cdc.gov/nchs/fastats/deaths.htm. (Accessed December 20, 2013)

3. Centers for Disease Control and Prevention. "NCHS Data on Obesity," NCHS Fact Sheet Web site. http://www.cdc.gov/nchs/data/factsheets/factsheet_obesity.htm. (Accessed December 20, 2013)

4. Robert Wood Johnson Foundation. "Chronic Care: Making the Case for Ongoing Care," Princeton, NJ: Robert Wood Johnson Foundation; 2010:16. http://www.rwjf.org/content/dam/farm/reports/reports/2010/rwjf54583. Accessed December 23, 2013.

5. American Heart Association. "Heart Disease and Stroke Statistics—2014 Update," AHA Statistical Update Web site. http://circ.ahajournals.org/content/early/2013/12/18/01.cir.0000441139.02102.80.full.pdf . (Accessed January 6, 2014)

6. National Cancer Institute. "Cancer Prevalence and Cost of Care Projections Web site," http://costprojections.cancer.gov/. (Accessed December 23, 2013)

7. American Diabetes Association. "The Cost of Diabetes Web site," http://www.diabetes.org/advocate/resources/cost-of-diabetes.html. (Accessed December 23, 2013)

PLANT-BASED DIET FACTS

1. Primitive Medicine. http://www.historyworld.net/wrldhis/PlainTextHistories.asp

2. BBC - GCSE Bitesize, Prehistoric Civilisation. "They have done this through a process of trial and error and natural selection".

3. Willcox, B. J. Willcox, D. C. Todoriki, H. et al. "Caloric Restriction, the Traditional Okinawan Diet, and Healthy Aging: The Diet of the World's Longest-Lived People and Its Potential Impact on Morbidity and Life Span," Annals of the New York Academy of Sciences 1114 (October 2007): 434–55.

4. Otten, Jennifer J. Pitzi Hellwig, Jennifer. Meyers, Linda D. eds, "DRI: Dietary Reference Intakes: The Essential Guide to Nutrient Requirements," Washington, DC: National Academies Press, c. 2006, http://www.nal.usda.gov/fnic/DRI/Essential _Guide/DRIEssentialGuideNutReq.pdf.

5. Vogel, Robert A. Corretti, Mary C. Plotnick, Gary D. "The Postprandial Effect of Components of the Mediterranean Diet on Endothelial Function," *Journal of the American College of Cardiology 36* (November 1, 2000): 1455–60. Blankenhorn, DH. Johnson, RL. Mack, WJ, el Zein, HA, Vailas, LI. "The influence of diet on the appearance of new lesions in human coronary arteries," JAMA. 1990 Mar 23-30;263(12):1646-52

6. Nordström, D. C. E. Friman, C. Konttinen, Y. T. Honkanen, V. E. A. Nasu, Y. Antila E. "Alpha-Linolenic Acid in the Treatment of Rheumatoid Arthritis. A Double-Blind, Placebo-Controlled and Randomized Study: Flaxseed vs. Safflower Seed," *Rheumatology International 14* (1995): 231–34; Allman, M. A. Pena, M. M. Pang, D. "Supplementation with Flaxseed Oil Versus Sunflowerseed Oil in Healthy Young Men Consuming a Low-Fat Diet: Effects on Platelet Composition and Function," *European Journal of Clinical Nutrition 49* (March 1995): 169–78; Namazi, M. R. "The Beneficial and Detrimental Effects of Linoleic Acid on Autoimmune Disorders," *Autoimmunity 37* (February 2004): 73–75; Purasiri, P. McKechnie, A. Heys, S. D.

Eremin, O. "Modulation in Vitro of Human Natural Cyto-toxicity, Lymphocyte Proliferative Response to Mitogens and Cytokine Production by Essential Fatty Acids," *Immunology* 92 (October 1997): 166–72; Hazlett, D. "Dietary Fats Appear to Reduce Lung Function," *Journal of the American Medical Association 223*, no. 1 (1973): 15–16; Welsch, Clifford W. "Relationship Between Dietary Fat and Experimental Mammary Tumorigenesis: A Review and Critique," *Cancer Research 52* (April 1992): 2040S–48S; Griffini Patrizia. Fehres, Olav. Klieverik, Lars. et al., "Dietary Omega-3 Polyunsaturated Fatty Acids Promote Colon Carcinoma Metastasis in Rat Liver," *Cancer Research 58* (August 1, 1998): 3312–19; Klieverik, Lars. Fehres, Olav. Griffini, Patrizia. Van Noorden, Cornelis J. F. Frederiks, Wilma M. "Promotion of Colon Cancer Metastases in Rat Liver by Fish Oil Diet Is Not Due to Reduced Stroma Formation," *Clinical & Experimental Metastasis 18* (September 2000): 371–77; Karroll, Kenneth K. "Experimental Evidence of Dietary Factors and Hormone-Dependent Cancers," *Cancer Research 35* (November 1975): 3374–83; Weisburger, J. H. "Worldwide Prevention of Cancer and Other Chronic Diseases Based on Knowledge of Mechanisms," *Mutation Research 402* (June 18, 1998): 331–37; Sauer, Leonard A. Blask, David, E. Bauchey, Robert T. "Dietary Factors and Growth and Metabolism in Experimental Tumors," *Journal of Nutritional Biochemistry 18* (October 2007): 637–49; Clement, IP. "Review of the Effects of Trans Fatty Acids, Oleic Acid, N-3 Polyunsaturated Fatty Acids, and Conjugated Linoleic Acid on Mammary Carcinogenesis in Animals," *American Journal of Clinical Nutrition 66* (December 1997): 1523S–29S.

Plant-Based Food and the Ancient Civilizations

ANCIENT CHINESE

1. Benn, Charles. *China's Golden Age: Everyday Life in the Tang Dynasty*, Oxford University Press. (2002)

2. Gernet, Jacques. *Daily Life in China on the Eve of the Mongol Invasion, 1250-1276*, Translated by H. M. Wright. Stanford: Stanford University Press. (1962)

3. Anderson, E. N. *The Food of China*, (illustrated, reprint, revised ed.). Yale University Press. (Retrieved 24 April 2014) (1988)

4. Crosby, Alfred W, Jr. *The Columbian Exchange: Biological and Cultural Consequences of 1492*, 30th Anniversary Edition. Westport: Praeger Publishers. (2003)

5. Gernet, Jacques. *Daily Life in China on the Eve of the Mongol Invasion, 1250-1276*, Translated by H. M. Wright. Stanford: Stanford University Press. (1962)

6. Engelhardt, Ute. "Dietetics in Tang China and the first extant works of material dietetica", in Elisabeth Hsü (ed.), *Innovation in Chinese Medicine*, Cambridge: Cambridge University Press. (2001)

7. Barnes, Linda L. "A World of Chinese Medicine and Healing: Part Two", in TJ Hinrichs and Linda L. Barnes (eds.), *Chinese Medicine and Healing: An Illustrated History*, Cambridge, Mass.: The Belknap Press of Harvard University Press. (2013),

ANCIENT SUMERIAN

1. Bottéro, J, *Everyday Life in Ancient Mesopotamia*, Johns Hopkins University Press. (1992)

2. Nemet-Nejat, K.R, *Daily Life in Ancient Mesopotamia*, Greenwood. (1998)

ANCIENT INDIAN

1. Prabhupāda, A. C. Bhaktivedanta Swami. *Bhagavad-gītā As It Is*, New York: Bhaktivedanta Book Trust. (1972)

ANCIENT EGYPTIAN

1. Pilsbury Alcock, J. *Food in the Ancient World*, Greenwood Publishing Group. (2006)

2. Weiss Adamson, M, Segan, F. *Entertaining from Ancient Rome to the Super Bowl: An Encyclopedia [2 volumes]*, - ABC-CLIO. (Oct 30, 2008)

3. *The Cambridge World History of Food, Volume 2*, University of Cambridge, Cambridge University Press. (2000)

4. Prance, G, Nesbitt, M. *The Cultural History of Plants*, Routledge. (2012)

ANCIENT MAYA

1. Mt. Pleasant, Jane. "The science behind the Three Sisters mound system: An agronomic assessment of an indigenous agricultural system in the northeast". In John E. Staller, Robert H. Tykot, and Bruce F. Benz. "Histories of maize: Multidisciplinary approaches to the prehistory, linguistics,

biogeography, domestication, and evolution of maize". Amsterdam. (2006)

2. Bronson, Bennet. "Roots and the Subsistence of the Ancient Maya". *Southwestern Journal of Anthropology* 22: 251–279. (1966)

3. Bogin 1997, Coe 1996, Montejo 1999, Tedlock. (1985)

ANCIENT BABYLONIAN

1. Bancroft Hunt, N. *Living in Ancient Mesopotamia*, Facts On File, Incorporated. (Jan 1, 2008)

2. E. H. Rustad, Martha. *The Babylonians: Life in Ancient Babylon*, Lerner Publishing Group. (2009)

ANCIENT AZTEC

1. Coe, Sophie D. *America's first cuisines*, University of Texas Press (1994)

2. Coe, Michael D, Koontz Rex. *Mexico: From the Olmecs to the Aztecs*, Thames & Hudson. (2013)

3. Arnot, Bob. *The Aztec Diet: Chia Power: The Superfood that Gets You Skinny and Keeps You Healthy*, Harper Collins. (2013)

4. Smith, Michael E. *The Aztecs*, Wiley Blackwell, 2nd ed. (2002)

5. Smith, Michael E. *The Aztecs*, John Wiley & Sons. (2013)

ORIGINS OF VEGETARIANISM

1. Davis, J. "Extracts from some journals 1842-48 - The earliest known uses of the word vegetarian".

2. Davis, J. "Extracts from some journals 1842-48 - The earliest known uses of the word vegetarian".

3. Spencer, Colin. *The Heretic's Feast: A History of Vegetarianism* Fourth Estate Classic House.

4. Reuters: http://uk.reuters.com/article/uk-pope-environment-idUKKBN0FA0BC20140705

5. Schmidt, A, Fieldhouse, P. *The World Religions Cookbook* Greenwood Publishing Group. (2007)

6. Editors of Hinduism Today. "What Is Hinduism?: Modern Adventures Into a Profound Global Faith" Himalayan Academy Publications. (Retrieved 2013) (2007)

7. "Apparitions of the Self: The Secret Autobiographies of a Tibetan Visionary" - Google Books. Books.google.com. (Retrieved 2015)

8. Esposito, J. *Islam: The Straight Path* (3rd ed.). Oxford University Press. (1998)

9. Shah, Umakant P. *Jaina-Rupa-Mandana* Abhinav Publications. (1987)

10. Bleich, J. D. *Contemporary Halakhic Problems 3* KTAV Publishing House. (1989)

11. Kook, Avraham Yitzhak, Cohen, David, ed. *A Vision of Vegetarianism and Peace* (PDF). (1961)

12. Schwartz, Richard H. *Judaism and Vegetarianism* Lantern Books. New York. (2001)

13. Kalechofsky, Roberta. *Rabbis and Vegetarianism: An Evolving Tradition* Micah Publications. (1995)

14. "Bal Tashchit" http://www.reformjudaism.org.uk/a-to-z-of-reform-judaism/contemporary-issues/bal-tashchit.html

15. Brook, Dan, Ph.D. "The Vegetarian Mitzvah"

16. Beskow, Per. *Strange Tales about Jesus: A Survey of Unfamiliar Gospels*. Fortress Press. (1985)

17. Young, Richard Alan. *Is God a Vegetarian?* Open Court Publishing. (1999)

18. Szekely, Edmond Bordeaux. "The Essene Gospel of Peace, Book One," International Biogenic Society. (1981)

19. Ehrman, Bart D. *Did Jesus Exist?: The Historical Argument for Jesus of Nazareth,* HarperCollins. (2012)

20. Jaeger, Werner *Early Christianity and Greek Paideia* Harvard University Press. (1961)

21. "Living an Orthodox Life: Fasting". Orthodoxinfo.com. (Retrieved 2010) (May 27, 1997)

The Enlightened Diet

COMMON QUESTIONS

1. LaSalle Jr, Leffall D, M.D, Kripke, Margaret L. "Reducing environmental cancer risk. What We Can Do Now". Rep. n.p.: U.S. Department Of Health And Human Services, National Institutes of Health, National Cancer Institute, n.d. Print.

2. Grein, Jonathan. "The Cognitive Effects of Iron Deficiency in Non-Anemic Children" Nutrition Noteworthy. (2001)

3. American Academy of Environmental Medicine (AAEM). https://www.aaemonline.org/gmo.php

4. Sjödahl, K. Jia, C. Vatten, L. Nilsen, T. Hveem, K. Lagergren, J. "Salt and gastric adenocarcinoma: a population-based cohort study in Norway," Cancer Epidemiol Biomarkers Prev. 2008 Aug;17(8):1997-2001.

5. González, CA. Jakszyn, P. Pera, G. Agudo, A. Bingham, S. Palli, D. Ferrari, P. Boeing, H. del Giudice, G. et.al. "Meat intake and risk of stomach and esophageal adenocarcinoma within the European Prospective Investigation Into Cancer and Nutrition" (EPIC). J Natl Cancer Inst. 2006 Mar 1;98(5):345-54.

6. González CA, Pera G, Agudo A, Bueno-de-Mesquita HB, Ceroti M, Boeing H, Schulz M, Del Giudice G, et.al. "Fruit and vegetable intake and the risk of stomach and esophagus adenocarcinoma in the European Prospective Investigation into Cancer and Nutrition" (EPIC-EURGAST). Int J Cancer. 2006 May 15;118(10):2559-66.

7. Esposito, K. Marfella, R. Ciotola, M. Di Palo, C. Giugliano, F. Giugliano, G. D'Armiento, M. D'Andrea, F. Giugliano, D. "Effect of a mediterranean-style diet on endothelial dysfunction and markers of vascular inflammation in the metabolic syndrome: a randomized trial," JAMA. 2004 Sep 22;292(12):1440-6.

8. Ryan, M. McInerney, D. Owens, D. Collins, P. Johnson, A. Tomkin, GH. "Diabetes and the Mediterranean diet: a beneficial effect of oleic acid on insulin sensitivity, adipocyte glucose transport and endothelium-dependent vasoreactivity," QJM. 2000 Feb;93(2):85-91.

9. Vogel, R. Corretti, M. Plotnick, G. "The postprandial effect of components of the Mediterranean diet on endothelial function". J Am Coll Cardiol. 2000 Nov 1;36(5):1455-60.

10. Rueda-Clausen, C. Silva, F. Lindarte, M. Villa-Roel, C. Gomez, E. Gutierrez, R. Cure-Cure, C. López-Jaramillo, P. "Olive, soybean and palm oils intake have a similar acute detrimental effect over the endothelial function in healthy young subjects" Nutr Metab Cardiovasc Dis. 2007 Jan;17(1):50-7.

11. Nordström, D. Friman, C. Konttinen, Y. Honkanen, V. Nasu, Y. Antila, E. "Alpha-Linolenic Acid in the Treatment of Rheumatoid Arthritis. A Double-Blind, Placebo-Controlled and Randomized Study: Flaxseed vs. Safflower Seed," Rheumatology International 14 (1995): 231–34; Allman, M. Pena, M. and Pang, D. "Supplementation with Flaxseed Oil Versus Sunflowerseed Oil in Healthy Young Men Consuming a Low-Fat Diet: Effects on Platelet Composition and Function," European Journal of Clinical Nutrition 49 (March 1995): 169–78; Namazi, M. "The Beneficial and Detrimental Effects of Linoleic Acid on Autoimmune Disorders," Autoimmunity 37 (February 2004): 73–75; Purasiri, P. McKechnie, A. Heys, S. Eremin, O. "Modulation in Vitro of Human Natural Cytotoxicity, Lymphocyte Proliferative Response to Mitogens and Cytokine Production by Essential Fatty Acids," Immunology 92 (October 1997): 166–72; Hazlett, D. "Dietary Fats Appear to Reduce Lung Function," Journal of the American Medical Association 223, no. 1 (1973): 15–16; Welsch, Clifford W. "Relationship Between Dietary Fat and Experimental Mammary Tumorigenesis: A Review and Critique," Cancer Research 52 (April 1992): 2040S–48S; Griffini, P. Fehres, O. Klieverik, L. et al, "Dietary Omega-3 Polyunsaturated Fatty Acids Promote Colon Carcinoma Metastasis in Rat Liver," Cancer Research 58 (August 1, 1998): 3312–19; Klieverik, L. Fehres, O. Griffini, P. Van Noorden, C. J. F. Frederiks, Wilma M. "Promotion of Colon Cancer Metastases in Rat Liver by Fish Oil Diet Is Not Due to Reduced Stroma Formation," Clinical & Experimental Metastasis 18 (September 2000): 371–77; Karroll, Kenneth K. "Experimental Evidence of Dietary Factors and Hormone-Dependent Cancers," Cancer Research 35 (November 1975): 3374–83; Weisburger, J. H. "Worldwide Prevention of Cancer and Other Chronic Diseases Based on Knowledge of Mechanisms," Mutation Research 402 (June 18, 1998): 331–37; Sauer, Leonard A. Blask, David E. Bauchey, Robert T. "Dietary Factors and Growth and Metabolism in Experimental Tumors," Journal of Nutritional Biochemistry 18 (October 2007): 637–49; Clement, IP. "Review of the Effects of Trans Fatty Acids, Oleic Acid, N-3 Polyunsaturated Fatty Acids, and Conjugated Linoleic Acid on Mammary Carcinogenesis in Animals," American Journal of Clinical Nutrition 66 (December 1997): 1523S–29S.

12. Chu, N. F. Spiegelman, D. Yu, J. Rifai, N. Hotamisligil, G. S. Rimm, E. B. "Plasma Leptin Concentrations and Four-Year Weight Gain Among US Men," International Journal of Obesity and Related Metabolic Disorders 25 (March 2001): 346–53; Chu, N. F. Stampfer, M. J. Spiegelman, D. Rifai, N. Hotamisligil, G. S. Rimm, E. B. "Dietary and Lifestyle Factors in Relation to Plasma Leptin Concentrations Among Normal Weight and Overweight Men," International Journal of Obesity and Related Metabolic Disorders 25 (January 2001): 106–14; Kuroda, M. Ohta, M. Okufuji, T. et al. "Frequency of Soup Intake and Amount of Dietary Fiber Intake Are Inversely Associated with Plasma Leptin Concentrations in Japanese Adults," Appetite 54, no. 3 (June 2010): 538–43.

13. Christensen, S. Viggers, L. Hasselström, K. Gregersen, S. "Effect of fruit restriction on glycemic control in patients with type 2 diabetes - A randomized trial". Nutr J. 2013 Mar 5;12:29.

GETTING STARTED

1. Willcox, B. J. Willcox, D. C. Todoriki, H. et al. "Caloric Restriction, the Traditional Okinawan Diet, and Healthy Aging: The Diet of the World's Longest-Lived People and Its Potential Impact on Morbidity and Life Span," *Annals of the New York Academy of Sciences* 1114 (October 2007): 434–55.

2. Calder, Philip C. "N-3 Polyunsaturated Fatty Acids, Inflammation, and Inflammatory Diseases," *American Journal of Clinical Nutrition* 83 (June 2006): 1505S–19S.

3. Otten, Jennifer J. Pitzi Hellwig, Jennifer. Meyers Linda D. eds. "DRI: Dietary Reference Intakes: The Essential Guide to Nutrient Requirements" Washington, DC: National Academies Press, c. (2006) http://www.nal.usda.gov/fnic/DRI/Essential _Guide/DRIEssentialGuideNutReq.pdf.

4. Mursu, J. Robien, K. Harnack, Lisa J. Park, K. Jacobs, David R. "Dietary Supplements and Mortality Rate in Older Women. The Iowa Women's Health Study," *Archives of Internal Medicine 171* (October 10, 2011): 1625–33.

5. Fortmann, Stephen P. Burda, Brittany U. Senger, Caitlyn A. Lin, Jennifer S. Whitlock, Evelyn P. "Vitamin and Mineral Supplements in the Primary Prevention of Cardiovascular Disease and Cancer: An Updated Systematic Evidence Review for the U.S. Preventive Services Task Force," *Annals of Internal Medicine 159* (December 17, 2013): 824–34.

6. Bjelakovic, G. Nikolova D. Gluud, Lise L. Simonetti, Rosa G. Gluud, C. "Mortality in Randomized Trials of Antioxidant Supplements for Primary and Secondary Prevention: Systematic Review and Meta-Analysis," *Journal of the American Medical Association 297* (February 28, 2007): 842–57.

7. Van Dusseldorp, Marijke. Schneede, Jorn, Refsum. Helga, et al, "Risk of Persistent Cobalamin Deficiency in Adolescents Fed a Macrobiotic Diet in Early Life," *American Journal of Clinical Nutrition 69* (April 1999): 664–71.

The Master Plants

1. Koyama, Satomi et al. "Pomegranate Extract Induces Apoptosis in Human Prostate Cancer Cells by Modulation of the IGF-IGFBP Axis." Growth hormone & IGF research : official journal of the Growth Hormone Research Society and the International IGF Research Society 20.1 (2010): 55. PMC.

2. Turrini, E. Ferruzzi, L. Fimognari, C. "Potential Effects of Pomegranate Polyphenols in Cancer Prevention and Therapy. Oxidative Medicine and Cellular Longevity," 2015;2015:938475. doi:10.1155/2015/938475.

3. Torres, MP. Rachagani, S. Purohit, V. et al. "Graviola: A Novel Promising Natural-Derived Drug That Inhibits Tumorigenicity and Metastasis of Pancreatic Cancer Cells In Vitro and In Vivo Through Altering Cell Metabolism," Cancer Letters. 2012;323(1):29-40. doi:10.1016/j.canlet.2012.03.031.

4. Pieme, CA. Kumar, SG. Dongmo, MS. et al. "Antiproliferative activity and induction of apoptosis by Annona muricata (Annonaceae) extract on human cancer cells," BMC Complementary and Alternative Medicine. 2014;14:516. doi:10.1186/1472-6882-14-516.

5. Dai, Y. Hogan, S. Schmelz, EM. et al: "Selective growth inhibition of human breast cancer cells by graviola fruit extract in vitro and in vivo involving downregulation of EGFR expression," Nutr Cancer 63:795-801, 2011.

6. Hamizah S, Roslida AH, Fezah O, et al: "Chemopreventive potential of Annona muricata L leaves on chemically-induced skin papillomagenesis in mice," Asian Pac J Cancer Prev 13:2533-2539, 2012.

7. Kopec, RE. Cooperstone, JL. Schweiggert, RM. et al. "Avocado Consumption Enhances Human Postprandial Provitamin A Absorption and Conversion from a Novel High–β-Carotene Tomato Sauce and from Carrots," The Journal of Nutrition. 2014;144(8):1158-1166. doi:10.3945/jn.113.187674.

Photo Credits

These photos are all courtesy of the stock agency 123rf.com, and were taken by the following photographers:

INDEX

A

Almond Milk, Classic, 260
Ancient civilizations, 16–28
Ancient wisdom, 13–14
Arugula
    benefits, 56
    Lasagna, Mediterranean Green, 126–127
    nutrients, 57
    Rucola Salad, Apulia, 124–125
Asparagus
    benefits, 58
    Damascus-Crusted Asparagus, 128–129
    Ishtar's Asparagus, 130–131
    nutrients, 59
Avocado
    Aztec Avocado Boats, 132–133
    benefits, 61
    Cashew e Pepe, 134–135
    nutrients, 61

B

Beans, cooking, 264
Beet
    Beet Chips, Marrakesh, 138–139
    benefits, 62
    nutrients, 63
    Ravioli, Cinque Terre Stuffed, 137
Bell Pepper
    benefits, 64
    Goulash, Columbus's Favorite, 143
    nutrients, 65
    Pepper Boats, Andean, 140–141
Beverages
    Milk, Classic Almond, 260
    Milk, Classic Hemp, 260
    Smoothie, All-Star Pregnancy, 259
    Smoothie, Bhutan Lemon, 205
    Smoothie, Cancer Fighter, 259
    Smoothie, Cleansing Kidney and Liver, 262
    Smoothie, Digestion Booster, 261
    Smoothie, Green Protein, 261
    Smoothie, Healing Mumbai Curcuma, 249
    Smoothie, Heart-Thriving, 261
    Smoothie, Man-Power, 262
    Smoothie, Persian Green Antioxidant, 238–239
    Smoothie, Tayrona's Secret, 234–235
    Tea, Holy Anti-Inflammatory, 187
Blueberry
    benefits, 66
    Cheesecake, Apache, 144–145
    nutrients, 67
    Parfait, Blueberry Hopi, 147
Brazil Nut
    benefits, 68
    nutrients, 69
    Pear Crumble, Carioca, 151
    Steaks, Amazon Nutty, 148–149
Broccoli
    benefits, 70
    nutrients, 71
    Soup, Emperor's Broccoli, 152–153
    Wings, Satay Broccoli, 155
Brown Rice, cooking, 263
Brownies, Olmec Fudge, 162–163
Bruschetta, Agrodolce Fig, 180–181
Buckwheat
    benefits, 72
    cooking, 263
    nutrients, 73
    Porridge, Monk's Cacao, 158–159
    Wraps, Nepal's Buckwheat, 156–157
Burgers, Demeter's Harvest, 209

C

Cacao
    benefits, 74
    Brownies, Olmec Fudge, 162–163
    nutrients, 75
    Pancakes, Caribbean Cacao, 161
    Porridge, Monk's Cacao, 158–159
Calcium, 44–45
Caps, Tibetan Creamy, 178–179
Carrot Cookies, 275
Carrot Wraps, Qi, 192–193
Cashew Cheese, 272
Cashew e Pepe, 134–135
Cauliflower, Ming's Roasted, 184–185
Cheese substitutes, 50
Cheesecake, Apache, 144–145
Chia
    benefits, 76
    Mousse, Chichén Itzá Blackberry, 164–165
    nutrients, 77
    Pudding, Chia, 276
    Pudding, Incan Mango, 167
Chickpea
    benefits, 78
    cooking, 265
    nutrients, 79
    Roasted Chickpeas, Jordanian, 171
    Stew, Lebanese Chickpea, 168–169
Chips
    Beet Chips, Marrakesh, 138–139
    Kale Chips, 268
    Plantain Chips, Spicy Baked, 267
Chocolate Spread, 275
Cookies and Bars
    Brownies, Olmec Fudge, 162–163
    Carrot Cookies, 275
    Hemp Bars, Steps to Heaven, 195
    Holy Bites, Pharaoh's, 214–215
    Macaroons, Ningxia Goji, 191
    Oat Cookies, Three-Ingredient, 276

    Quinoa Cookies, Machu Picchu's, 225
Cookware, 51–52
Crackers, baking, 268
Croquettes, Turmeric Vedic, 250–251
Crumble Cream, Ming's Raw, 217

D

Date Sauce, 275
Date Turmeric Dressing, 258
Desserts and Sweets. See also Cookies and Bars
    Cheesecake, Apache, 144–145
    Chocolate Spread, 275
    Crumble Cream, Ming's Raw, 217
    Date Sauce, 275
    Ice Cream, El Dorado's Golden, 233
    Mousse, Chichén Itzá Blackberry, 164–165
    Parfait, Blueberry Hopi, 147
    Pear Crumble, Carioca, 151
    Pie, Babel Fig, 172–173
    Pie Crust, Naked, 276
    Pudding, Chia, 276
    Pudding, Incan Mango, 167
    Pudding, Shiva's Antioxidant, 222–223
Diets
    of ancestors, 11–13
    of ancient civilizations, 16–28
    enlightened diet, 37–42
    GMO-free diets, 40
    modern diet, 11–13
    oil-free diets, 41–42
    organic diets, 38–39
    plant-based diets, 16–28
    salt-free diets, 40–41
    sugar-free diets, 42
Dips and Spreads. See also Sauces
    Cashew Cheese, 272
    Chocolate Spread, 275
    Guacamole, Naked, 273
    Mayo, Naked, 272
    Pâté, Fig, 272

Pâté, Keobab Kelp, 200–201
Pesto, Mesopotamian Kale, 197
Pico de Gallo, 273
Pico de Gallo, Zen Persimmon, 218–219
Ragù, Sunday's Italian, 246–247
Sofrito, 274
Disease, causes of, 12–15
Dressings
    Date Turmeric Dressing, 258
    Lemon Dressing, 258
    Ranch Dressing, 258

E

Eating habits, 11–14
Egg substitutes, 50
Enlightened diet, 37–42
Essential recipes, 257–276

F

Fatty acids, 46
Fig
    benefits, 80
    Bruschetta, Agrodolce Fig, 180–181
    nutrients, 81
    Onion Tarts, Goddess's Baked, 175
    Pâté, Fig, 272
    Pie, Babel Fig, 172–173
Fish, 45–46
Food sources, 43–44
Food substitutions, 50
Fungi
    benefits, 82
    Caps, Tibetan Creamy, 178–179
    nutrients, 83
    Risotto, Kyoto Fungi, 176–177

G

Garlic
    benefits, 84
    Bruschetta, Agrodolce Fig, 180–181
    nutrients, 85
    Veggies, Kazakh Sautéed, 183
Gazpacho, Essenes, 254–255
Ginger
    benefits, 86
    Cauliflower, Ming's Roasted, 184–185
    nutrients, 87
    Tea, Holy Anti-Inflammatory, 187
Glossary, 278–283
GMO-free diets, 40
Goji
    benefits, 88
    Macaroons, Ningxia Goji, 191
    nutrients, 89
    Rice, Himalayan Goji, 188–189
Goulash, Columbus's Favorite, 143
Grass-fed animal products, 47
Guacamole, Naked, 273

H

Healthy lifestyles, 12–14
Hemp
    benefits, 90
    Carrot Wraps, Qi, 192–193
    Hemp Bars, Steps to Heaven, 195
    Hemp Milk, Classic, 260
    nutrients, 91
Hummus, Sweet Potato, 270

I

Ice Cream, El Dorado's Golden, 233

K

Kale
    benefits, 92
    Chips, Kale, 268
    nutrients, 93
    Pesto, Mesopotamian Kale, 197
    Salad, Persepolis Kale, 199

Kelp
    benefits, 94
    nutrients, 95
    Pâté, Keobab Kelp, 200–201
    "Tuna" Salad, Madagascar, 203
Kitchen essentials, 51–52
Kitchen sustainability, 53
Kitchen tools, 51–52

L

Lasagna, Mediterranean Green, 126–127
Lemon
    benefits, 96
    Dressing, Lemon, 258
    nutrients, 97
    Smoothie, Bhutan Lemon, 205
    Tarts, Tantric Lemon Bliss, 206–207
Lentil
    benefits, 98
    Burgers, Demeter's Harvest, 209
    cooking, 266
    nutrients, 99
    Risotto, Plato's Lentil, 210–211

M

Macaroons, Ningxia Goji, 191
Mango Pudding, Incan, 167
Marinara Sauce, 127
Master plant recipes, 123–255
Master plants, 55–121
Mayo, Naked, 272
Meat substitutes, 50
Milk, Almond, 260
Milk, Hemp, 260
Milk substitutes, 50
Millet, cooking, 264
Modern diet, 11–13
Mousse, Chichén Itzá Blackberry, 164–165

N

Nutty Steaks, Amazon, 148–149

O

Oats
    benefits, 100
    Holy Bites, Pharaoh's, 214–215
    nutrients, 101
    Oat Cookies, Three-Ingredient, 276
    Oatmeal, Nile's Pan-Seared, 213
Oil substitutes, 50
Oil-free diets, 41–42
Omega-3s, 46
Onion Tarts, Goddess's Baked, 175
Onions, Valle d'Itria's Roasted, 228–229
Organic diets, 38–39
Organic products, 47

P

Pancakes, Caribbean Cacao, 161
Pancakes, Pan-Seared Oatmeal, 213
Parfait, Blueberry Hopi, 147
Pasta substitutes, 50
Pâté, Fig, 272
Pâté, Keobab Kelp, 200–201
Pear Crumble, Carioca, 151
Pepper Boats, Andean, 140–141
Persimmon
    benefits, 102
    Crumble Cream, Ming's Raw, 217
    nutrients, 103
    Pico de Gallo, Zen Persimmon, 218–219
Pesto, Kale Mesopotamian, 197
Pico de Gallo, 273
Pico de Gallo, Zen Persimmon, 218–219
Pie, Babel Fig, 172–173
Pie Crust, Naked, 276
Pkhali, Fabulous Mediterranean, 220–221
Plantain Chips, Spicy Baked, 267
Plant-based foods, 16–28

Plant-based substitutions, 50

Pomegranate
    benefits, 104
    nutrients, 105
    Pkhali, Fabulous Mediterranean, 220–221
    Pudding, Shiva's Antioxidant, 222–223

Porridge, Monk's Cacao, 158–159

Potato, Sweet
    benefits, 114
    Hummus, 270
    Layered Bake, Polynesian, 241
    nutrients, 115
    Sacred Potatoes, Samoa, 242–243

Potato Salad, 269

Potato Soup, Classic, 271

Protein, 44–45

Puddings
    Antioxidant Pudding, Shiva's, 222–223
    Chia Pudding, 276
    Mango Pudding, Incan, 167
    Mousse, Chichén Itzá Blackberry, 164–165

Q

Quinoa
    benefits, 106
    Breakfast Bowl, Manna Quinoa, 253
    Cookies, Machu Picchu's Quinoa, 225
    cooking, 265
    nutrients, 107
    Quinoa Bowl, Quechua, 226–227

R

Ragù, Sunday's Italian, 246–247

Ranch Dressing, 258

Ravioli, Cinque Terre Stuffed, 137

Recipes, 123–276

Rice
    Brown Rice, 263
    cooking, 263
    Goji Rice, Himalayan, 188–189
    Spinach Rice, Armenian, 237

Risotto, Kyoto Fungi, 176–177

Risotto, Plato's Lentil, 210–211

Rosemary
    benefits, 108
    nutrients, 109
    Onions, Valle d'Itria's Roasted, 228–229
    Rosemary Roast, Sumerian, 230–231

Rucola Salad, Apulia, 124–125

S

Salads
    Avocado Boats, Aztec, 132–133
    Dressing, Date Turmeric, 258
    Dressing, Lemon, 258
    Dressing, Ranch, 258
    Kale Salad, Persepolis, 199
    Potato Salad, 269
    Rucola Salad, Apulia, 124–125
    "Tuna" Salad, Madagascar, 203

Salt substitutes, 50

Salt-free diets, 40–41

Satay Sauce, 155

Sauces. *See also* Dips and Spreads
    Date Sauce, 275
    Marinara Sauce, 127
    Satay Sauce, 155

Seitan, 50

Shopping list, 48–49

Smoothies
    Antioxidant Smoothie, Persian Green, 238–239
    Cancer Fighter Smoothie, 259
    Cleansing Smoothie, Kidney and Liver, 262
    Digestion Booster Smoothie, 261
    Healing Smoothie, Mumbai Curcuma, 249
    Heart-Thriving Smoothie, 261
    Lemon Smoothie, Bhutan, 205
    Man-Power Smoothie, 262
    Pregnancy Smoothie, All-Star, 259

Protein Smoothie, Green, 261

Secret Smoothie, Tayrona's, 234–235

Sofrito, 274

Soups and Stews

Broccoli Soup, Emperor's, 152–153

Chickpea Stew, Lebanese, 168–169

Gazpacho, Essenes, 254–255

Potato Soup, Classic, 271

Watermelon Soup, Chilled, 271

Soursop

benefits, 110

Ice Cream, El Dorado's Golden, 233

nutrients, 111

Smoothie, Tayrona's Secret, 234–235

Spinach

benefits, 112

nutrients, 113

Rice, Armenian Spinach, 237

Smoothie, Persian Green Antioxidant, 238–239

Steaks, Amazon Nutty, 148–149

Stews. *See* Soups and Stews

Stuffed Tomatoes, Mayan, 245

Substitutions, 50

Sugar substitutes, 50

Sugar-free diets, 42

Supplements, 46–47, 51

Sweet Potato

benefits, 114

Hummus, 270

Layered Bake, Polynesian, 241

nutrients, 115

Sacred Potatoes, Samoa, 242–243

T

Tarts, Lemon Bliss, 206–207

Tarts, Onion Baked, 175

Tea, Holy Anti-Inflammatory, 187

Tempeh, 50

Tofu, 50

Tofu Steaks, 148–149

Tomato

benefits, 116

nutrients, 117

Pico de Gallo, 273

Ragù, Sunday's Italian, 246–247

Sofrito, 274

Stuffed Tomatoes, Mayan, 245

"Tuna" Salad, Madagascar, 203

Turmeric

benefits, 118

Croquettes, Vedic Turmeric, 250–251

Dressing, Turmeric Date, 258

nutrients, 119

Smoothie, Healing Mumbai Curcuma, 249

V

Vegetarianism, 15, 29–36

Veggies, Kazakh Sautéed, 183

Vitamin B12, 47, 51

Vitamin D, 45, 51

W

Watermelon Soup, Chilled, 271

Wheatgrass

benefits, 120

Breakfast Bowl, Manna Quinoa, 253

Gazpacho, Essenes, 254–255

nutrients, 121

Wings, Satay Broccoli, 155

Wraps, Nepal's Buckwheat, 156–157

Wraps, Qi Carrot, 192–193

Y

Yucca, Traditional-Style, 270